LINGUISTICS AND INFORMATION SCIENCE

KAREN
SPARCK JONES
Computer Laboratory
University of Cambridge
Cambridge, England

MARTIN
KAY
Department of Information
and Computer Science
University of California
Irvine, California

FID publ. no. 492

ACADEMIC PRESS   New York and London   1973

A Subsidiary of Harcourt Brace Jovanovich, Publishers

ACADEMIC PRESS, INC.
111 Fifth Avenue, New York, New York 10003

United Kingdom Edition published by
ACADEMIC PRESS, INC. (LONDON) LTD.
24/28 Oval Road, London NW1

Library of Congress Cataloging in Publication Data

Sparck Jones, Karen, DATE
    Linguistics and information science.

    "Commissioned by the Committee on Linguistics in
Documentation of the Fédération internationale de
documentation."
    Bibliography: p.
    1.   Information storage and retrieval systems.
2.   Linguistics.   I.   Kay, Martin, joint author.
II.   International Federation for Documentation.
Committee on Linguistics in Documentation.
Z699.S635   029′.9′41   72-12198
ISBN 0–12–656250–4

CONTENTS

Chapter 4   **Language in Documentation**   45

Chapter 5   **Syntax**   79

FOREWORD

Most information is expressed in language and most language conveys information. So information science and linguistics should have much to learn from one another. But how much interpenetration of these two fields has there been?

To answer this question two qualified specialists, Karen Sparck Jones of Cambridge University, well known for her work in library and information science, and Martin Kay of the Rand Corporation, recognized for his contributions to linguistics, undertook this study. Both are members of the recently formed Committee on Linguistics in Documentation of the Fédération Internationale de Documentation, and it was at one of the first meetings of the Committee that they accepted the suggestion of another member, Dr. Hans Karlgren of Sweden, that they undertake a survey of current work.

Some areas which they have examined are the application of linguistic theory to the structure of knowledge; the application of phonology, morphology, syntax, and semantics to the organization, storage, and transmission of information; and computational linguistics as applicable to information handling, for example, automatic morphological and syntactic analysis, machine-aided transla-

ix

tion and machine translation, automatic indexing, abstracting, the machine preparation of indexes (both regular and inverted), thesauri, and statistical studies.

Though some of these topics have been treated briefly in the journal literature, this is the first comprehensive study of United States and foreign work. Sparck Jones and Kay set forth the present state of the art and explore those avenues for research which look most fruitful in a readable, informative, challenging book which should appeal to students of linguistics and library and information science.

WILLIAM N. LOCKE

Emeritus Director of Libraries,
the Massachusetts Institute of
Technology
Former Chairman, Committee on
Linguistics in Documentation, FID

PREFACE

This study was commissioned by the Committee on Linguistics in Documentation of the Fédération Internationale de Documentation (FID). It is concerned with the linguistic aspects of information science, and in particular with the linguistic components of document analysis, description, and retrieval. We have attempted to relate linguistics and information science by considering the theories and techniques linguistics has to offer, and how far these have been, or could be, exploited by information scientists. We have examined these questions within the context of automated language processing and automated documentation. The use of computers for linguistic operations presents special challenges as well as interesting possibilities, and we have chosen to approach the field from this particular point of view. We believe that a state of the art survey in this area is of value now because major developments have taken place in linguistics in the last decade, and computers have become familiar aids to research and practice in documentation, as in other fields. We have concentrated on the literature of the five years up to 1971, and have hopefully not omitted too many relevant references, though we have not aimed at total exhaustivity.

Our thanks are due to the FID itself for providing the necessary expenses of preparation; to the members of the Linguistics in Documentation Committee for their advice and support; and to the Chairman, Professor William N. Locke, and Secretary, Dr. A. Hood Roberts, in particular, for their continuing help and encouragement.

KAREN SPARCK JONES

MARTIN KAY

1

INTRODUCTION

Linguistics and information science are natural bedfellows. At least, both are centrally concerned with texts in ordinary language so that there is a strong common bond of interest to unite them. But there has been relatively little contact between the two fields and the number of people who are professionally active in both is infinitesimal. If there is justification for a review surveying what has been done over the past twenty years in the common ground between linguistics and information science, especially one of this size, it is presumably because the level of activity has been more than negligible. We are motivated in writing this report by curiosity. We are impressed by the great overlap in the subject matter of linguistics and information science and, at the same time, by the lack of interpenetration between the fields and we ask ourselves: is this an unfortunate accident of history? Is it that both fields are young and insecure? Is the situation likely to change and what, if anything, should be done to make it change?

It is important to be clear at the outset what we understand the terms "linguistics" and "information science" to mean and to set some boundaries for the field we intend to survey. It would be possible, without stretching the usual meanings of the terms too grossly, to treat information science as a proper part of applied linguistics on the grounds that it deals primarily with records or documents of one sort or another, that documents consist mainly of text, and that text is also the stuff of linguistics. On the same grounds, one could claim hardly less plausibly that linguistics ought to be considered part of information science. But there is nothing to be gained by debasing the terminological coinage in this way, and it is certainly not our intention to survey the activities of the past twenty years in linguistics and information science as wholes.

"Information science" may be interpreted very broadly as having to do with storage, retrieval, and transmission of information of any kind, in any way. It is thus concerned with a primary human activity. As Shera (1971) puts it: ". . . we have been transferring information all our lives without knowing it, like Molière's bourgeois gentleman." But since language is such a major vehicle for the transfer of information, information science may be regarded as chiefly concerned with linguistically encoded information.

Within the field of information science, thus interpreted, effort has been mainly devoted to information retrieval. This will be our concern here. Our specific interest is thus in the problems that arise in characterizing the content of documents and information requests in such a way that the characterizations can be used in an automatic process which can assess the relevance of the document to the request. This is surely the area in which information sicence presents the greatest challenge to linguistics. We are not concerned with the kind of request that can be satisfied by a formal library catalog, automated or otherwise. Requests in terms of author, title, publisher, date, and the like present no comparable challenge and they will be ignored in what follows. There may be somewhat greater linguistic interest in such tasks as catalog design and formation or the training of library staff, but the most interesting parts of these subjects will be dependent on our main subject, and the rest would lead us, at best, into an amorphous series of essentially uninformative anecdotes. We do not mean to suggest that information retrieval is the only important aspect of information science or the only one with genuine intellectual content. But we do believe that it provides the setting in which the relevance of linguistics to the field as a whole is most clearly to be seen.

We understand the term "linguistics" to refer to the science that attempts to explain how language works, that is, just what it is that small children are able to learn with so little instruction that enables them to convey and understand such an immense variety of ideas. To the extent that linguists are successful in explaining how language works, they can expect to find applications for their theories in such fields as language teaching, translation, and possibly information science.

While a common interest in textual data is sufficient to justify the interest that linguists and documentalists have in one another's affairs, it was the advent of computers that made it important to exploit this interest. What linguists are concerned to describe and explain is a natural human faculty—the faculty of language—which is taken for granted by documentalists no less than by other nonlinguists. It is true that information retrieval involves sophisticated operations that must be carried out on texts, but it is not true that one must necessarily be able to analyze these operations in detail in order to perform them any more than it is true that one must understand mechanics in order to ride a bicycle. But it has become clear that if information scientists want to have their place in the computer revolution, they will be forced into a new self-consciousness. Much of what must be explained in order to make information science amenable to computer techniques belongs to what linguists have undertaken to explain for quite independent reasons.

There are various reasons that could be adduced for the lack of communication between linguists and information scientists. One claim that might be made is that linguistics is still in too primitive a stage of development to provide a firm basis for the kinds of practical activity that information scientists are involved in. Linguistic theories are in a continual state of flux, and there is hardly time to begin fleshing out one theoretical skeleton before it is replaced by another. Furthermore, the best developed parts of linguistic theory are usually concerned with the sound system of languages, which have little or no relevance for information science, and with syntax, which is relevant only to the extent that it is associated with an equally well-developed theory of semantics. But semantics has only become a matter of primary concern to linguists during the last five years, and it is therefore still in a highly speculative stage of development. Computational linguistics is dependent on linguistics, so that it can hardly be less primitive.

Paradoxically, it is also possible to claim that any tools linguists might develop would be far too fine, expensive, or elaborate for the needs of information scientists. There has been almost no work in linguistics on units of text larger than a sentence. The structure of sentences and smaller units of text is studied microscopically so as to uncover every phonological nuance, or grammatical subtlety, or logical idiosyncracy that they may contain. But the primary matter that documentalists must handle consists of complete texts, and the main problems that face them are problems of volume rather than detail. It is true that requests must sometimes be presented that are highly specific and which cannot be adequately treated by a system that is not capable of making the finest distinctions. But it may never be possible to construct a system that will be capable of taking these requests in its stride while still being cost effective. The designer of an indexing system must make some assessment of the kind of request that it will be expected to satisfy; he must have some idea of the angles from which users are likely to approach the document collection. Only if the collection is large enough to warrant a sophisticated system and if there is to be no limit on the specificity of requests, is there also no limit on the demands that are imposed on the imagination of the system designer. What is wanted, then, if this view is correct, is a theory of langugage which makes it possible to make fairly gross statements about large units of text, and this is a matter on which linguistics has had very little to say.

A linguist might say that there is little of value that he can contribute to information science until that field develops theories commensurate with his own. Over the last forty years, and especially since 1957, linguistic interest in abstract theories and mathematical models has increased tremendously. The extent to which these theories and models have provided new insight into the working of language, or provided keener edges to the tools that linguists can bring to practical problems, is a matter for debate. But many linguists now consider themselves to be scientists of the purest kind and they are often impatient with anything that smacks of engineering or practical applications. This is as true of language teaching and lexicography, which are traditionally thought of as belonging to the field of linguistics, as it is of information science, which is not. Linguists do not talk to one another; it is hardly surprising, therefore, that they do not talk to information scientists. Computational linguists, who are concerned with finding ways of furthering the linguistic enterprise with the help of computers, are second-class citizens in the linguistic community for the same reason. Computation is at best applied science, and at worst engineering. But it presumably is from computational linguistics that information scientists must expect to obtain their most immediately usable tools.

It is far from our purpose in this report to prophesy remarkable advances in linguistics or information science that would come with a more determined effort to exchange problems and results. Our purpose is only to chronicle what has been done. However, we believe that, while there is no drama in the story we have to tell, there is evidence of greater scientific maturity and theoretical self-consciousness in both disciplines and that further exchange agreements can be expected to be at least as fruitful as any in the past.

Chapters 2 and 3 are devoted to an overall view of information retrieval and linguistics respectively, attempting to draw out the main lines of development over the last ten years and to identify the areas in each that have relevance for the other. In Chapter 4, the uses of language in information retrieval are discussed in an attempt to disengage questions that turn on an understanding of how natural languages work from those that are concerned with artificial languages and notations. Chapters 5 and 6 are given over to the two branches of linguistics that are of greatest importance for information science, namely syntax and semantics. These chapters each contain a brief summary of the most recent theoretical developments followed by a discussion of the applications of them that have been made, or that might be made, in information science. Chapter 7 contains a summary of some recent work in fact retrieval and Chapter 8 summarizes the report and attempts to draw some conclusions.

Finally, some points need to be made on the relation between this report and the literature, or more strictly between the report and the work being reported, that is, on what we take the state of the art to be. In the background surveys (Chapters 2 and 3) and also in the final summary (Chapter 8) we shall simply refer to the more obvious literature. In the main chapters we shall naturally attempt to be more comprehensive, and will concentrate on more recent work. We shall not, however, try to describe or even list as many relevant pieces of work as possible in an attempt to be exhaustive. For one thing, the field we are concerned with is sufficiently large to make this a crushing enterprise; for another, we wish to restrict references to transient items like progress reports or in-house documents which are often relatively inaccessible, except where these are the only sources of information for interesting work. Furthermore, we feel that volumes of the *Annual Review of Information Science and Technology* over the last five years function extremely effectively as detailed and exhaustive listings, and there is no need for us to attempt to do the same thing. More positively, we believe that this report will be more useful if we try to pick out and discuss the main points concerning linguistics and information science, supporting these with the most important references where appropriate, or with fairly arbitrarily selected examples in cases where many similar sources are available. For example, faceted classification is now well established, and a large variety of individual faceted schemes have been set up for special purposes. These are well documented, so that, in examining faceted schemes, we will do well to confine ourselves to the main references on principles, and to convenient selected examples.

Our indebtedness to the *Annual Review of Information Science and Technology* (Cuadra, 1966–1970) will be evident throughout. We must also acknowledge a greater debt than is betrayed by individual references in the text to a number of detailed and comprehensive publications, namely, by Cleverdon and his collaborators (Cleverdon *et al.*, 1966); Gardin and his colleagues (Bely *et al.*, 1970; Coyaud, 1966; Coyaud and Siot–Decauville, 1967; Cros *et al.*, 1964; Gardin, 1965); Lancaster (1968a, b); Salton and members of the SMART Project (Salton, 1966–1969, 1968a); Sharp (1965); Stevens (1965); and by the authors of the volumes in the Rutgers series on systems for the intellectual organization of information (Artandi, 1964–1966).

Earlier general surveys by Berul (1965) and Lipetz (1966) should be mentioned, and the *Encyclopedia of Library and Information Science* (Kent and Lancour, 1968–) of course provides a comprehensive, though currently far from complete, survey of all aspects of the field. A thorough review of the computational side of the field is given by Stevens (1970). Some indication of ongoing work in a geographical area not well represented in the *Annual Review* is provided by the survey by Voskobojnik *et al.* (1969) and other papers presented at the 1967 Moscow conference on information retrieval and automatic processing of scientific and technical information (*All-Union Conference*, 1969), by the set of surveys by Kraus (1968a–e), and for the related area of machine translation, Rozencvejg (1968). An overall review of automated retrieval systems is given by *Aspects* (1970a). A discussion and survey of work

on information retrieval languages is given in Šreider *et al.*
(1969a), and the linguistic problems of scientific information are
analyzed in Šreider *et al.* (1969b); on this theoretical side the very
important subject of the nature of information science, or informatics, as a whole is analysed by Mixailov and his colleagues
(Mixailov *et al.*, 1968, 1969b), and other relevant papers are to
be found in Mixailov *et al.* (1969a). A useful survey of this area is
also provided by Foskett (1970).

More specifically, an overview of automatic language processing up to 1966 is supplied by Borko (1967a); automatic extracting
is examined in Wyllys (1967), and automatic indexing has been
surveyed by Batty (1969), Borko (1967b), and most recently,
Salton (1970a). Question answering systems have been reviewed
by Simmons (1965, 1970) and also by Kasher (1966). The current
state of conventional classification is described by Mills (1970).

Finally, some key collections of conference papers should be cited,
namely those of the FID/CR meeting on classification of 1964
(Atherton, 1965), the National Bureau of Standards symposium
on mechanized association methods (Stevens *et al.*, 1965), and the
symposium on relational factors held at the University of Maryland in 1966 (Perreault, 1967a).

2

INFORMATION RETRIEVAL
BACKGROUND

The current state of information retrieval is interesting in some ways, and depressing in some ways. Its character has been determined by two factors, namely, the so-called information explosion, and the advent of computers. The undoubted increase in the rate of publication, creating Mixailov's "Himalayas of libraries" (*All-Union Conference,* 1969) has encouraged an interest in new methods of handling documents, simply because the old ones have become unworkable. In its most obvious form, this problem appears at the level of shelf arrangement. In a small library, books can be crudely grouped by subject on shelves, because seeking and browsing users look about them; if the total number of books is not large, even quite simple groupings will bring relevant books near enough for them to be spotted. With very many more books we cannot rely on so haphazard a plan. Everyone is familiar with the problems which arise when conventional systems burst at the seams because there are too many documents to be properly processed: on the human side we encounter the consistency and communicaton problems of large staffs, while on the system side, the failure comes in classifications which are inadequate because they are too crude or too inflexible.

Computers in Information Retrieval

When gloom about the information explosion was deepening in the 1950s, the arrival of computers seemed like a gift from the gods, at least to some people. The decade 1955–1965 was the honeymoon of mechanized information retrieval research, but it was followed by a fairly serious collapse in those areas in which the use of computers seemed to constitute the most striking innovation, namely sophisticated, fully automatic indexing and searching. The parallel history of machine translation is well known, though the collapse there was much more dramatic, presumably because the scope of the enterprise is much greater; and there has been no follow-up in the use of computers for more limited subtasks, such as occurred in the documentation area.

In general, the enthusiasm for mechanized information retrieval was not shared by traditionally trained librarians. The idea of using a computer for analysis and searching seemed too farfetched, and even now the suggestion that one could form classes of indexing terms automatically by using distributional information is regarded with suspicion. It is significant that most of the original workers in automatic retrieval in this period did not start out from the viewpoint of the librarian; the conventional library wisdom was neglected, and most of the work done was characterized by simplifying assumptions about the use of libraries, and by optimistic beliefs about the capacities of computers as substitutes for human beings.

These attitudes were not wholly unjustified. You have to neglect the conventional wisdom to get new ideas off the ground. Equally, the attempt to approach the problems of document analysis and retrieval in new ways must depend on models of the processes involved, and if these are initially somewhat simple, this is acceptable so long as they are satisfactory in principle. Again, while we may doubt whether computers can replace human beings if the analysis of content involves understanding in any strong sense, it remains an open question whether computers can process documents as effectively for retrieval purposes as human beings, though doubtless by different methods. Bar–Hillel's attacks on the more pretentious and utopian claims of the period were indubitably justified, but we may now have better reasons for thinking that computers can make more positive contributions to information retrieval, within certain limits, than he was prepared to allow (Bar-Hillel, 1960, 1963). Salton's (1968a, 1969a, 1970a) comparisons between manual and automatic keyword extraction are a case in point.

Mechanized Documentation since 1965

The situation has changed substantially in the last five years. Now the traditional librarians are making a comeback, on the one hand because they are beginning to use computers, and on the other because the advocates of new methods recognize that they have something relevant to say about information retrieval. It is true that the conventional librarians are using computers primarily for the most obviously clerical sides of their work—the preparation, maintenance and circulation of basic catalog material—but more ambitious forays into retrieval proper are also being undertaken; the two sides are exemplified by the Marc and Medlars projects, respectively, and Project Intrex is an extremely ambitious attempt to combine the two using a multiaccess computing system (Austin, 1968; Avram, 1968; Avram *et al.,* 1968; Lancaster 1968a, 1969; Overhage and Harman, 1965; Overhage and Reintjes, 1969; Reintjes, 1969). The important point, however, is that computers are being treated here as helpful and modest rather than as alarming and omnipotent.

The original computer people, on the other hand, have become disillusioned with the difficulties of analysis and retrieval, as they have discovered the complexities of real library use. It is noteworthy that many of the contributors to the 1964 Washington Symposium on Statistical Association Methods for Mechanized Documentation (Stevens *et al.*, 1965), which can be regarded as the culmination of the period of enthusiasm for the new approaches to the central problem of document description by statistical techniques, are no longer actively engaged in research in this area. The effort involved in performing serious retrieval experiments has contributed to the marked diminution of enthusiasm. The need to test bright ideas, when combined with a growing awareness of the complexity of a retrieval system, and higher standards of experimentation, brought research workers up against the prospect of long hard labor with a very uncertain outcome. The Cranfield 2 project was not really a large scale one of the kind which is now regarded as mandatory, but it took several years (Cleverdon *et al.*, 1966).

At first sight the situation as a whole might, therefore, be regarded as fairly healthy: the old-style librarians are becoming more modern, while the new-style information scientists are becoming less brash. There is, moreover, little doubt that the introduction of computers, even at the level of routine tasks, forces system and consistency on notoriously unsystematic and inconsistent human beings; at the same time, bringing research workers down from the blue sky to face the very real complications and ill-understood problems of information retrieval must be regarded as an advance. Unfortunately, the situation is not, in our view, a really satisfactory one.

Aspects of Mechanization

As we said earlier, there are two roles that mechanization can play in library work:

1. Mechanization which is confined to purely clerical operations, like the derivation of alternative and subcatalogs from a main file

as part of a project for circulating information about a library's holdings. Much of the work involved in this sort of activity is very tedious, but provided the aims are moderate, and suitable controls are imposed on the inputs, reasonable results can be expected. For example, though elegant approaches to KWIC indexing lead to nasty linguistic difficulties, more limited ones can produce perfectly acceptable and very useful results. It is true that if wholesale mechanization is attempted, the whole is liable to become exceedingly expensive. The Marc Project Report (Avram, 1968) can be taken as an illustration of this kind of work, and some relevant points about storage costs are made by Locke (1970). Clerical mechanization of this sort is often combined with traditional indexing using a subject classification, and in particular the UDC.

2. Mechanization related to the document analysis and retrieval operations of libraries. This is really hybrid or partial mechanization in most cases, since it typically combines the manual analysis of documents and requests with the mechanized execution of searches. Here the computer is used primarily as a device for scanning the document file, or more precisely the file of document descriptions, where the speed and power of the machine makes some elaboration of the process possible, say in the pursuit of subsearches and the ordering of output. There seems to be a trend towards the establishment of library systems of this sort, particularly in specialized fields, which offer both retrospective search and selective dissemination services. We feel that this development should be treated with more reserve than is usual, simply because the main activities of analyzing and characterizing documents and queries are usually done uncritically in a conventional way. These systems as a whole tend to be based on descriptor lists or thesauri but may also involve traditional subject headings or the UDC (Caless and Kirk, 1967; Freeman, 1967, Freeman and Atherton, 1968; Mesnik, 1969; Schneider, 1968). These systems often offer access to documents by a variety of keys, sometimes exploiting several indexing languages, and may operate on an impressively large scale. There is a mass of literature describing systems of this sort; some random examples are the

Euratom system (Rolling, 1966; Rolling and Piette, 1968); Medlars (Austin, 1968; Lancaster, 1968a); the Scandinavian POLYDOC system (Holst, 1970); the Swedish ABACUS system (Tell *et al.*, 1970); the United Kingdom Chemical Information Service System (Kent, 1970); and the variety of systems appearing in *All-Union Conference* (1969), such as those described by Goroxov (1969) and Nadtočij, (1969), and in Kraus (1968a–e). An information retrieval system for chemistry is described in *Aspects* (c. 1970) (see also Ivanova *et al.*, 1969), and automatic indexing for patents by Kravec and Šenderov and their colleagues (Gerasimova *et al.*, 1967; Giršberg and Šenderov, 1970; Kravec *et al.*, 1966; Vasilievskij and Kravec, 1970; and other papers in *Experim.* 1970).

This is not to imply that the traditional modes of analysis and retrieval are wrong. The point is rather that experiments with alternative procedures are usually impracticable in existing libraries, so that the response to the manifest inadequacies takes the form of patching or gradual modification. Again, existing libraries usually have many purposes, so that a form of document description which is adapted to a particular mode of machine searching but is incomprehensible to a physically present user, is unacceptable. Automatic keyword classifications, for example, are often intended to be not merely constructed but used within a wholly mechanized system; so there is no need for the classes to have natural names or be related in any simple way. But if the classification is to be displayed for inspection by uninitiated users, it may have to be substantially edited. Even so, it is depressing to see how little traditional concepts, particularly in the classification area, have been questioned by those concerned with initiating mechanized schemes for new collections.

This problem is well illustrated by the Medlars project (Austin, 1968). Lancaster's evaluation of the National Library of Medicine retrieval system, and the conclusions he draws about the way it works are of great interest, but he approaches the problem from within (Lancaster, 1968a). He is concerned, that is, with how well the Medlars system works, and not with whether another system would do better. There is, of course, nothing objectionable in this; his brief, which was to investigate the Medlars system with particular reference to its failures and possible ways of avoiding these, is clearly stated. In the course of the discussion, however, the fact that the whole project is based on some apparently unexamined assumptions about the need for a controlled indexing vocabulary. becomes apparent.

Key Questions

The two questions which emerge are:

1. Can traditional methods of characterizing and retrieving documents be really effective?
2. Does the use of computers open up new possibilities?

As subsidiary questions it becomes interesting to ask whether the construction of hierarchical subject classifications is a useful approach to the design of indexing languages, or is relevant only in particular situations, and whether the formation of distributionally based word classifications, which is not something free human agents willingly undertake, is useful for a computer based system. These are in fact questions which were asked more than ten years ago, and though, as we shall see, some progress in answering them has perhaps been made, it is still the case that information retrieval systems largely depend on plausible but unexamined assumptions about the purpose and character of indexing.

This is evident to anyone who embarks on research in this area. It soon becomes clear that surprisingly little is known about how information retrieval systems in general work, though individual systems may be very well understood, and that assertions are made about the merits and demerits of different indexing and searching devices, which appear to be general but are in fact severely limited. Thus, as far as the first point goes, there are some reasonably solid generalizations, like that asserting the inverse relation of recall and precision, but they are not very powerful because they are not tied, in a manner useful to the designers of new systems, to specific system devices. Thus, while it is apparent that, on the whole, matches on more descriptive items raise precision, there are restrictions on the choice of the items. The disagreement about the use of syntactic encodements illustrates the second point very well: there are many who believe in the need for syntactic constraints on index descriptions, and it is easy to find examples like "exports from Britain to America" versus "exports from America to Britain" in which the syntax is very effective in rejecting unwanted documents. However, it seems that when the performance of syntactic and nonsyntactic indexing systems as wholes is compared, the differences are not marked, and the syntactic techniques do not produce the expected gains. This result has been obtained independently by Melton (1966), the SMART Project (Salton, 1968a; Salton and Lesk, 1968), and at Western Reserve University (Comparative Systems Laboratory, 1968). Related results for descriptor as opposed to conventional subject systems are reported by Grinina and Sokolova (1970) and by Popova and Jakubson (1969).

In this situation, therefore, it can be maintained that mechanizing current information retrieval procedures is a fairly dangerous undertaking, unless the limitations on the whole are well understood. Clearly, automated KWIC indexing is something which is safe enough, and automating an existing manual system with proved maximally satisfied users is equally unobjectionable. Many of the mechanized projects are, moreover, initially experimental to some extent. Again, setting up a mechanized system because it will be manifestly more efficient or economical than its manual counterpart, or for which a manual counterpart is impracticable, is justifiable even if its foundations are not as solid as they should be. Generally speaking, if the needs a mechanical system are to satisfy are clear, and if there are good grounds for thinking that the proposed system will satisfy them, then there is no base for criticism. But unfortunately one suspects that the needs are often not well defined and, more importantly, that the ability of the proposed system to satisfy them is not established. In these cases mechanization is only a gratuitous coat of icing on a very soggy cake.

At the same time, if we regard the mechanization of a library as an occasion for rethinking its indexing and retrieval procedures, and so condemn the failure to be radical, then we cannot really blame librarians for not taking advantage of the findings of research in information retrieval. In general, research over the last decade has not come up with answers to the fundamental questions that must be asked about the correct approaches to indexing and searching; and the new machine-oriented techniques, like those based on statistical information, have not been sufficiently developed or tested for them to be taken seriously as alternatives to traditional methods. But conventional documentalists can perhaps be accused of not taking more notice of the ideas of research workers and of some of their findings, however tentative or limited they may be. It is, however, worth pointing out that the coordinate indexing revolution which was made possible by the very primitive mechanization inherent in punched cards—as Lancaster (1968b) described it—has been accepted by the trade.

Relevance of Linguistics

In examining the relation between linguistics and information science, we have two rather different, though obviously connected, aspects of the relation to consider. One is the extent to which indexing and retrieval implicitly involve language, and so are concerned with the same problems as linguistics. The other is the extent to which linguistics and information retrieval as currently practiced made explicit reference to one another. On the one hand we consider the extent to which a librarian is concerned with the meaning or message of a document, and on the other, we look at the attempts which have been made by documentalists to apply specific techniques, like those of generative grammar. The recent history of research in information retrieval is of interest, however, not only because some of this research has been concerned either with examining implicit linguistic problems, or with proposing explicit linguistic solutions to them; it is also of interest because the difficulties which have been encountered in designing and evaluating retrieval experiments show that identifying the real characteristics of a particular indexing or searching device is a major problem. In making comments on the current state of the art, therefore, we must bear this point in mind.

Experiments in Information Retrieval

In general, over the last ten years, experimental work in information retrieval has been characterized by a greater awareness of the complexities of retrieval systems as wholes, of the problems of measuring performance, and of the need for well-designed experiments and statistically reliable results. See, for example, Cleverdon *et al.* (1966), Comparative Systems Laboratory (1968), Fairthorne (1965), Giuliano and Jones (1966), Goffman and Newill (1966), Lancaster (1968b), Lancaster and Climenson (1968), O'Connor (1964), Rees (1965, 1967), Saracevic (1967), Saracevic and Rees (1967), Salton (1968a, 1970c), Salton and Lesk (1968), and Sokolov *et al.* (1969). Many experiments have been neither well enough controlled, nor on a large enough scale, to support valid conclusions about the devices which were nominally being compared. From the purely organizational point of view, there are two major difficulties facing the research worker. One is the very large number of factors entering into a system, which make it extremely difficult to isolate a given factor for study and very tedious to carry out experiments involving a variety of values for several variables. The second is the problem of scale. Some areas, like document clustering, necessitate fairly large collections and, more generally, comparisons between devices should be carried out for several realistically large collections. In addition, the behavior of some variables cannot be properly studied unless a substantial range of alternative values is examined. Unfortunately this implies not merely a large amount of work in the actual conduct of the tests, but a major effort in the supporting compilation of relevance judgements which are required to evaluate performance, even if a sampling rather than exhaustive procedure is used. This point is well illustrated by the approaches using samples or extrapolating from them, adopted by Lancaster in evaluating the Medlars project (Lancaster, 1968a), by Giuliano and Jones (1966), and by Vaswani and Cameron (1970) in dealing with 10,000 and 12,000 abstracts respectively. Typically, if a variety of tests are carried out, the union of the relevant output from them all is taken as the relevance set, as in the Comparative Systems Laboratory (1968) experiments.

The more important point, however, is that retrieval experiments rely on relevance judgements, and the problem of relevance is, of course, the central one of information retrieval. There is a large literature on this whole topic, distinguishing forms of relevance and investigating the reliability of relevance judgements, reasons for variation in them, the connection between relevance judgements and document texts, and so on. See, for example, Barhydt (1967), Comparative Systems Laboratory (1968), Cuadra and Katter (1967a, b), Cuadra *et al.* (1967), Gifford and Baumanis (1969), Hillman (1964a, 1964b), Kuznecov (1970), Lesk and Salton (1969), O'Connor (1967, 1968a, b, 1969), and Rees and Saracevic (1969). It must be accepted that relevance is necessarily subjective, that is ultimately inaccessible, but for experimental purposes sets of relevance judgements can be obtained which are sufficiently solid to be used as a base for index language testing. Naturally, the hypothesis which is being tested in any information retrieval system is that certain specified document characteristics are correlated with relevance; thus, if we partition a collection using, say, extracted keywords, we assume that the clusters of documents we obtain by looking for common keywords are also clusters of documents relevant to different requests or request sets.

Most research projects have relied on extensive simplifications in setting up test systems as wholes, to avoid getting completely swamped. They have typically concentrated on one type of collection, or one type of user, or one type of query, and they normally disregard the question of costs which are of interest to those evaluating existing systems or proposing operational ones. These self-imposed limitations are, of course, not necessarily objectionable in themselves. Conclusions drawn from experiments with one form of request may be valid for that form of request, and may therefore be acceptable as long as their limitations are recognized; and a disregard for costs may be reasonable because the optimal organization of a system designed purely for test purposes may well be quite different from that appropriate to its regular use. Even so, the amount of effort involved in anything more than trivial experiments is very large. There are, for instance, many aspects of a retrieval system as a whole which have not been investigated by the SMART Project, and there are many options within the area which has been studied which have not been examined. Yet, as Salton (1968a) points out, hundreds of experiments have been carried out under the project.

The more important evaluation experiments over the last twenty years have been surveyed by Cleverdon (1970), following an earlier review by Brownson (1965), and recent work is covered by the relevant chapters of the *Annual Review.* Some of the more serious experiments, primarily concerned with index languages, but all suffering from limitations of some kind, are described in Aitchison *et al.* (1970), Altmann (1966, 1967), Altmann and Reissler (1969), Blagden (1966), Cagan (1970), Cleverdon (1967), Cleverdon *et al.* (1966), Comparative Systems Laboratory (1968), Fangmeyer and Lustig (1969, 1970), Lancaster (1968a, 1969), papers by workers at Arthur D. Little (Giuliano and Jones, 1966; Jones *et al.*, 1967, 1968), Montague (1965), O'Connor (1967, 1968a, b, 1969), Shaw and Rothman (1968), SMART Project publications (Lesk, 1968; Salton, 1966–1969, 1968a, 1969a; Salton and Lesk, 1968), Sparck Jones (1971), Sparck Jones and Jackson (1970), Vaswani (1969), and Vaswani and Cameron (1970). Also of interest are Grinina and Sokolova (1970), Ivanova *et al.* (1969), Lazarescu (1969), Popova and Jakubson (1969), Šemakin (1969), Sokolov (1965), Sokolov *et al.* (1969), Tomasik-Bek (1970), and Vaxabox *et al.* (1969).

The main general points which emerge from this and the related literature are as follows.

Experimental Methodology

It seems that the factors involved in an information retrieval system, and the relations between them, are being sorted out. Some relevant discussions appear in Cleverdon *et al.* (1966), Comparative Systems Laboratory (1968), Fairthorne (1967), Giuliano and Jones (1966), Lancaster (1968b), Lesk (1968), Martyn and Vickery (1970), Salton (1968a), Salton and Lesk (1968), Saracevic and Rees (1967), Vickery (1968), and Wall (1967). At the same time, research workers tend to underestimate the degree of refinement in distinguishing variables and of control in varying them that is needed for reliable experiments. For instance, when examining keyword classification techniques, it is necessary to distinguish not merely different cluster definitions but any changes in subordinate threshold parameters as well. In principle all the combinations of all the values of all the variables should be tested, but this may well be impracticable. At least a subset of tests should be chosen from which reliable inferences can be drawn about the results of tests which were not carried out.

It is very difficult to draw useful conclusions, especially at the detailed level, from the published results of some projects, because the differences in retrieval performance cannot be attributed to particular factors. Of course broad conclusions based on different projects can often be arrived at, and individual experiments may be of interest in their own right. It is only when we seek to analyze results and compare explanations for them at the detailed level, in order to determine how particular devices work and why they work in this way, that we get into difficulties because we are unable to be systematic. For instance, we may observe that two different projects have produced different results concerning the performance, say, of automatic keyword classes as opposed to unclassified terms, and we may be fully informed about the respective characteristics of the classifications involved. But we may be unable to attribute the differences in performance to specific differences in the classifications, if these appear in more than one point. For example, we may find that alternative methods of forming both the underlying keyword similarity matrix, and deriving classes from this, are involved; and in this case we may not be able to determine which is responsible for the performance variation. The same considerations apply to sets of experiments carried out by individual projects, but they are more obtrusive in comparisons between projects. This point is also important because in some areas, like keyword classification, it seems that apparently trivial changes in the values of individual variables seem to lead to large changes in retrieval performance.

Performance Measures

There is still great uncertainty about performance measures and subsidiary related questions like the correct method of treating the information on which they are based, as in averaging over sets of requests and so on. This is a fraught subject, as is apparent from the discussions in, and different measures adopted by, among others: Brookes (1968a), Černjavskij and Laxuti (1970), Cleverdon *et al.* (1966), Comparative Systems Laboratory (1968), Cooper (1968), Fairthorne (1964), Giuliano and Jones (1966), Goffman and Newill (1966), Jordan (1968), Kagalovič (1969), Keen (1967a), King and Bryant (1970), Königova (1968), Kurbakov and Boldov (1968), Lancaster (1968a), Meetham (1969), Pollock (1968), Robertson (1969a, b), Romerio and Cavara (1968), Rothenburg

(1969), Salton (1968a), Sokolov *et al.* (1969), Swets (1969), and Vaswani and Cameron (1970).

Part of the difficulty stems from what is being measured, that is, what components, and behavioral aspects, of the system should be taken into account: should we, for instance, attempt to allow for the nature of a collection as well as its size, and are we interested in the cost of indexing a document as well as the form of the indexing? We must decide which system variables to consider and, broadly, whether we are interested in effectiveness or efficiency. But there are also more formal problems about characterizing and relating the selected information in a mathematically acceptable, yet nontrivial, way. (Getting a measure off the ground presupposes a working interpretation of relevance, but this of course itself presents thorny problems, particularly where operating retrieval systems are concerned.) In addition there is some controversy about the diagnostic purpose of a system performance measure, usually taking the form of arguments about the propriety of single numbers as overall measures of system merit.

This is not the place for a detailed examination of this question but its implications for the discussion of our main topic should be noted, since the variety of approaches to the measurement of performance adopted by different projects makes it very difficult to relate the conclusions they draw about the relative merits of indexing and search procedures, even if these are of the same or similar types. This difficulty is usually compounded by other variations. For example, if two projects are investigating keyword classifications, they may use their classifications in similar ways to characterize documents and requests, but carry out searches differently, say to produce outputs ordered by ranking and coordination levels. It may therefore be very difficult to decide whether any differences in the results obtained by projects investigating a particular form of indexing or search device are due to differences in the device which is primarily being investigated, differences in such items as the test collections which, though not central, are relevant, or differences in such items as averaging or measuring procedures, which are strictly irrelevant. Further difficulties may arise over such things as different search procedures, when these are not primary but are determined by the form of the indexing language, so that comparisons confined to differences in the indexing language alone could not be set up. However, what may be described as gratuitous differences are especially trying when different projects are actually using the same test collection. It must also be remembered that even when the same **performance** measures are used, and this is quite common, given the persistent popularity of recall and precision, the results may be based on different averaging processes and so not be strictly comparable.

In consequence, it is necessary for the reviewer to consider individual projects in detail and in isolation, and to exercise caution in drawing comparative conclusions. We can say, for example, that both Cleverdon (Cleverdon *et al.*, 1966) and Salton (Salton and Lesk, 1968) find that the use of syntactic information in descriptions, in the form of complex terms, is not particularly profitable, and that they each give the same general reason for their result. But in investigating their experiments in more detail, we must be very careful about more refined comparisons and making inferences for them.

Current State of Experiments

When all these points are taken into account it will be evident that the more specific comments on work relating to linguistic aspects of information retrieval should be seen against the background of an insufficiently imaginative approach to retrieval on the part of conventionally based documentalists, and of an over-simple attitude to experiments on the part of computationally minded research workers. The normal assumptions about indexing and searching have not been critically examined on the grounds that they are confirmed by experience, while the newer ideas have not been adequately tested on the grounds that they are intellectually convincing. Further, for these and other reasons, we are faced with the fact that comparatively few experiments have been done, given the range of questions for investigation, and that those which have been published are often vitiated by their incompleteness and by their idiosyncracy. The situation is improving in the sense that the need for well-designed experiments is becoming more accepted, but serious system comparisons are still depressingly few and far between.

It must be emphasized that these remarks apply to basic research. In some sense the amount of information retrieval research which is being done is very large, but our point is that a relatively small proportion of it is basic research. This is obviously relevant to our main concern. The character of index descriptions and the form of the language used in them are the crucial topics of documentation, and they have to do with the extremely fundamental subjects of language and information in general. Research on these aspects of our subject, if properly conceived, is therefore basic research, both in terms of documentation itself, and in terms of the wider field of information science. From this point of view it is evident that many investigations in the documentation area do not count as basic research at all; tests on an SDI system, for example, can be characterized as applied research; studies of given indexing languages can perhaps be described as advanced research, since the languages themselves presuppose certain models of information organization and description, though such studies may also be used as vehicles for approaching the underlying issue of basic research, namely what should an indexing language be like.

It is possible that to achieve successful results in implementing the relatively limited form of information apparatus represented by a document retrieval system, we do not need a full understanding of the way language and information processing in general work. If we do, we clearly have a very daunting prospect. In a sense we can describe the present report as an attempt to throw some light on this question indirectly. Nevertheless, our general ignorance of the way document retrieval systems really function means that we cannot be sure of what the limits are within which we should work, and consequently of how we should work within them.

Information Retrieval Models

The distressing absence of productive formal models of information retrieval which can be used to tackle our research problems is only too evident. Even if any proposed models turned out to be inadequate or wrong, their existence might make it easier to organize our experiments. But unfortunately it seems that such general models as have been put forward are too obviously merely descriptive, or involve too many simplifying assumptions, to be really helpful. Hillman's work in this area perhaps represents one of the most successful attempts to develop a general theory (Hillman, 1965, 1968; Hillman and Kasarda, 1969). Some suggestive formal models of particular features of retrieval systems have been put forward, for example in connection with searching, by Goffman (1965, 1968), and file organization, by Leimkuhler (1967), but more usually as supports for performance measures, as by King and Bryant (1970) and Rothenburg (1969). Those features of a system which have a Zipf distribution may be more rigorously characterized (Brookes, 1968b, 1969; Fairthorne, 1969; Kozačkov, 1969b; Leimkuhler, 1968), but it is not always obvious how such a distribution, say of index terms, is to be profitably exploited. For some suggestions, however, see Sparck Jones and Barber (1971), Toma (1969), and Vaxabov (1970b).

Nevertheless, it is still not clear, for instance, how classificatory models can be set up which do not simply characterize the properties of a given set of documents, terms, requests, retrieval and relevance classes in a relatively general manner, but enable one to construct classifications which will have desired properties. Similarly, in considering Salton's (1968a) discussion of retrieval in terms of matrix operations, we can distinguish a useful way of characterizing some specific operations, which is what he provides us with, from a model which would enable us to develop wholly new and fruitful ways of thinking about the indexing and retrieval problem. Generally speaking, the models which have so far been proposed can be characterized by analogy with the Katz and Fodor (1963) model of semantic sentence analysis: this can be presented as an argument to the effect that, since discourse analysis relies on a conceptual classification, if you have the right classification you can do discourse analysis. This does not, however, mean that good notations are not helpful.

Recent Developments

Finally, two recent developments deserve comment, both of which might be regarded as somewhat alarming. One is the growing emphasis on costs in contexts in which we have too little information for proper estimates. There are many aspects of documentation systems for which costing is both desirable and proper; but the attempt to evaluate, say, index languages on a cost basis is in a sense premature, because we still know so little about their detailed effectiveness. Of course, if a given list of alternatives is taken to represent a closed area of choice, relative costing is legitimate. But though it seems to be true that greater care in document processing is not automatically accompanied by performance improvements, we are not well enough informed about the best ways of doing things simply. Or at least, one can regard the success of KWIC indexes, in relation to their extreme simplicity, as constituting a challenge. Are there other, more sophisticated but still comparatively simple ways of describing and looking for documents which give disproportionately good performance returns in such a handsome way, though on a consistently higher level? The use of citations is an interesting approach of this kind (see Chapter 6), but there may be others.

The other development is a consequence of the introduction of multiaccess on-line computing. This has suggested both iterative search methods of relatively simple kinds, and more elaborate modes of user–library interaction. These alternatives are discussed, for instance, by Salton (1968b, 1969b), the former being represented by the "relevance feedback" techniques studied by the SMART Project, where the user's intervention is confined to relevance judgments about the output of a search and requests are automatically modified for further searching on the basis of this information (Brauen, 1969; Ide, 1969); in the latter the user exploits a variety of aids which are displayed by the computer, to formulate and control his search strategy. Borko and Burnaugh's BOLD system at SDC and Massachusetts Institute of Technology's Project TIP represent early work on this approach, which is currently being pursued on a large though not yet effective scale by Project Intrex (Borko, 1968; Burnaugh, 1967; Keenan and Terry, 1968; Kessler, 1965b, 1967; Mathews, 1967; Overhage and Harman, 1965, Overhage and Reintjes, 1969; and Reintjes *et al.*, 1969). Related projects are described by Curtice and Jones (1969), Hillman (1968), Hillman and Kasarda (1969), and Parker (1968). Question answering or fact retrieval systems naturally exploit on-line facilities. This will be discussed further in Chapter 7. In addition such facilities readily lend themselves to indexing and editing, including index language maintenance (Bennett, 1969).

It must, however, be recognized that on-line retrieval, though a fashionable idea, has not been taken up to the extent that its proponents originally suggested, presumably because of its expense, which, in turn, is associated mainly with the file problem presented by real collections. From a purely practical point of view, the more limited approaches may be more successful, for a successful system may not necessitate actual on-line facilities, but only a good off-line one. In any case, one important point about these suggestions must be remembered. In general they have been welcomed because they have seemed to provide an escape from the intractable problems of obtaining a satisfactory retrieval performance in noninteractive, simpleminded, straight-from-cold searching. This is bound to fail in those cases where requests are radically ill formed, and it unfortunately does not provide good enough results even for the average sensible request. Referring to users who can presumably be stimulated into producing really well-formulated requests which are tailored both to their needs and to the collection at hand, looks like a way out of what has come to seem more of an impasse. But the whole process still implies document descriptions of some sort and all the apparatus of indexing languages and search algorithms; and while the keen user may be able to remedy some of the inevitable defects of these system components, there is clearly going to be a limit to how far he can go in kicking a thoroughly bad, or even only mediocre, system into giving him the goods.

Present State of Play

The reader might conclude from the foregoing that our view of the current state of information retrieval proper is a somewhat negative one. But this would be a mistake: for while those working in the field may sometimes feel, from better acquaintance with them, that the really fundamental problems are highly intractable, considerable progress has been made in sorting out questions to be investigated, in clarifying the overall picture of an information system, in developing research techniques, and in providing a variety of suggestions or results for discussion. It may be that the optimism based on the sensation of a better understanding of the issues involved is unjustified, because it is the result simply of replacing old terminologies by modern ones. But it also appears that more positive gains have followed the introduction of computers, since they have suggested new approaches to the basic problems, and this is of value in itself.

In conclusion, therefore, it will be useful to list some of the points that have become evident over the last decade, and which are relevant in some way to our main concern. The following is an indicative partial list:

1. Indexing based on abstracts may be as good as indexing based on full documents, but indexing based on titles is very inferior.

2. Greater indexing effort is not necessarily associated with better performance.

3. Automatic keyword extraction is both feasible and competitive with manual.

4. Documents may be classified by requests as well as index descriptions, that is postcoordination may be as valuable as precoordination.

5. The indexing language used may not be a major influence on system performance.

6. The statistical properties of an indexing vocabulary are important, especially in relation to specificity and exhaustivity.

7. Index term classifications may be precision or recall devices.

8. Automatic keyword classification is feasible and may be competitive with manual.

9. It is doubtful whether we can escape the inverse relation between recall and precision, or analogous features of performance.

10. Mechanized systems may be as effective as manual ones.

3

LINGUISTICS

In this chapter we give a brief characterization of the field of linguistics, attempting to show what the main questions are that provide its motivating force. There are many important subfields of linguistics, such as historical linguistics and sociolinguistics, that receive no treatment here because of their slight relevance to the problems of information science. The major stress will be on the generative, or transformational, view of linguistics, not because we believe that it is the only one worthy of attention, but because its insistence on strict formalisms makes it more apt than most other contenders for computer applications. For a more complete introduction, see Bach (1964), Bloomfield (1933), Dinneen (1967), Gleason (1961), Hockett (1958), Jacobs and Rosenbaum (1968), Lyons (1968), and Robins (1964).

Theoretical Linguistics

Linguistics is the scientific study of language. It is concerned with such questions as: what characteristics, if any, distinguish human language from other actual or imaginable languages, and what are the mechanisms that make it possible for human beings to communicate a presumably infinite variety of ideas using only the finite set of words provided in the dictionary of their language? Some linguists deny that the first question, that of so-called linguistic universals, is a real question. They claim that human languages have no distinguishing characteristics, but that they are chosen essentially at random from the total set of imaginable languages. For the members of the school of transformational, or generative, linguistics, on the other hand, the search for linguistic universals is the primary matter of concern. As to the second question, there are linguists who hold that their subject can, and if it is to maintain a proper scientific objectivity must, eschew all reference to the notion of meaning. However, the number of these linguists is rapidly diminishing and the prevalent view is now that meaning is an essential part of the very notion of language, and the claim that one can study any part of language in isolation from meaning is incoherent.

For one reason or another, almost all linguists are prepared to accept on behalf of their discipline the responsibility of providing a finite, and preferably succinct, account of the infinite variety of sentences that make up a language, giving rules for distinguishing sentences from other sequences of words, sounds, or letters which are not part of the language. In other words, they are concerned with the grammars of languages. As we have said, most linguists agree that a grammar should not only provide a means for distinguishing sentences from nonsentences, but that it should also provide a description of each sentence that is somehow revealing about what the sentence means. Since every ordinary language contains an effectively infinite number of sentences, we must assume that people associate them with the proper meanings by dissecting them into parts, each of which is drawn from a finite repertory, and by using the arrangement of these parts in the sentence to dictate operations that yield the meaning of the sentence as a whole. An adequate grammar of the language must show what the parts of a sentence are and must classify the kinds of relations that can be constructed by these parts so as to influence the meaning of the whole in one way or another. This is the primary purpose of grammar.

Natural languages are notorious for the extent to which they admit ambiguities of all kinds. Theories of grammar differ in the amount of ambiguity they attempt to account for and in the extent of the responsibility that they assume for accounting for it. However, the notion of ambiguity arises naturally in almost every theory of grammar, not to mention semantics, because it will almost invariably happen that there are sentences whose presence in the language is accounted for in the grammar in more than one way so that there will be typically more than one way of dividing them into meaningful parts, or more than one set of relations that the parts enter into. Consider, for example, the sentence

He saw that gas can explode.

This can mean either that he observed the explosion of a gas can or that he perceived that it was possible for gas to explode. In the first case, the word "gas" functions as an adjective modifying the noun "can." In the second case, "can" is an auxiliary, or modal verb which goes together with the infinitive "explode." The first sentence has the same grammatical structure as

He saw that gas bottle explode

whereas the second sentence is analogous to

He saw that gas may explode.

When two or more sentences with different structures happen to fall together in this way, the result is said to be grammatically ambiguous.

While the grammatical analysis of a sentence may frequently reveal ambiguities in the sentence as a whole, it is equally important in reducing the number of interpretations of individual parts of the sentence. In

He saw that gas may explode

the word "saw" can only be interpreted as a verb, whereas in the sentence

He cut the log with a saw

it can only be interpreted as a noun.

Views of Grammar

Theoretical linguists, the linguistic scientists par excellence, are concerned more with the form that the grammar of a language should take than with producing grammars of actual languages. American linguists, and particularly those of the school of generative grammar founded by Chomsky, are concerned with formalism to an extent unprecedented in the history of language study. For them, a grammar is a calculus whose form is dictated by the same kind of strict rules as apply to algebra or symbolic logic. The reason for this insistence on formalism is twofold: first, it is claimed that the true value of an informal acount of how language works can never be properly assessed because it will always be prey to hidden circularities. This is because the description employs the same linguistic devices that it purports to describe. Only by adhering to a strict formalism can a grammar be tested in a completely mechanical way against sentences that speakers of the language are actually observed to use. Secondly, if the formalism is sufficiently restricted, it is sometimes possible to show mathematically that there could be a language whose grammar it would be utterly unable to accommodate. If a formalism could be found that would accommodate the grammars of all natural languages but which would demonstrably not accommodate the grammars of a large class of theoretically imaginable languages, then a very significant claim would have been made about the nature of human language, that is, about linguistic universals.

Other linguists are less concerned about the question of exactly what form a grammar should take. To be sure, grammars written by the members of one school will show a family resemblance. But these linguists are more concerned with making detailed statements about particular languages, claiming that, with no more goodwill than it is normally reasonable to expect, it will be clear what these statements mean and there will be no serious difficulty in judging how well they conform to actual data. If these linguists are interested in universals at all, then they expect them to emerge after the fact. In other words, they expect linguistic universals to be perceptible only by examining fairly complete grammars of a large number of languages.

A grammar intended to show the relationship between an infinite set of possible meanings and an infinite set of possible sentences can be based on a number of alternative strategies. It could be what Hockett (1961) has called a grammar for the hearer, which shows how to obtain the meaning of any given sentence. The grammar may contain a separate component to indicate whether the string of words presented to it is in fact a sentence, or it may reject a proposed sentence only when it discovers that the process of obtaining a meaning for it cannot be carried through successfully. Another strategy is adopted in a grammar for the speaker. This accepts meanings as input and provides rules for obtaining sentences that express them. Yet another strategy is that used in transformational grammar. The grammar is a set of rules by which pairs consisting of a sentence and a corresponding meaning can be generated. The sentences that make up the language are those that occur in at least one generable pair, and a sentence has as many meanings as there are generable pairs to which it belongs. It is important to realize that a grammar of one of these kinds is, in general, not automatically convertible into a grammar of one of the other kinds. It is perhaps unfortunate for the practical applications we are considering here that those linguists for whom the exact form of the grammar is most important should have chosen to concentrate neither on grammars for the hearer nor grammars for the speaker. A large amount of the efforts expended on computational linguistics has gone to the development of production and recognition devices which, though they must necessarily employ other formalisms, profit from the insight of generative grammarians.

Components of Grammars

So far, we have concentrated on that part of linguistics that is now usually referred to as syntax. Some linguists use the word "grammar" interchangeably with "syntax," but more modern usage subsumes syntax, phonology, semantics, and possibly morphology, under the heading of grammar. Phonology is the study of sound systems from a linguistic point of view. By saying that the study is from a linguistic point of view, we mean simply that it is concerned less with acoustics and the positions taken up by various parts of the mouth in the course of speech than the ways in which speakers themselves tend to classify sounds. The acoustic properties of languages are studied in acoustic phonetics and the use of the mouth in articulatory phonetics, both of which are usually regarded as outside linguistics. Whereas phoneticians, of one kind or another, use categories like frequency, wave form, harmonic composition, muscle tension, shape of the oral cavity, and the like, phonologists talk in terms of vowels, voiced and unvoiced consonants, syllables, stress, and so on. In any case, none of these fields will have any application to the problems of documentation until attempts to build machines that can produce and recognize speech have progressed much further. At present, speech production by machine is possible but uneconomic; speech recognition is not foreseeable at all.

Morphology is the study of word formation. The fact that the final "-y" of "entry" is changed to "-ie" in the plural form "entries" is a fact about English morphology.* Languages differ greatly in the complexity of the morphological processes they employ. It is

---

*Strictly speaking, it is a fact about English *orthography*. Linguists usually base their distinctions on the spoken rather than the written form of the language.

usual to distinguish between inflectional morphology, which is concerned with the changes that large classes of words, such as nouns, adjectives and verbs, undergo when they are used in sentences, and derivational morphology which refers to the ways in which new words, possibly with new meanings, are derived from old ones. The change of the final "-y" in the plural form of "entries" is a fact of inflectional morphology; the fact that there is usually a noun ending in "-tion" corresponding to every English verb ending in "-ate" is a fact about derivational morphology. Thus, "inflation" corresponds to "inflate."

Languages differ radically in the complexity of the morphological processes they employ. Morphology is relatively simple in English and most other Indo-European languages, which is not to say that the inflectional morphology of Russian and Latin is not more complex than that of English and French. The inflectional morphology of Hungarian, Turkish, and Eskimo is considerably more complex than that of Indo-European languages. In Japanese, it is considerably simpler, and in Chinese and Vietnamese, it is nonexistent. In English, most of the inflections are suffixes; in Russian, there is a large number of prefixes and some languages, such as Arabic, can introduce so-called infixes inside the word. In some languages, like Turkish and Eskimo, a single word can have more than one inflection attached to it at once, whereas that does not happen in English. In some languages like Hungarian the form of a word may change somewhat when certain kinds of inflection are added. This occasionally happens in English and the word "entries" is a case in point. The introduction of umlauts in German is another example. Some languages are rich in derivational morphology, whereas others, like Chinese, have virtually none. German is famous for the way in which it allows the creation of words like *Lebensversicherungsgesellschaftsangestellter* ('life insurance company employee').

Morphology is clearly important in almost any application of computational linguistics. A computer program that is to process material in a natural language must first identify the words in the material by looking them up in a dictionary. If the language has little or no morphology, then it is at least thinkable to provide a dictionary which contains the inflectional variants of all words, though this may more than double the size of the dictionary. If the same solution were adopted for a language like Russian, Finnish, or Arabic, the dictionary would be expanded by an even greater factor, say ten or twenty. For a language like German where compound nonce words are common, it is hardly thinkable to provide a dictionary entry for each.

In recent years, fairly general solutions have been proposed to the problem of morphological analysis which are effective for most languages (see Chapin and Norton, 1968; Kay and Martins, 1970). Almost all languages have morphologically exceptional words like "manly" which looks as though it should be an adverb formed from the adjective "man," or "scissors" which, in some dialects at least, is singular. These are taken care of by looking words up in a list of such exceptions before any attempt is made at morphological decomposition. Morphological ambiguities are relatively rare and they can usually be resolved in later processes. However they are commoner in some languages than in others. A rare example in English occurs in the phrase "an untieable knot" which is presumably either a knot which cannot be tied, or a knot which cannot be untied.

The other major area of linguistics which concerns us is semantics—the study of meaning and reference. This is a topic to which a later section will be devoted. We shall see that semantics has recently become a major center of interest for linguists of all schools. We shall see that there is contention between those who hold that it is right to approach meaning before anything else in linguistics because meaning is, in a very obvious sense, at the heart of the matter, and those who believe that it can only be tackled coherently when other relatively simple matters are fairly well under control. Within the latter camp there is contention between those who regard semantics as a simple extension of syntax and those who think of it as a separate problem with its own categories and methods.

Computational Linguistics

The term "computational linguistics" has been coined to refer to those linguistic activities in which a computer plays a central role (see Hays, 1967). These fall under three main headings:

1. *Grammar testing* (see Friedman, 1969; Gross, 1968; Londe and Schoene, 1968).   It has come to be realized that a modern formal grammar is far too complicated for a person to be able to decide at all easily whether it assigns to sentences just the structures that the linguist intended, whether it covers all the sentences it was meant to cover, and whether it accepts as sentences some strings of words that it ought to have excluded. Programmers have learned by bitter experience that a program of even very modest complexity can only be made to operate correctly by having it actually applied by a computer, correcting it, running it again, and so on, sometimes for many cycles. The grammatical formalisms proposed for the description of natural languages are, in some ways, fundamentally more complex than programming languages, because the processes that must be carried out to certify them are nondeterministic. In other words, whereas an instruction in a programming language causes some determinate operation to take place, a rule in the grammar of a natural language is frequently designated as optional so that it is thenceforward necessary to consider two cases, the one in which it is applied, and the one in which it is not applied. Furthermore, a given rule, whether it is optional or obligatory, may be applicable in the current situation in more than one way, and the effects of each of these must be considered individually. When this nondeterminism is put together with the fact that grammatical formalisms are, in general, very rich in expressive power, the need for automatic devices for verifying the accuracy and coverage of grammars becomes abundantly clear. These devices take the form of generators, which follow the rules in a given grammar to produce sample sentences more or less at random, and parsers, which accept and reject sentences offered to them, assigning struc-

tures to the accepted strings, in accordance with the rules of a grammar.

2. *Modeling.*   Under this head belong computer programs that are intended to simulate some or all aspects of human linguistic behavior. This work is based on the belief that something so complex as the human linguistic faculty is unlikely to be reproducible in a machine without also reproducing some of the detailed mechanisms and constraints that are built into human beings. Suppose that a machine could be built which understood English perfectly, that remembered what it was told about as well as human beings do, that could respond to questions, and so forth. Suppose, in other words, that it was able to demonstrate reasonable command of human linguistic competence. There would be no necessary connection between the inner structure of the machine and the way humans operate, but the prima facie case for such a connection would be strong and compelling. Most models of this kind that have actually been proposed or are being worked upon make use of a formal grammar of one kind or another and of sentence-generation and parsing techniques. To this extent, they belong to the same field of endeavor as grammar testing.

3. *Practical systems.*   The earliest work in computational linguistics was aimed at the production of computer programs to translate text from one natural language into another. This is still a very important, but by no means the only, application of techniques developed by computational linguists. We just postulated a machine that would be designed to emulate human linguistic performance. Such a machine would have to be capable not only of analyzing the grammatical structures of sentences, storing some representation of their meaning and producing grammatically acceptable output sentences, but it would also have to be programmed to forget the kinds of things that humans forget about as often as they forget them and to recall some of them later under different circumstances. Left to itself, the computer store retains what is put into it, perpetually, and in complete detail. Early versions of such a machine, while they were still far from imitating human beings

at all convincingly, might therefore be used as convenient filing devices. They could be given information in a natural language, or in a reasonably comfortable subset of one, and caused to respond in the same language to questions about what they had been told. Such so-called question-answering systems have, in recent years, become a major research interest of computational linguists. Once again, it is clear that such systems require, among other things, the ability to perform certain kinds of linguistic analysis.

ALPAC Findings

In April 1964, the National Academy of Sciences of the United States established the Automatic Language Processing Advisory Committee (ALPAC) under the chairmanship of John R. Pierce to advise certain agencies of the federal government on the current state of computational linguistics, mechanical translation, and other related fields which had been, and might expect to continue to be, supported largely by these agencies. The findings of this committee have become widely known. There was no way to tell whether it would ever be possible to construct computer programs that could produce translations in technical or everyday language that would be comparable in quality to those made by a good human translator. The twenty million dollars that the federal government was conservatively estimated to have spent had certainly not resulted in such a system and, given the current state of knowledge, it would be less than honest to undertake to construct a usable, fully automatic translation system in the foreseeable future. What was required was a great deal more fundamental research on all aspects of linguistics and computational linguistics. The committee looked more favorably on the possibility of practical language-processing systems, whether for translation or other purposes, constructed with more modest aims in view. These might include machine aids for the technical translator, computer editing programs, and the like.

Since 1964, a considerable amount of worthwhile work has been done in linguistics and computational linguistics, but, in our view, a great deal more needs to be done before the situation described by the Automatic Language Processing Advisory Committee will have been changed in any essential way. It is as clear today as it was then that computer programs that can respond in sophisticated ways to ordinary textual material are a long way off, and a great deal of basic research has still to be done before we shall be able to say with any confidence even that the construction of such programs is theoretically feasible.

However, there has been one change of major importance which opens the way to the construction of various kinds of semiautomatic language processors that might be of immediate practical use. A great many devices now exist for enabling the human being to communicate directly with a computer, and programming techniques have been devised so that large numbers of people can be connected to the same computer in such a way as to give each of them the impression that he has the machine's undivided attention. This means that we are now in a much better position to arrange for men and machines to collaborate smoothly on a single job. The detailed work of carrying out a linguistic analysis can be taken on by the machine which works quickly and accurately and is not easily overtaken by boredom. But, when ambiguities and like difficulties arise, the machine can appeal to its human partner for help and advice. The results of the analysis can, when necessary, be checked by the human member of the team before the machine engages on the next step. In this way, the human translator, for example, can be relieved of the necessity of making frequent searches in large technical dictionaries and the user of an automatic question-answering system can verify that his questions have been properly understood before the search for an answer is undertaken. In short, interactive computer systems may be such as to compensate sufficiently for the ambiguities and inaccuracies about which science has so far found nothing to say and which render fully automatic systems infeasible.

Contributions to Information Science

We are now in a position to consider the kinds of contribution that linguists, and especially computational linguists, can be expected to make to information science both in the short and the long term. They can be collected under five headings as follows:

1. *Naturalness.*   Documents are in natural languages and the person seeking information from a document collection will almost always find it easiest to put his request in the language of everyday discourse. There is therefore a clear case for making ordinary language the initial means of communication with any documentation system. But, unless a great number of arbitrary restrictions are put on the ways in which things can be said, so that the language is no longer ordinary language, but an artificial language whose sentences happen to coincide with those of an ordinary language, the sentences must undergo a considerable amount of linguistic processing before they can be used in logical operations. In particular, there must be ways of reducing to some relatively well-disciplined form the great variety of ways in which a given thing can be said in everyday language.

2. *Ambiguity.*   Sentences are, in general, ambiguous; and individual words are ambiguous even more often. Linguists have shown that the formal processes of syntactic analysis can do much to reduce ambiguity, and progress that has been made on comparable semantic processes can be expected to continue.

3. *Precision.*   A description of, or a request for, a document, or indeed anything else, which takes the form of an essentially unordered list of terms, whether or not they are chosen from some agreed list, is fundamentally imprecise. Whether it is intolerably imprecise is a matter for debate, and one we shall take up again later. If some kind of syntax is defined over a set of terms, it is clear that they can be made to go much further. Suppose that I want my information service to give me the recipe for *sole bonne*

femme but that I do not remember the name of it. I might ask for a recipe for "poached fish with an egg sauce." If the information system worked with an unordered list of keywords, my request could have a form something like "poach, fish, egg, sauce." But this might equally well retrieve information on poached eggs with fish sauce, a dish with which I am not familiar but which might be intriguing. If the order of words can be made to have its usual force in the system, that is, if the system is sensitive to syntax, then I stand a better chance of getting only what I want.

4. *Semantic structure.*   Any information system is bound to be afflicted with the problems of synonymy and ambiguity in individual terms as well as in phrases and sentences. As we shall see, there are two principal lines of attack that can be made on these problems, one involving the establishment of a set of semantic primitives, and the other appealing to so called structural semantics. Documentalists have almost invariably taken the first approach, establishing thesauri, authority lists and the like. Whichever approach is taken, the establishment of a workable semantic structure on which to base an information system is a task requiring a great amount of linguistic sophistication.

5. *Decoupling.*   It is highly desirable, especially in the early stages of work on an information system to separate, to the extent possible, the language that must be used to communicate with the system from the data store and the logical operations needed to manipulate it. This is not only because it may be desirable to use different languages on different occasions and for different purposes, but also because languages continue to develop while documents remain unchanged in the archive.

4

LANGUAGE
IN DOCUMENTATION

Before embarking on a detailed discussion of the treatment of syntax and semantics in information science, we can usefully attempt a more refined analysis of the linguistic aspects of documentation which will serve as a framework for the subsequent discussion.

Linguistic Components
of Information Retrieval Systems

The conventional view of the documentation process is that it involves "the analysis of each document's content, a formulation of this content in a set of descriptors, and an organization of descriptors such that enquirors can match their search requests and not miss any documents relevant to that request [Hutchins, 1967]."

We accordingly distinguish:

1. an informal interpretation of the document;
2. a formal representation of this interpretation;
3. the manipulation of the representation in searching.

Points of linguistic interest arise:

1. in the treatment of the text of the document;
2. in the formulation of the description text;
3. in the treatment of the description text.

Another view is that there are two parallel processes: the handling of the document text, and the handling of the index description text. In the first case the text is in a natural language and, in the second, in a language which is more or less artificial. The linguistic operations involved in the two processes may thus not be the same in detail, though there will be some level on which they are comparable, or there would be no justification for calling an indexing language a language.

Natural and Indexing Languages

Indexing languages are generally parasitic on natural language, that is, are derived from or dependent on it; but they are intended to be in some sense more logical, whether or not they are also much simpler. Indeed, we sometimes encounter impassioned pleas, of the kind associated with the seventeenth century writers on a Universal Character, for the use of index languages confined to terms with single well-defined meanings and constructions with equally regular and unambiguous forms (see, for example, Moss, 1967). But though not many attempts have been made to scale this dizzying logical height, the general consensus is that effective indexing depends on indexing languages being logical in a general sense, that is, reasonably tidy and systematic. The relations between the logic of an indexing language and the logic of the natural language used in documents input to the indexing system, on the one hand, and between these and symbolic logic, on the other, are clearly not simple ones. We are here concerned with the first and, to the extent that indexing languages take over the established notions of symbolic logic, with the second. But this clearly is not an appropriate place for a direct attack on the relationship between formal logic and natural language.

We are interested in the relation between the input language of a document and the index language used to characterize the document, recognizing that there is a large variety of index languages ranging from the wholly natural to the highly formal, but with the great majority characterized by some degree of artificiality. We shall not regard any language which explicitly makes use of standard logical or mathematical forms as special.

Input Texts and Index Descriptions

The major feature of the conventional view of the information retrieval process is the replacement of a long and complex linguistic entity, the entire document text, by a greatly abbreviated description. The use of such a summary is not solely a consequence of practical constraints on the amount of material that can be stored and inspected in searching. It may also be desirable in principle, since the function of the description is to bring out the essential features of the document. The summary, then, functions as a device for emphasis which is essential for effective searching. This is particularly important because the description is not merely a representation of the document, but the means of relating the document to the remainder of the collection. The description provides information of a more uniform kind than is directly given by the document alone.

Now it has been suggested, mainly by more euphoric, computationally oriented workers in information retrieval, that retrieval systems should be based on full document texts, functioning as their own descriptions. Sooner or later, they say, the hardware will be available that will make the storage of, and rapid access to, such vast quantities of matter feasible. A scheme of this kind supposedly has the advantage that it avoids the omissions and distortions inevitably associated with index descriptions. But it ignores the positive role of the summary index description. It is true that full text searching may be desirable in special circumstances, say in establishing legal references (see Borkowski *et al.*, 1970; Furth, 1968; Niblett and Price, 1970). Occasionally the text may be usefully replaced by a somewhat simplified paraphrase rather than a summary. But there will always be circumstances in which summaries are used for reasons of convenience as well as economy, and we can therefore continue to assume that document retrieval systems typically involve the substitution of a shorter text for a longer one. It must, however, be emphasized that though this role of an index description as a summary is widely accepted, sophisticated analyses of the relation between such a summary and its source text, or indeed between summaries and sources in general, are lacking. A purely quantitative study is reported by Lynn (1969).

This argument does, however, point to an important distinction. Consider, for instance, a system in which document titles are taken as descriptions, without any processing, and are manipulated directly in searching. Compare this with a system in which titles are processed in some way, say to extract keywords, and the selected lists of keywords are used in searching. From the viewpoint of the overall documentation process presented earlier, these alternatives can be looked at in different ways. In the first case, it is as though either the full document had been analyzed and the title set up as its description so that the indexing language happens to be the natural language of the document, or alternatively, that the title is treated as though it were the document, which is then taken as its own description. In the second case the title is treated just like a source document, and a description of it is set up.

The fact that we may either not go through the two steps of analyzing a document and providing a description for it, as two separate processes, or may choose not to set up a description of a text which differs from it in any way, should not obscure the logical character of the processes involved. A description is derived from a given text which is used in searching. The fact that the input may not be the full document but may be a surrogate, like an abstract or a title, has no direct effect on our linguistic interests, though it may well have an indirect effect, because a retrieval system based on such document surrogates may be relatively ineffective as a device for retrieving the documents themselves.

The fact that the process of deriving a description from an initial interpretation may be the trivial one of transcribing it does not alter the fact that the status of the piece of text in question has been changed. Whether the input is a full document or a surrogate like an abstract or title is only indirectly relevant. Some approaches to indexing, like that adopted by the SYNTOL group (Bely *et al.*, 1970), produce a transformation rather than a summary of the input document. The experiments of this group have typically used abstracts as input, and whether their approach would be helpful in retrieval if full texts were used instead is an open question. The choice of input may also have other indirect linguistic consequences since a retrieval system based on document surrogates may be relatively ineffective as a device for retrieving the documents themselves, if the form of the indexing language is not adapted to the nature of the input. For example, selecting keywords on a frequency basis would not be sensible if titles were used as input.

More generally, the choice of what is input to the indexing process is highly significant. In particular, the performance of a system which is intended to retrieve documents, including the performance of the indexing techniques within the system, must be influenced by the form in which the documents are presented to the system. This unfortunately makes for a disagreeable complication in the evaluation of retrieval systems, which is normally based on their ability to select relevant documents as wholes, and not relevant surrogates. While from the strictly linguistic point of view we may confine our interest to the relation between the index description and whatever form of the document it is derived from, we are obligated to take any distinction between one form of the document and another with respect to the system into account because the object of the indexing language is to aid retrieval and its merits are judged in the light of its ability to obtain relevant documents. It may, of course, be that this does not matter as much as one might expect. Experiments by Cleverdon *et al.* (1966), Salton and Lesk (1968), and Aitchison *et al.* (1970), for instance, suggest that though titles are inferior as surrogates, the use of abstracts as opposed to full texts does not noticeably lower performance level for a given indexing language. For purely practical reasons the level of performance attainable with titles as input is of interest, but results here are somewhat variable. They were somewhat low for Bottle (1970), but higher for Cleverdon *et al.* (1966). This is also an example of the whole class of related factors, to which the character of requests or relevance judgements also belongs, which interlock to determine system performance and should therefore in principle be taken together, but which we have necessarily excluded as subjects for detailed discussion in this report.

We are, moreover, concerned only with the analysis, description, and manipulation stages of the documentation process to the extent that these are open to any kind of inspection. For example, to use the earlier illustration, to regard the title of a document as the result of an analysis of the full text, which is a wholly plausible informal approach, is not an analysis technique which is in any serious linguistic sense open to further investigation. In such a system we can only look at the subsequent two stages, and, more generally, we must confine ourselves to processes which are not opaque in this way.

Linguistic Problems

The linguistic questions we are faced with are:

1. What units of input text should we look at in analysis, and what semantic and syntactic features of them should we take into account?

2. What should be the units of description, and what syntactic features should they have?

3. What semantic and syntactic devices are available in the index language for manipulating descriptions during searching?

Units of Input and Description

At this stage, "unit" is being used very informally, since its interpretation will be one of the main topics of discussion. But examples of units for use in analysis might be the individual words of the input text, word sequences, sentences, or even the text as a whole. We may choose to have more than one unit of description, and to have a range of possible forms of unit. Thus if we have a keyword list as a description, the individual keywords may be regarded as units, so that we have an n-unit description. If we have a subject characterization of the traditional kind like "manufacture of kettledrum skins from elephant hide," this entire specification constitutes a unit and will probably be the only one for the document. Alternatively, if we take the abstract of a document as its description, we may take its component sentences as units of description. What we regard as units is determined by the analysis and description procedures.

We also have to consider the components of a unit. The question of minimal components will be examined in greater detail later; it is sufficient for the present purpose to assume that they will be something very like words. However, the treatment of the input text may involve some morphological analysis, in which case subverbal items may be explicitly considered. Furthermore, indexing languages may confine themselves to standard forms of a word, typically nouns. Of course, whether or not a thing which looks like a word in a natural language behaves or is intended to behave, in an index description, like its natural-language counterpart is an important question. Some degree of vocabulary control is very common, so that index language words are used in a manner which corresponds to a subset of their ordinary meanings, and in languages hankering after logical purity, words may be used as concept labels in a manner which is connected with their regular use only in a tenuous or arbitrary manner.

In fact, the process of removing suffixes is a case where the correspondence between the components of the input document and its description is not one to one, though the latter are derived from the former and are very closely related to them. But though this is merely an example of the relation between document and description, some particular points about it must be kept in mind. These are illustrated by the very common use in indexing languages of source text phrases as minimal units. For example, one indexing language may contain the two terms "engine" and "steam" to allow for documents dealing with engines of nature unspecified, or steam engines. The further introduction of, say, "diesel," allows additional distinctions to be made. An additional term like "performance" makes it possible to refer to the behavior of a variety of engines. In another language, the interest may be less in steam engines as opposed to diesel engines than in steam engines as opposed to horses. In this case "steam engine" can be adopted as a term, so that descriptions could refer to the performances of steam engines and horses. In this second case the indexing language does not record any relations between "steam" and "engine" which are in some sense preserved in the first case. Nevertheless the fact that something about the relation between "steam" and "engine" is preserved, though it is only implicit in the term "steam engine," may influence the retrieval performance of the system of which the language forms a part, and not necessarily to the same effect as follows from the language in which "steam" and "engine" are explicitly related.

The fundamental point here is, of course, a familiar one for documentalists, but it is useful to look at it specifically from the linguistic point of view. In the context of this report we are interested in the relation between the unit of description as a whole and the unit of the source document from which it is derived;

this relationship involves the relations between the components of the two units and is itself involved, for sources or descriptions containing more than one unit, in the relations between the source and description as wholes. We must allow for relations between units where more than one occurs in either source or description, but the focus of interest is clearly the individual unit.

The relation between source and description units is the relation we have to consider initially. We are of course also forced to consider the secondary relations holding between the descriptions of one document and another, and between a document and a request. Unfortunately, though the relations are different in kind, we cannot treat the relations between documents and their descriptions and between one description and another as independent, particularly since how document descriptions are related and how documents and requests are related are two sides of the same coin. For retrieval in general implies document selection, and while the selection of one document and rejection of another by means of their descriptions will be achieved primarily if the descriptions reflect the genuine differences between them, it will also be influenced by conscious decisions about the way the language is used to characterize the whole collection, since an indexing language is an artificial creation. This is clearly illustrated by the way in which descriptor vocabularies are often developed, namely on the basis of an inspection of a collection sample. The choice and allocation of descriptors, though it is primarily determined by the content of individual documents, must also take into account the relations between documents.

Information Retrieval Needs and Linguistic Solutions

While bearing all this in mind we still have to consider the most important point about the relation between descriptions and documents. Suppose that we have the descriptive unit "manufacture of kettledrum skins from elephant hide," which has been derived from an inspection of a source document as a whole, and that it constitutes the complete description of the document, in other words, that we have proceeded in a manner which is typical of conventional subject indexing as it is practiced in a very large number of libraries. In looking at the relation between this description and its hypothetical source document we are brought face to face with one of the basic questions concerning the relation between linguistics and documentation.

This question is this: is the kind of drastic compression of content that must be done to provide a document with an index description a process about which linguists can reasonably be expected to have anything to say? It might be that though the documentalist's practical objective is of no concern to the linguist, he may invoke linguistic techniques as aids; the question then would be one of selecting the appropriate techniques, or perhaps of developing or modifying them. But the possibility we have to allow for is that the linguist could have nothing essential or material to offer, given not only the object of the documentalist's indexing but also its form. To put the question somewhat simplistically, should one expect the linguist to tell one how to replace five thousand words by five? This is not a question we can hope to answer here. But we can hope to accumulate some ammunition for the future.

Analysis, Description, and Searching

We should now look at the documentation process as we have outlined it in more detail. We originally separated three processes, namely analysis, description, and searching, though we have hitherto concentrated mainly on the relation between source and description. But we can alternatively characterize information retrieval in terms of two analogous activities—the handling of document texts and the handling of description texts. This has the advantage from an aesthetic point of view in that in each case we have text which is typically processed with the aid of a lexicon and discourse rules, the lexicon in the first case consisting of any specified index vocabulary list, and in the second of any form of classification of the index terms. Clearly the parallelism does not hold in detail, since matching a request against a file of document texts is not quite the same as generating descriptions from source documents, but the analogy holds at the general level.

The tripartite division does, however, represent a common view of documentation; and while it might be sensible from one point of view to consider the structure of the index language as a whole, and hence a component of it like a term classification, in connection with index descriptions, the structure of the language is mainly relevant to searching. We shall therefore consider the structure of the language, and specifically its classificatory structure, in connection with searching.

Solutions to our three problems can be categorized as follows:

1. In analysis we can compare approaches which seek to make features of the input text explicit with those where they are merely implicit in the information extracted from the text.

2. In the description we can contrast maximal and minimal control over the form of a description.

3. In searching we can oppose elaborateness and simplicity in the indexing language and hence in the means for correlating a request with items in the file.

Some differences are perhaps merely terminological and others may be due primarily to different views of documentation based on, say, a particular tradition of librarianship and computational training respectively. But it is evident that there are genuine differences of approach, as summarized here, among those who are agreed on the overall objective of the enterprise. At the same time, a question of major interest, given the lack of any real understanding of information retrieval and hence of adequate instructions for going about it properly, is whether radically different approaches, as currently implemented, in fact lead to significant differences in retrieval performance. The conclusion to be drawn from some series of experiments is that different approaches do not produce significant performance differences, and in particular that very careful indexing and the use of a sophisticated language do not make for a substantive improvement over much cruder techniques. It does not follow that differences of approach could not influence performance profoundly. It must in any case be emphasized that these experiments have been very limited, that the results tend to hold for the best representatives of each type of language, where surprisingly large variations can be obtained for a given form of language, and that they are couched in terms of a certain interpretation of performance.

Indexing and indexing languages may fulfill a variety of functions and hence be evaluated by a variety of criteria. Discussion of the merits of specific approaches tend to assume specific purposes, or modes of system use, so that simpleminded comparisons between languages may be quite improper. The division between those whose document descriptions are actually going to be looked at by human beings in searching and those whose descriptions are concealed in a computational black box is substantial. In the present context, we consider different languages primarily within the framework provided by the assumption that we are making a single blind search and that performance is evaluated in terms of some relative objective relevance judgements.

Strong and Weak Approaches

The contrasts just made under the three headings for the documentation process act as useful guidelines in the detailed examination of particular projects. As regards the first there are, on the one hand, those who believe in the analysis of content, or the discovery of what a document is about, who talk in terms of subjects and concepts as the matter with which descriptions are concerned. In contrast, there are those who say that we need not ask what a document as a whole is about as long as we can obtain, by whatever means, suitable content indicators or tags; these people eschew even subjects, let alone concepts, and tend to talk about keywords.

Under the second heading there are those who believe in controlled indexing vocabularies, that is, in carefully designed thesauri, descriptor or factor lists, and, since a more complex descriptive unit than the simple list item is generally assumed, in well-defined rules for the organization of a descriptive unit. The opposite camp does not attempt really rigorous term control and may be either less interested in systematizing the structure of descriptions or work with units without any structure at all.

In the third case we can contrast those who believe in vocabulary classification systems and structure-modifying rules with those who do not regard them as essential. In fact, in this case in particular, but in the others to a considerable extent, the division is not an absolute one, but rather one of emphasis, or of degree in the sophistication and completeness which is regarded as desirable in providing a structure for the indexing language, and especially a classification for the vocabulary.

For convenience we can call the members of the two parties formalists and naturalists, though it must be recognized that two slightly different contrasts are involved. Strictly we can contrast controlled and uncontrolled indexing languages, exemplified by the use of a keyword thesaurus with cross-references, and that of a simple keyword list, respectively; and we can contrast the use of artificial and ordinary indexing languages, exemplified by, say, the Western Reserve University Semantic Code and any statistical keyword classification, respectively. But controlled and artificial shade into one another, as do uncontrolled and ordinary.

The arguments of both parties are familiar, the former advocating languages which are in some sense more accurate and explicit than our own, the latter claiming that our own is just as good as it may be. The first point of view is presented by, for example, the members of the Classification Research Group (Classification Research Group, 1969), Farradane (1967), Farradane *et al.* (1966), Hillman (1965, 1968), Perreault (1967b), Ranganathan (1965,

1967), the SYNTOL group (Bely *et al.*, 1970; Cros *et al.*, 1964; Gardin, 1965), and Western Reserve University (Comparative Systems Laboratory, 1968; Melton, 1962). Surveys of approaches under this head include those by de Grolier (1962) and Soergel (1967, 1969), and it is generally represented by contributors to the symposium on relational factors in classification (Perreault, 1967a). The form of the classification of knowledge is of course the traditional preserve of the librarian (for a recent survey see Mills, 1970). The second point of view is particularly associated with those advocating automatic extracting and classification procedures, from Luhn (Schultz, 1968a) and the other workers surveyed by Stevens (1965), or represented at the symposium on statistical association methods (Stevens *et al.*, 1965), to more recent workers such as Cagan (1970), Curtice and Jones (1967, 1969), Dennis (1965, 1967), Salton (1968a, 1970a), and Sparck Jones (1971). The picture is filled out by the many languages based on one principle or the other used in operating documentation systems. The major classifications are examples of the former, as are the *Medical Subject Headings* list (National Library of Medicine, 1968) and thesauri like the *Thesaurus of Engineering and Scientific Terms* (Project LEX, 1967); faceted schemes like those discussed by Vickery (1966) or presented by Broxis (1966), to take a random example; and hybrids like the thesaurofacet (Aitchison, 1970; Aitchison and Day, 1969). Under the latter come the many title-based systems of the basic kind now widely established, and also systems using relatively uncontrolled and simple thesauri.

There is one aspect of indexing languages that should be mentioned, though we shall not consider it in detail: this is their role as interlinguas, or devices for characterizing documents in different natural languages. The design of an indexing language may be affected by the need to use it to represent information given in different input languages. This presents problems which in principle are not those of choosing a suitable linguistic code for the indexing language itself, though they are liable to turn out the same in practice. Generally speaking one would expect a language to become more artificial to match its interlingual ambitions. Similar problems arise with second-order switching languages intended for transferring descriptions from one index language to another (see Coates, 1970; Gardin and Lévy, 1969; Lévy, 1967).

In general, there is a strong correlation between those who believe in what may be called the thoroughgoing approach to document analysis and those who advocate strict description control and language organization. For obvious reasons these also tend to be the workers in the field who maintain that there must be a substantial human intellectual contribution to the documentation process, primarily, and also continuously, in the analysis of documents, also initially in the design of the language, and to some extent continuously in the updating of the vocabulary. Their opponents may have been forced into their position partly by economic pressures, though they may also maintain that there is not sufficient evidence for the notably superior performance of the manual systems, at least in the restricted senses usually tested. We should, however, distinguish among the members of what may be called the informal or minimal school, those who take a humble view of their systems, regarding them as poor relations of the proper systems they cannot afford, and those who more arrogantly assert they are just as good.

We have natually emphasized these contrasts for the sake of argument, but in practice systems representing all kinds of intermediate positions have been implemented. In particular, individual systems may combine quite different approaches in the treatment of their semantic and syntactic components. For example, if we regard an absence of structure in a descriptive unit as the limiting case of lack of control over the structure, we find systems with a carefully controlled vocabulary and extensive vocabulary classification combined with unstructured descriptions or with a relatively simple bracketing structure imposed by links. Alternatively, we sometimes find a strict unit format combined with moderate vocabulary control and an absence of any vocabulary classification. The word "thesaurus" in particular covers index term lists ranging from the most carefully designed descriptor sets to barely modified lists of extracted keywords.

Linguistic Implications

The approaches contrasted under the three heads obviously have different linguistic implications. If the process of document analysis involves the explicit identification of the content or message of a document, that is, the discovery of what it is really about, the analysis operation can be expected to be a delicate and exacting one. As noted, the assumption is that it is something that a human can do relatively successfully and noncontentiously, but which a machine could not do wholly or even sufficiently adequately. In any case, any attempt to substantially assist or replace human beings in the explicit interpretation of documents will clearly necessitate a fairly sophisticated semantic and syntactic analysis procedure. The requirements of an approach which seeks simply to identify more important terms, primarily on statistical grounds, will presumably be much more modest, though the choice of the items to be looked at and the justification for the procedures adopted rest on linguistic assumptions. Again, stricter control over the vocabulary and form of a description depends on a model of topic specifications which will be more complete, and hence more difficult to design, while the more elaborate language organization which is desired under the third head presupposes a detailed identification of the relations between the terms and structures of the language.

Available Linguistic Tools

These are requirements we can make in principle. We get a rather different view of the situation and, in addition, another distinction between semantics and syntax, if we consider the extent to which linguistics is currently capable of being exploited to satisfy the requirements just listed. We can also distinguish attempts to exploit linguistic models from the use in a more or less ad hoc manner of linguistic information. An example of the former would be the application of a transformational grammar to input analysis; the latter is evident when, say, prepositions or inflections are used to identify word groups.

In the analysis of source texts linguistic models have been used explicitly for syntactic purposes; Salton's application of the Predictive Analyzer (Salton, 1968a) is an example. Quasi-linguistic techniques with at most implicit references to linguistic models are evident in procedures like those initially proposed by Lynch (1966) and Armitage and Lynch (1967), though perhaps most strikingly in the far more extensive set of procedures used for text analysis by the SYNTOL group (Bely *et al.*, 1970; Coyaud and Siot-Decauville, 1967). Both of these projects exploit the occurrence of prepositions, for example.

Finally there is the wholly nonlinguistic, that is, unformalized or rule-based approach represented by the average human subject indexer. It must, of course, be emphasized that the linguistic models more or less consciously exploited in analysis may be neither the most fashionable contemporary ones, nor particularly satisfactory, whether viewed as general models for textual analysis or as special documentation oriented models. We are concerned simply with whether some analysis rules couched in currently recognizable language underlie the document analysis operations of particular systems. From this point of view the "kernelizing" and predicate logic approaches to analysis and description primarily studied by workers in fact retrieval (see Simmons, 1970; and Chapter 7) are of interest since they involve a type of powerful linguistic model which is nevertheless simpler than transformational grammar, for example. In documentation Hillman and the SYNTOL group have worked along these lines (Bely *et al.*, 1970; Hillman, 1968; Hillman and Kasarda, 1969), but have not carried the formal development of the description language so far.

As far as semantics goes, the situation is somewhat different, both in its structural and lexical aspects. Broadly speaking, no attempts have been made to apply semantic theories explicitly, because none are sufficiently developed for application. But an implicit reference to some theory of discourse structure, and of lexical characterization, though of a very simple kind, is involved in automatic extraction procedures. The great majority of library systems depend, however, on manual selection, where the identification of the topic of a document and the selection of important words or phrases is not rule-governed at all.

The state of description and manipulation is different again. The use of syntactic structure in descriptive units and the operations on it for retrieval represented, for example, by the replacement of specific relations by more general ones, seem to owe little to contemporary linguistics. More reference, though often in a vague or modified way, is made to logic. Equally, in the control of vocabulary and in the construction of term or subject classifications, the principles or theories involved are not obviously linked with current linguistics but are affiliated with a long and respectable historical series of vocabulary, conceptual, and scientific classifications. The lack of linguistic support on the semantic side is comprehensible enough, but the apparent failure to exploit recent syntactic developments at all noticeably is interesting because it bears on the question raised earlier concerning the different objectives and hence different character of linguistics and information science.

We can thus distinguish those points where linguistics currently offers techniques which may be exploited from those where there are gaps in linguistic theory and hence an absence of the techniques that might otherwise be exploited. But we also have to decide, as information scientists, whether the techniques which exist are suited to our purposes. For example, some apparatus for parsing natural language text exists, though it is not wholly adequate. Does this give the amount and kind of information to achieve a good retrieval performance? The difficulty about the semantic aspects of analysis, description, and searching, on the other hand, is that we cannot decide whether linguistic techniques are suited to our retrieval purpose, since these techniques are simply not available.

Characteristics of Indexing Languages: Coyaud

Further insight into the relationship between linguistics and documentation can be gained from Coyaud's (1966) description of indexing languages, which uses linguistic terms rather than comparatively informal ones like "unit" and "structure." Coyaud brings out the characteristics of indexing languages in relation to natural languages. His discussion further serves to introduce a more detailed separation of semantics and syntax, which has hitherto been maintained very informally. At the same time, Coyaud's approach is limited in an important sense. He seeks to characterize and relate the members of an apparently very heterogeneous collection of indexing languages by using a common descriptive framework referring to lexemes, syntagms, and so on. This is very valuable as a means of viewing indexing languages, but though a detailed description of a language should provide the rules governing its use, Coyaud does not consider the input to the indexing process, and neglects, therefore, the difficult problem of how index descriptions are derived from documents. The characterization of the language used to generate index descriptions does not tell us which items we select for encodement.

Coyaud's mode of description also raises again the question of whether it is right to expect to use the same framework of description for the natural input and artificial index languages of documentation. The language of input documents is certainly complicated, though it may be possible to extract information from them which is sufficient for retrieval purpose without requiring a full-scale grammar. Automatic keyword extraction procedures, for example, may depend on sets of rules which hardly constitute a grammar. Index languages, though they vary considerably, are also enormously simpler than natural languages: they normally possess a reduced and less finely structured vocabulary and permit relatively few forms of descriptive unit.*

Whether an indexing language is the same kind of animal as a natural language, though with fewer spots, is not clear from Coyaud's description. The apparatus he uses to describe indexing languages is relatively simple, but provides only a broad categorization of the features of the languages he examines. Equally, though the individual headings may also be used for natural language, the whole apparatus is clearly inadequate as a means of describing natural language.

Coyaud's characterization is nevertheless helpful as a guide in approaching indexing languages, and we shall therefore summarize it here.

Starting with the notion of *moneme* or minimal unit, Coyaud distinguishes lexical and functional monemes called *lexemes* or *morphemes,* respectively. Lexemes are the documentalist's terms, and morphemes are terms relations, which are always binary. Coyaud then distinguishes *analytic* or a priori relations established between index terms before they are used and *synthetic* relations established in indexing. This is similar to Lancaster's (1968b) analytico-synthetic subject classification for the organization of descriptions. Under syntax Coyaud distinguishes the minimum independent unit, or *word*, and the *syntagm.* The word may be either a lexeme accompanied by a synthetic morpheme indicating its function, or a set of lexemes characterized by a particular analytic relation. A syntagm, on the other hand, consists of a pair of lexemes or words combined by a synthetic relation. A descriptive unit, or *énoncé*, is rather loosely defined as the smallest unit making sense from the point of view of documentation, that is, the smallest unit that could constitute a request. Associated with the notion of descriptive unit in some languages is that of *expansion.* This is a device for generating other related units from a given unit. Finally, the descriptive units that describe a document combine to form a *discourse.*

*Chemical and drug nomenclatures form special closed systems.

Coyaud does not regard indexing languages without synthetic relations as of much interest, but concentrates on those that have them, dividing them according to whether the syntax permitted by the language is free or rigid. Examples of the former are the UDC (Mills, 1964), SYNTOL (Gardin, 1965), Selye's Symbolic Shorthand (Selye, 1966), and WRU's Semantic Code (Melton, 1962), whereas Ranganathan's Colon Classification (Ranganathan, 1965) and faceted schemes like Vickery's for soil science (Vickery, 1966) are examples of the latter.

Some Examples

Coyaud's framework allows him to characterize a wide variety of indexing languages and to bring out their common features. For example, in the UDC a lexeme is a numerical symbol corresponding to some natural language word or word group, such as 491 *"langues indoeuropéennes diverses"*; each digit of the symbol is itself a moneme indicating an analytic relationship. The analytic relations in the UDC form a multivocal classification, since concepts appear in different locations, and also a multidimensional one, since the governing inclusion relation has in fact a variety of interpretations. The UDC also includes the synthetic relations represented by ":" and "+" interpretable as logical product and logical sum, respectively.

The Semantic Code of Western Reserve University is more complex. The lexemes of the language are the 200-odd semantic factors, representing concepts of varying generality, like "digestive system" and "tissue"; the classes they define contain terms to which infixes and suffixes indicating participation and neighbor relations are attached. The morphemes indicating analytic relations are represented either by the infixes marking, for example, composition, production, or negation, or by the semantic code representing the multivocal classification of the semantic factors through relations indicating states, processes, substances, and so on. Synthetic relations are represented by a series of prefixed role indicators concerned with, for instance, properties attributed to, or studied in, something. The Semantic Code carries the development of units of description much further than the UDC, which essentially provides only for words and syntagms. In the Semantic Code the word is a collection of lexemes linked by analytic relations and provided with a role indicator. As an example, illustrating the degree of conceptual reduction typical of the Code, we may cite the representation of "telephone" (without role) as a Machine *for* Transmission *of* Information *by* Electricity, that is, by a sequence of four factors each with an infix. A syntagm resembles an ordinary phrase. An énoncé is a group of words associated by role indicators, which represents one of several forms of proposition concerned, say, with processes or products, as in "X was obtained by reduction of Y by Z"; several énoncés can be further combined via roles to give a "phrase," and a complete discourse is represented by the telegraphic abstract for a whole document.

These two are examples of indexing languages with free syntax. One example of a rigid language is provided by Vickery's faceted classification for soil science. Terms with facet codes are lexemes; analytic relations are represented by hierarchical structures of terms within facets organized, for example, by soil origin and soil texture; synthetic relations linking terms from different facets concern soil structures, constitutes, and processes, for instance. Syntagms are generally represented by two terms from different facets linked as indicated.

Coyaud also considers two documentary languages of this type developed for special fields, which are of interest in referring more directly than the previous ones to mathematical logic. One is the semantic language for mathematics (LM) presented in Gladkij *et al.* (1962), and the other is the language for geometry (LG) found in Kuznecov *et al.* (1962).

The LM is developed in an algebraic manner; it permits operations like intersection and union and contains a variety of support elements like person, action, subordination, coordination, mental category, interrogation, and theory, satisfying certain formal conditions. Lexemes representing lexical classes are supplied with indicators showing whether they are terms in a mathematical sense. There is a large range of both analytic and synthetic relations. The former include three levels of support elements, the categorization of lexemes as terms or nonterms, and the grouping of lexemes into types, say of activity represented by "examine," "verify," "generalize," or of text segment like "paragraph," "chapter," or "book." The many synthetic relations are defined as to subordination or coordination, examples of the former being "*a* belongs to *b*" and "*a* satisfies *b*," and of the latter "*a* equals *b*." There are complicated rules for forming expressions, essentially determining syntactic and semantic well-formedness; as Coyaud notes, the languages is distinctive in having a very restricted lexicon but allowing complicated operations.

In the LG lexemes are either variables or predicates, representing the analytic relations defined by the classes of objects and qualities. There are four synthetic relations, including "and" and "or." A formula applying predicates to variables resembles a syntagm, and a proposition consisting of formulae connected by synthetic relations constitutes an énoncé. The whole leans heavily on orthodox logic.

The detailed analysis of the various languages Coyaud considers is followed by a comparison between them from certain linguistic points of view. Some of these, such as the character of the code used, are not our concern here; the most interesting include the degree of motivation of the documentary lexicon, or degree of logical reduction in the characterization of concepts. Some languages are highly motivated in being confined to a relatively small number of general or basic terms, whereas others are much less so. Coyaud comments on the difficulty of pitching on the right level of conceptual generality for terms and also on the persistent hankering after what amounts, in the form of a highly motivated indexing language, to a Universal Character. The Western Reserve University Semantic Code is a prime example of a strongly motivated indexing language [and it is therefore interesting to note that its performance in the Comparative Systems Laboratory tests was not distinguished (Comparative Systems Laboratory, 1968)]; the UDC is only weakly motivated.

As far as the analytic relations are concerned, the question of interest is how many and which of these are useful. Coyaud maintains that a total absence of such relations, so that even synonymy is not allowed for, is a mistake, and that documentary languages may therefore be grouped according to whether they have one analytic relation corresponding to one notion, or one for several, or several for one. Most documentary languages are of the second kind, which is illustrated by the use of the inclusion relations in the UDC, or intrafacet inclusion in Vickery's faceted scheme. The Semantic Code infixes are an example of the third. Synthetic relations in documentary languages may be considered as nonspecified, formal, or real, where the last may be static or dynamic. The UDC ":" illustrates the first; coordination and comparison relations, which appear in several languages, exemplify the second; and again, most languages exhibit both static and dynamic real relations: Western Reserve's role indicator for composition is an instance of the former, and the LM "result of" relation is an example of the latter.

In attempting to compare structures across the different languages, Coyaud notes that not all of the documentary languages have words or syntagms; it is difficult to discover a common view of what an énoncé should consist of, and there are equally few common approaches to expansion. At the level of discourse, Coyaud notes that synonymous expressions may occur, though these are excluded at the lexical level, and that, in general, context is represented by the organization of the lexicon.

These comparisons are summarized in an overall classification table of the documentary languages by their resemblance to natural language, under the relevant heads. The most striking feature of the classification table is the occurrence of particular languages at quite different points on the like-unlike scale, for different components. For example, LM is like natural language in its morphemes, but quite unlike it in discourse; the Semantic Code is moderately like natural languages in its morphemes, and very like it in énoncé and discourse. The table indeed brings out the distinctive feature of documentary languages in general, compared with natural languages. This is their heterogeneity or unevenness. Natural languages are complex all round. Documentary languages are typically highly complicated in some respects—usually the lexical ones—and very simple in others—generally the syntactic ones.

In conclusion Coyaud considers the relation between indexing languages and natural language. In his view they share the same fundamental properties: they both have a referential function, and they are both constructed for the same purpose, *"assurer la communication, sans regarder aux moyens."* On the other hand, indexing languages lack many specific features of natural languages: Coyaud's list includes, for example, the absence of synonymy, missing categories like pronouns, no provision for forms of text like imperatives, and so on, so that the overall picture of an indexing language is of something very much less rich than a natural language.

Coyaud's detailed analysis is useful just because it brings out this relative simplicity. The difference between natural and indexing languages tends to be obscured by the apparent transfer of words or phrases from the former to the latter, and by the natural appearance of many subject descriptions. This suggests that an indexing language is simply a natural language with half the words left out and sentence forms unused. Some words appear in the indexing language only with some meanings or senses, but this appears to be a natural consequence of the scope of the document collection.

But it is evident that the situation is not so straightforward. For example, problems arise where particular natural language words are used in a controlled way, say as indicated by thesaurus scope notes, or as labels for the nodes of a classificatory hierarchy. In these cases, for instance, "chemistry" may not function quite like its English counterpart. Of course an indexing language has to have words in a logical sense; and it is convenient, to say the least, if librarians do not have to learn a quite new set of symbols; but whether there is a necessary connection between the words or the one and those of the other because index descriptions are derived from document texts, or some more uncertain connection because indexing is based on document content, is a major problem. Moreover, if the latter is the case, do we expect the document and description languages, though genuinely different languages, whatever common written symbols they possess, to be languages of the same sort?

An artificial language is no less artificial because its words are borrowed from a natural language or because some or all of its sentence forms coincide with those of a natural language. Coincidences of this kind occur because natural languages are an obvious source of inspiration for the language designer and because it is argued that the user of the language will be able to profit from analogies he can draw with a language he already knows. But, as Watt (1968) has pointed out, these analogies can be treacherous because of the inevitable temptation to assume that they extend further than they do. It can be quite as difficult to restrict what one says to an artificially constrained subset of a known language as to learn one that is entirely new.

Coyaud's descriptive framework is most easily applied to well-developed indexing languages. But there are some aspects of the use of an indexing language which it does not bring out, and it is therefore useful to compare it with the more traditional view exemplified, for example, by Sharp (1965).

Specification and Classification
in Indexing Languages: Sharp

Sharp's (1965) approach to documentation is from the notion of subject. In this case analysis is concerned with identifying the subject of a document, description with characterizing it, and searching with picking up documents on the subject specified in a request. This is wholly familiar, but it does serve to emphasize the functional aspect of an indexing language. If an individual description represents a subject, the set of descriptions for the collection constitutes the indexing language; the organization of the language as a whole is viewed in terms of its capacity to establish correct subject relations between documents and requests.

The fact that an indexing language is not merely a means of describing documents but is intended to describe them in a way which facilitates searching has important consequences. This point has been touched on already. It is possible to argue that there is no need to represent the content of a document particularly accurately, as long as different documents are discriminated from one another, and document descriptions can be matched with requests to give satisfactory results. It is clearly unlikely that this can be achieved without a fairly close relationship between a description and its document, but the open question is the extent to which the description of an individual document should be related to the nature of the collection as a whole.

There are two requirements an indexing language should satisfy: the first is probably obligatory, whereas the second may be optional. The first function of an indexing language is as a normalizing device, and the second is as a display device. If an indexing language is to be effective, it must take account of the fact that two documents, or a document and a request, are about the same thing, though they are couched in different language. Further, an indexing language may take account of the fact that two documents or a document and a request are about related subjects.

These two requirements can be associated with two views of an indexing language reflecting the need to access a subject, and the need to browse among subjects respectively. In the one case the aim is to reach a subject, and hence a document, from whatever angle, and in the other, to examine neighboring subjects. A particular feature of a language may be a help in both; term classification, for example, may either lead to or from a focal point, but the objectives are logically distinct and they are satisfied by different devices. The problems presented by these requirements, and especially the first, appear in their most acute form when seen from the point of view of retrieving current documents for remote future requests .

The normalizing function of an indexing language is exhibited in the constraints imposed by the language on the vocabulary and form of a description. Thus any reference or phrase of the form "see . . . ," or correlation of words in an entry vocabulary with terms in an indexing vocabulary, contributes to normalization. That is to say, any device which says that the terms "x," "y," and "z" in the source or initial interpretive text are represented by the index term "P" is a normalizing device. Notice that from this point of view, whether the adoption of a standard form is explicit in the formation of the description of the document, or is implicit in that correlation is only established in searching, for different index forms, is immaterial.

Equally, the replacement of, say, the English expression "unripe pears as a cause of stomachache" and "stomachache due to unripe pears" by the description "PAIN, Stomach ← CAUSE ← PEARS, Unripe" where we have an ordering of topics by importance and formalized relations, constitutes normalization. Similarly, any devices which establish structural equivalence among index descriptions in the course of searching are normalizing ones.

This aspect of an indexing language is most conspicuous where a glossary defining equivalences, or set of rules for converting extracted document text items of the kind considered in the automated SYNTOL encodement experiments, is provided. But it must be emphasized that in any indexing language with a defined vocabulary or set of relations, though without a translation apparatus, normalization is implicit, since one can only characterize documents by the given means.

Now an indexing language which contains normalizing devices is still restricted to what Sharp calls "subject specification" because the object of such devices is only to replace whatever initial interpretations are made of the subjects of documents by more systematic ones, with hopefully better consequences for retrieval. The mere characterization of a given subject may, however, not be sufficient for retrieval. To start with, if we assume that the specifications are alphabetically listed, and that the subjects are at all complex, it will be necessary to provide some means of access which makes it possible to approach individual subjects from different angles. The most obvious is to provide multiple entries for a subject under each of its components, but other devices are available.

However, it may also be desirable to investigate documents on related subjects, and for this purpose some sort of classification, whether of the older enumerative or newer faceted type is required. The classification, which constitutes an arrangement of subjects, acts as a device for displaying the relations between subjects. It is indeed possible to treat a classification as a normalizing device because, in moving up a level in a hierarchical classification, for example, previously differentiated subjects come to be treated as the same. But since the initial index formulations were distinct, it is more useful to emphasize the other aspect of classification, namely that it indicates relationships between subjects which are recognized to be distinct.

The difficulties which inevitably arise in handling complex subjects in classification are cogently described by Sharp. They are essentially those which arise when a variety of alternative arrangements are equally plausible and helpful, but when implementing them all is grossly uneconomic. The problem of distributed relatives, that is, a wide scattering in a classification or subject list of related notions, is indeed one which affects both the access and display capacities of a language.

The foregoing is of course a very much simplified account. In practice marked differences appear in systems which are in principle comparable. For example, Sharp points out that enumerative and faceted classifications can be essentially equivalent, though this is by no means obvious. It is also true that individual systems may be complicated aggregates of devices, or alternatively make use of single devices for a variety of purposes. The thesaurus, in particular, is a good example of a thoroughly ambiguous documentary notion, and descriptors are another. A thesaurus may be primarily an authority list of terms, but as soon as it incorporates cross-references, or specifically BTs, NTs, and RTs (Broad Terms, Narrow Terms, and Related Terms), it contains a classification of some sort. Again, a thesaurus is normally confined to terms or single vocabulary items, but more complex terms, that is, subject specifications, creep in. Finally, there is a conflict between the idea of a thesaurus as a glossary and the older idea of a thesaurus as a word classification which may then fulfill a variety of functions. It must, however, be recognized that this complexity in indexing languages comes from the fact that they face two ways, for they are used by both indexers and searchers, though not necessarily in the same way.

In some cases, the problems of constructing a classification satisfying a heterogeneous collection of customers is so great that it is either only attempted in a relatively unambitious way, or abandoned altogether. The problems of gaining access to individual subject specifications—which are combinatorial ones of greater or lesser severity—nevertheless remain; and the fact that these may still be so daunting explains the enthusiasm with which postcoordinate systems have been adopted. The effect of mechanization on information science is indeed most clearly seen in the postcoordinate revolution of the 1950s, though the guise in which it first appeared was so humble: with simple punched cards concepts can be easily and variably coordinated in searching. The only competitor in value for money is the KWIC index.

Postcoordination

The main point about this revolution is the effect the change in the means of access to a subject specification has had on the form of the specification and on the language used for it. The logic of postcoordinate techniques emphasizes the component elements in a description rather than the structure of the whole. It has therefore been associated mainly with the use of simple keyword or descriptor lists. The interesting consequence of the use of postcoordinate term combinations rather than precoordinate ones, however, has been the effect it has had on the view of a subject specification. Postcoordination rather than precoordination of terms was initially regarded as a means of obtaining access to subjects, that is, as a device for manipulating rather than generating subject description. But the hospitality of postcoordination as an access device seems to have been responsible for a much more flexible view of subject description. In this respect, the suggestion that UDC headings should be used as descriptors (Druk, 1968; Otradinskij and Kamalov, 1969), is perhaps symbolic.

Whether the list of keywords or descriptors characterizing a document is regarded as an aggregate of the descriptive units represented by the individual keywords or descriptors, or whether the list as a whole is treated as a single unstructured unit, is to a considerable extent a matter of choice. The important point is that the list of keywords for a document, especially if it is at all long, can be regarded as an open or comprehensive indication of the subject area of the document, which allows not merely access from different points of view, but different interpretations, associated with subsets of the keyword set as a whole. We thus obtain a more flexible view of subject specification.

The interest of this development is in the light it throws on a question which has been fairly acrimoniously argued, especially in the earlier literature of mechanized retrieval. This is whether computers can provide users with new information about documents. The argument is suggestive of rabbits and hats, and the more extravagant claims have been correctly condemned on the grounds that the rabbit has in fact to be put into the hat before it can be got out. On the other hand, experience shows that, while a keyword list may have been built up with words which were presented in a certain order or grouping in a document, effective retrieval can result from matches representing other groupings. Thus if we have the list "*A, B, C, D, E,*" where "*A,*" "*B,*" and "*C*" go together in the document, we may find that the document is of interest in relation to a request grouping *"A," "B,"* and *"E."* Postcoordination does not give us new information, but it allows us to look at documents from new points of view, which may be the same thing.

The opposite case is represented by combinations of words or descriptors that are permitted but either unhelpful or false. Full-blown postcoordinate systems produce problems which are either explicitly or implicitly avoided in precoordinate ones. The two approaches have complementary merits and defects. The consequence for postcoordinate systems has been the introduction of the devices for organizing descriptions used in precoordinate systems, in forms compatible with their mode of use, as roles and links.

This account of postcoordinate indexing serves to bring out the final general point to be made about document characterization, namely, the tendency, even with quite long and detailed descriptions, to jettison syntactic information and to concentrate on the semantic aspects of a document description. The same piece of information may of course be conveyed by different means in different languages, say by the choice of terms in one case and of relational structure in another, as in "plastic tube" versus "tube COMPOSED plastic"; or by treating a relationship as analytic or synthetic (see Lévy, 1967).

Relations in Indexing Languages: Šreider *et al.*

This point is emphasized by Šreider *et al.* (1969a) in *Development and Application of Information Retrieval Languages,* and this survey provides a third overview of information languages.

The general presumption is that adequate formal languages are required for effective information processing, but though the explicit use of mathematical logic is rare, the authors note that ordinary information retrieval languages for semantic notation may, if they have a structure, implicitly provide the object–predicate characterization of information typical of logical languages. The survey therefore considers the former from the point of view of their structural characterization.

The initial component of such a notational language is its term set, and the various statistical and lexical requirements to be satisfied are examined (Černyj, 1968). Successive steps in the indication of semantic relations between terms, given the inadequacy of pure keyword coordination, are then considered. These relations may be expressed paradigmatically or syntagmatically, but the authors note that this is a formal distinction, since the same predicate may be used either way. A generic relationship, for example, may be indicated paradigmatically or syntagmatically; equally, an associative relation, though usually represented syntagmatically, may, if it is constant, be expressed paradigmatically.

Systems indicating relations paradigmatically may be divided into those having only a single relation, either undifferentiated or of a certain kind; those where relationships are defined quantitatively; and those having several different relations. An example of the first, illustrating systems with an undifferentiated relation, is the "Pusto-Nepusto" system (Bernštejn *et al.*, 1963; Černjavskij *et al.*, 1966) in which terms are subordinated to one another in a way reflecting the utility of their substitution in retrieval. The other form of single relation is exemplified by any language having a true genus–species organization. The second class is illustrated by statistical association languages, on the one hand, and by languages characterizing terms by predicates or factors, on the other. An example of the latter is Skoroxod'ko's RX language (Griaznixina *et al.*, 1964; Skoroxod'ko, 1967, 1969, 1970), in which term proximity is measured by overlap in predicate strings. The third class includes both the many thesauri having generic and associative relations only, and systems with a greater variety of relations, like the part–whole one.

Syntagmatic relations represent progressive modifications of simple descriptor coordination, which is represented by the "Pusto–Nepusto" system just mentioned, and by the systems of Bud'ko *et al.* (1966) and Dobrovol'skij (Dobrovol'skij and Verevčenko,

1967; Dobrovol'skij *et al.*, 1969). Thus we may proceed from undifferentiated one- and two-place predicates, that is, roles and
links, to the more complicated use of, say, several two place predicates, as in SYNTOL, or of multiplace predicates. Faceted systems exemplify undifferentiated multiplace predicates, while differentiated ones are illustrated by Stokolova's "standard phrases"
in which terms are organized in a variety of patterns. (Stokolova
and Tonijan, 1970; Stokolova and Vleduc, 1966a, b; Vleduc and
Stokolova, 1969).

Taken together, the three analyses by Coyaud, Sharp, and Šreider *et al.* throw light on many features of information languages
and their relationships with natural languages. Some other discussions may also be mentioned, for example, those of documentary
languages by de Grolier (1962), Soergel (1967), and Van Slype
(1969), and those of the relation between documentary and natural
languages by Langleben (1967) and Moskovič (1967a, b). The linguistic problems of scientific information are also considered by
Šreider *et al.* (1969b).

As the basis for dividing the content of the two following chapters,
we can characterize the semantic and syntactic aspects of the
activities associated with the three stages of the documentation process as follows. Under the heading of analysis we distinguish the
attempt to identify significant words, or strings to be treated as
units, occurring in the input text, from the attempt to discover
the relations holding between them. In description there is the
treatment of terms as a semantic activity and their organization
in a description, and specifically the indications of relations among
them, as a syntactic one. Finally, under searching comes any form
of term classification as the semantic component of the indexing
language, and any devices for modifying the structure of descriptions as the syntactic component.

5

SYNTAX

Syntax in Natural Language

Syntax, as we have seen, is that part of linguistics which studies (1) formal mechanisms for distinguishing members of the presumably infinite set of sentences in a language from the infinite set of sequences of symbols which are not sentences, and (2) the structures of those strings that are admitted as sentences. Exactly what is meant by a structure differs from one theory to another, but usually it takes the form of a tree with labels on the nodes. Generative grammarians distinguish deep from surface structures, and the deep structures are regarded as more fundamental because they reveal more about the logical relations expressed in the sentence.

That syntax is crucial for the complete understanding of natural sentences is clear, if only because a given set of words can be strung together differently to give different sentences with different meanings. The fact that "Brutus killed Caesar" has a different meaning from "Caesar killed Brutus" is sufficient indication that there is importance in the arrangement, as well as the choice, of words. Furthermore, it seems clear that, in a sentence like "The American ambassador to Israel signed the treaty at two o'clock this afternoon," the phrase "the American ambassador to Israel" constitutes a unit in a way that the sentence "to Israel signed the treaty at" does not. The phrase "the American ambassador to Israel" refers to a single individual and it could be replaced by another phrase, such as simply "the ambassador," without disturbing the integrity of the sentence.

It is facts such as these, and many others, that are accounted for by the syntax of a language. A computer program that must do anything comparable to what humans do when they understand a sentence must, therefore, be capable of performing a syntactic analysis of sentences in the language it is designed to process. What is not so clear is just how far it is necessary to go in the direction of modeling human comprehension in order to achieve useful results in the kinds of task that are of central interest to information scientists. It is certainly not difficult to construct examples of information requests that could be met only by a librarian who knew not only the library collection and the subject matter of the request intimately, but who was also able to appreciate subtleties in the way the request was posed. But this is not to say that these subtleties are important for the general run of requests that libraries must satisfy or that the cost of making the necessary provisions in an automated procedure could be justified. All the automated methods of performing syntactic analyses of natural sentences that have been proposed are exceedingly costly in computer time and space. What is more important is that the linguistic theory underlying these methods is remarkably complex and it is not yet sufficiently well developed to provide reliable results. Different information retrieval applications will doubtless require different standards of performance to make them cost-effective and, if the necessary linguistic theory improves sufficiently, then there will be a place for it in automatic information retrieval systems.

Given that syntactic analysis is to play a role in an automatic information retrieval system, there are various ways in which it might be used, each with an associated cost. It may be considered necessary to analyze the entire text of each document in the system and either to store the analysis as it stands or to use it as a step on the way to obtaining some representation of the document that is more useful for the retrieval process. To carry out this analysis each time the document is considered as a candidate for retrieval would be unthinkably expensive. A second alternative would require that only the title, the abstract, or some short representation of the document be analyzed in this kind of detail. If syntactic analysis is used at all in an information retrieval system, then it will certainly be applied to the information request and, indeed, this may be the only place at which it is used.

Phrase Structure and Dependency

The kinds of grammatical formalism that have been proposed for use in automatic analysis systems fall into two classes. The first contains phrase-structure grammars, and a variant of them called dependency grammars, and the second contains various types of transformational grammar. Grammars belonging to the second class make a distinction between deep and surface structure, assigning to each sentence in the language one or more deep structures, one for each of its grammatical interpretations. No such distinction is made in grammars belonging to the first class.

The sentence "the dog chased the cat" might be analyzed by a phrase-structure grammar to give a result somewhat as shown in Fig. 5.1. The symbol S stands for "sentence", and it occupies the topmost position—the so-called root—of the tree. Extending down the root are two lines leading to nodes labeled NP and VP, respectively. NP stands for "noun phrase" and VP stands for "verb phrase." The node labeled S is said to dominate the two nodes labeled NP and VP, respectively. The claim made by this part of the structure is that the sentence consists of two parts, the noun

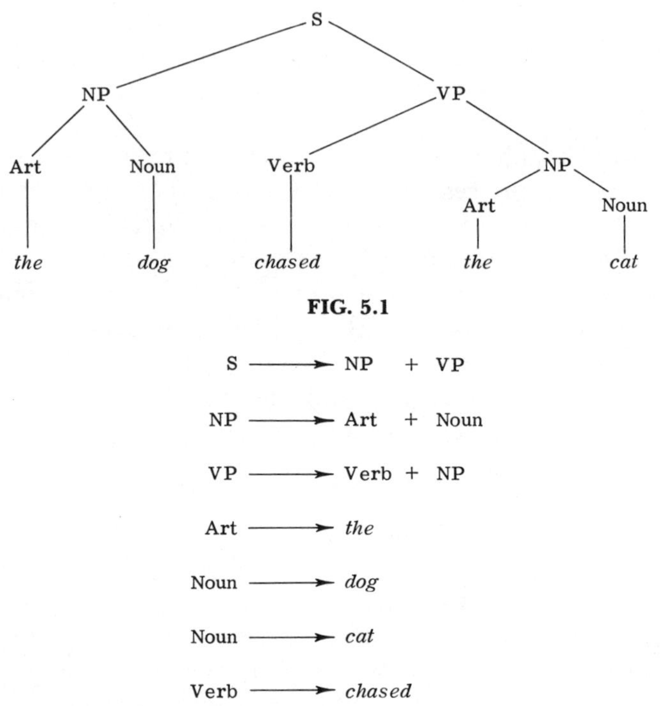

FIG. 5.1

$$S \longrightarrow NP + VP$$

$$NP \longrightarrow Art + Noun$$

$$VP \longrightarrow Verb + NP$$

$$Art \longrightarrow \textit{the}$$

$$Noun \longrightarrow \textit{dog}$$

$$Noun \longrightarrow \textit{cat}$$

$$Verb \longrightarrow \textit{chased}$$

FIG. 5.2

phrase "the dog" and the verb phrase "chased the cat." This part
of the structure is sanctioned by a phrase-structure rule which
is written as follows:

$$S \rightarrow NP + VP.$$

This says that, in general, sentences may consist of noun phrases
followed by verb phrases, though there also may be other rules
allowing other possibilities.

In the example, the noun phrase is claimed to consist of an
article and a noun, and the article is the word "the" and the noun
is the word "dog." The node at the root of the tree also dominates
these nodes, though not directly. In the same way, the verb phrase
is said to consist of a verb, namely the word "chased," and a noun

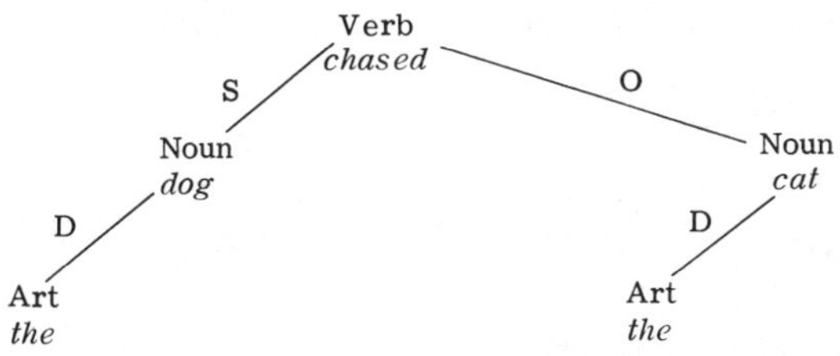

FIG. 5.3

phrase with the same structure as that of the subject of the sentence. The complete set of grammar rules that need to be invoked in constructing this structure is as shown in Fig. 5.2.

A dependency structure for the same sentence might be as shown in Fig. 5.3. Here every node of the tree is labeled with a word of the original sentence and, if the words are read from the tree from left to right, the order is that of the original sentence. The nodes may also be labeled, as in this example, with the names of the grammatical classes to which the words belong. In addition, each line segment in the tree is labeled to show the kind of grammatical relationship it represents. Thus, for example, the line connecting "chased" to "dog" is labeled S, for subject, indicating that "dog" is the subject of "chased." The first word of the sentence belongs, in a sense, to the subject of the sentence, but it is a dependent of the subject, a fact which is indicated by its position beneath it in the tree. Grammatical relations like subject and object are not usually represented by explicit labels in a phrase-structure tree. Instead, a convention is established to the effect that, whenever a noun phrase is directly dominated by a node labeled "sentence," the noun phrase is the subject of the sentence. The object of the sentence, on the other hand, is a noun phrase which is directly dominated by a node labeled "verb phrase."

We have put phrase structure and dependency together in the same class because it is easy to show that the differences between them are trivial from almost every point of view (see Gaifman, 1965). It is also possible to write grammatical rules in a suitable notation which describes a single language and which assigns to each sentence of that language both phrase-structure and dependency trees (see Kay, 1965; Robinson, 1967). In this paper, we shall make no further specific references to dependency grammar, intending what we say about phrase-structure grammar to be understood as applying also to dependency with occasional minor modifications.

Phrase-structure grammars are of interest not only to linguists and people who have cause to write computer programs to process ordinary language, but also to computer scientists who construct programs to translate the statements in a programming language into instructions in the language of a particular computer. There is much interest in compilers, as these translation programs are called, which are not restricted in their application to one programming language. A so-called syntax-directed compiler accepts two kinds of input: a set of programs which it will be expected to translate, and a formal description of the language in which those programs are written. Other kinds of compilers accept only the first kind of input, the description of the language being built into the very fabric of the compiler.

The syntax of a programming language is usually written in a variant of BNF (for "Backus–Naur form" or "Backus normal form") which is nothing more than a way of writing context-free phrase-structure grammars. The term "context-free" can be misleading. It should certainly not be taken as implying that such a grammar takes no account of context—context is the main business of grammar. Consider once again the following rule:

$$VP \rightarrow V + NP.$$

It says that a verb phrase can consist of a verb followed by a noun phrase, completely regardless of the environment this verb phrase occurs in. Wherever the grammar specifies a verb phrase, then, one of this kind will do. Suppose, however, that the grammar said that a verb phrase could take this particular form only, say, following a noun phrase. The rule might be written somewhat as follows:

$$VP \rightarrow V + NP/NP ____\,.$$

The original rule is here followed by a slash and a string in which the underline character represents the position that the verb phrase must occupy if this rule is to be applicable. In this case, the underlined character follows NP so that the rule can be applied only if the verb phrase occurs immediately after a noun phrase. If a grammar contains one or more rules involving conditions of this kind, it is said to be context sensitive. A context-free grammar is one which contains no rules of this kind. It is possible to show mathematically that context-sensitive grammars are, in general, fundamentally more powerful than context-free grammars. What this means is that there are languages, though not necessarily natural languages, which can be described by grammars containing context-sensitive rules but for which it is impossible to construct an adequate context-free grammar. Nevertheless, the formalism of context-free grammars is already so powerful, and a procedure necessary to process context-sensitive grammars is so complex, that the context-free formalism is preferred by linguists and computer scientists alike.

Automatic Phrase-Structure Analysis

As a result of the interest on the part both of compiler designers and computational linguists in phrase-structure grammars, techniques for causing computers to analyze, or parse, sentences with grammars of this kind are very well understood. Several algorithms are now available and there is a growing literature on the theory of such algorithms which concentrates on their relative efficiency measured in terms of the computer time or space that they consume (see particularly Earley, 1970; Griffiths and Petrick, 1965). There have been two large-scale projects aimed at showing how effective context-free phrase-structure grammar can be in the automatic analysis of ordinary language. The first resulted in the Predictive Analyzer of Kuno and Oettinger (see Kuno, 1965; Kuno and Oettinger, 1963). The second project was carried out at the

Rand Corporation by Robinson and Marks (1965) using the PARSE program. In both cases a grammar was written consisting of some thousands of rules. Both programs were applied to large numbers of sentences, additions and corrections made to the rules, and the cycle repeated many times.

The results of the experience were interesting but by no means encouraging. Perhaps the most important thing that was discovered was that it is virtually beyond human capacity to discover how well a grammar describes a particular language without using a computer and conducting this kind of experiment. Equally important was the discovery that context-free phrase-structure grammar, despite its undoubted power, is far too weak an instrument for the description of natural languages. The difficulties were of two kinds. First, it is difficult to decide in any but an entirely ad hoc manner which of various possible structures for a sentence should be considered correct, and, second, even if ad hoc decisions are made on a massive scale, it proved impossible to prevent the machine from obtaining large numbers of structures for apparently innocent sentences. The difficulty, then, was not so much to obtain a correct solution as somehow to limit the total number of solutions, correct or incorrect. In its final form, Robinson's procedure obtained no less than 106 solutions for the following sentence:

> An exploratory investigation is undertaken to survey the extent to which the idea of undetermined coefficients can profitably be used in practice for root-extraction with polynomial equations.

Robinson (Robinson and Marks, 1965) comments as follows:

> The major source of multiple parsings is the presence of prepositional phrases and other adverbial modifiers. The problem of correctly specifying when such constraints should be attached to the sentence as a whole or one of several elements within it appears to have no easy solution. All sentences ending with two or more prepositional phrases or with a prepositional phrase following a noun object will receive multiple parsings; and if they may be attached to several verb forms, the multiplication

of analyses is compounded further. This source alone accounts for most of the analyses obtained in sentence twenty-eight [above], whose three final prepositional phrases are attached in various permutations to each other and to the preceding verb phrases headed respectively by *undertaken, survey,* and *used.*

Kuno and Oettinger's (1963) program obtained 136 analyses of the sentence

Gravely concerned with spreading racial violence, President Kennedy used his press conference to issue counsel to both sides in the struggle.

Parsing Strategies

There are innumerable strategies on which an automatic procedure to parse sentences with a phrase-structure grammar can be based. This is not the place to go into them in detail, and an excellent introduction can be found in Hays (1966) or Hays (1967, Chapter 6). For our present purposes it will be sufficient to note that there are two broad classes of strategies which, following Hays, we may call target strategies and morsel strategies, respectively. The Predictive Analyzer of Kuno and Oettinger (1963) is an example of a program using a target strategy, and the algorithm due to John Cocke and used in Robinson's PARSE program was the earliest published example of a program using a morsel strategy.

A program based on a target strategy establishes for itself the goal of finding a set of rules in the grammar which, when applied in the appropriate order and at the appropriate place in the structure so far developed, will deliver as a result the sentence which it is required to parse, together with a structure for it. It will then retrace its steps and attempt to find a point in the process at which an alternative move could have been made and then go forward from that point, attempting, in this way, to find each of the possible structures of the sentences in turn. At any given moment, the program is working on one particular hypothesis about the structure of the sentence before it, and is attempting to find rules in the grammar which can be applied in such a way as to complete the validation of that hypothesis. Each time a rule is found which can be applied, or against which there is as yet not sufficient evidence, it is added to the bottom of a list with an indication of the position in the structure at which it is required. If a hypothesis proves untenable, that is, if there are no rules in the grammar that are compatible with the list as already constructed, then rules are removed from the bottom of the list, one by one, and an attempt is made to find an alternative for each so that a modified version of the hypothesis can be explored. Notice that exactly the same moves are made when an hypothesis is abandoned as when it is finally validated, except that a validated hypothesis is preserved as a current solution whereas an abandoned one is not.

So-called backtracking strategies of this kind are part of the programmer's stock in trade, and they have innumerable applications in and outside linguistics. In its simplest form it is the strategy required to explore a maze. We begin by taking an essentially random path, remembering which alternative we choose wherever there is an alternative. Whenever our way is blocked, or when it becomes clear that the present path will not lead to our goal, we return to the last intersection, mark a path from which we just returned so that we shall not take it again, and try another one. Eventually all the paths from that intersection will be marked as having been tried, and we return to do likewise at the preceding intersection. It is easy to see that this policy will lead us to the prize wherever in the maze it may be or, if there is no prize, will lead us to explore the entire maze.

At any given moment in the operation of a program based on a morsel strategy, it is not possible to say that one particular hypothesis about the structure of the sentence is being explored. On the contrary, a collection of partial structures is being assembled, using current members of the collection as the basis on which to construct new ones, in such a way that, when the process is complete, all the admissible structures of the sentence will be in the collection.

An efficient program of this kind must be designed so as to keep the collection as small as possible while insuring that it contains the material necessary for building all the admissible structures of the sentence being analyzed. There are many ways in which this can be done. One way is to examine each word in the sentence in turn and to add to the list of structures all those phrases allowed by the grammar which could be formed from this word and those preceding it in the sentence. This policy insures that, if a phrase ending in a certain word contains as parts other phrases involving earlier words in the sentence, then these other phrases will necessarily have been added to the collection previously. The program can therefore be sure to find all the material it needs for constructing a new phrase already in the collection. When the final word of the sentence is reached, it is to be hoped that one or more structures will be added to the collection which involve both the first and the last word of the sentence and which bear the label "sentence." These are the correct structures of the string, and any others now in the collection which did not prove useful in constructing these can be forgotten.

It is not clear that one of these strategies is markedly better than the other under all circumstances. Where the language is highly ambiguous, there is much to be said for the morsel strategy, whereas when ambiguities are few or entirely absent, as in the case of most programming languages, a target strategy is to be preferred. The reasons for this are easy to see. Consider, for example, the sentence "Drinking water can cause an increase in the severity of this condition." Any phrase-structure grammar of English is likely to find this sentence highly ambiguous. It consists of a subject, "drinking water" and a predicate "can cause an increase in the severity of this condition." But both the subject and the predicate are ambiguous and the number of interpretations of the sentence as a whole is the number of interpretations of the subject multiplied by the number of interpretations of the predicate. The subject can be construed as a noun phrase consisting of an adjective followed by a noun, which is the only possible interpretation in the sentence "the drinking water can cause an increase in the severity of this condition." The great number of interpretations of the predicate comes from the fact that there is no straightforward way to decide what each of the prepositional phrases modifies. Are there any criteria that could be reasonably stated in the terms of phrase-structure grammar that would show whether "of this condition" modifies "cause," "increase," or "severity"? The answer is presumably "No," especially in view of the fact that the same grammar must presumably provide a structure for the sentence "Drinking water can cause an increase in the severity of two degrees" for which the most naturally appealing structure is different.

A program based on the standard target strategy would choose one interpretation of the subject first and then rehearse each of the possible structures of the predicate, putting them together with the chosen interpretation of the subject to form a complete structure for the sentence. It will then find the second interpretation for the subject and will construct complete interpretations of the sentence by repeating considerable amounts of work that it has already done on the ambiguous predicate. This kind of multiplication of effort will be unavoidable wherever there is more than one interpretation of some words that occur toward the beginning of the string, and the amount of work that has to be repeated grows with the length of the string following that ambiguous part. Following a morsel strategy, the various interpretations of the subject and the predicate would be developed independently and added to the collection. Only then would an attempt be made to construct interpretations of the sentence as a whole and to add them to the material already in the collection, and the work would be done only once.

The disadvantage of the morsel strategy is that phrases are often added to the collection which are grammatically incompatible with anything that precedes or follows them. For example, the sentence "Drinking water can cause an increase in the severity of this condition" contains the sequence "water can" which could occur as a noun phrase in a sentence like "He could not find the water can." This would be added to the collection of structures along with everything else, but it would go unnoticed by a target strategy.

An algorithm was recently proposed by Earley (1970) that combines the advantages of the target and morsel strategies while exhibiting some additional attractive properties. The plan adopted here is to work on particular hypotheses about the structure of the sentence as in a target strategy, but to work on them in parallel, conflating two or more of them whenever they predict the same thing for the part of the sentences that remains to be examined. Applied to the sentence in our example, the program would be working on two separate hypotheses by the time it reached the second word. But, once it decided that the first two words constitute a noun phrase, it would establish only one hypothesis about the remainder of the sentence, namely that it consists of a verb phrase in spite of the fact that there are two different ways of constructing the initial noun phrase. There is very little doubt that Earley's algorithm is the best that has been proposed.

If phrase-structure grammars have been abandoned by most computational linguists, it is not because of a lack of suitable analysis algorithms. The programs of Kuno and Oettinger and of Robinson would doubtless have been less expensive in computer time and storage space if Earley's algorithm had been available, but the inherent deficiencies of phrase-structure grammar would not have been in any way affected, and they would still have attained large numbers of uninformatively different structures for apparently innocent sentences. For more fundamental reasons, phrase-structure grammar has also been abandoned by large numbers of theoretical linguists who have turned instead to one variant or another of transformational or generative grammar.

Transformational Grammar

As a formal device, transformational grammar is considerably more complicated than phrase-structure or dependency grammar. Transformational grammar contains a number of components, the

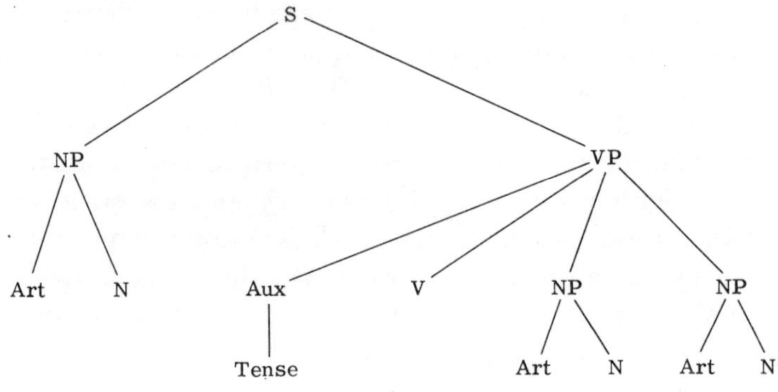

FIG. 5.4

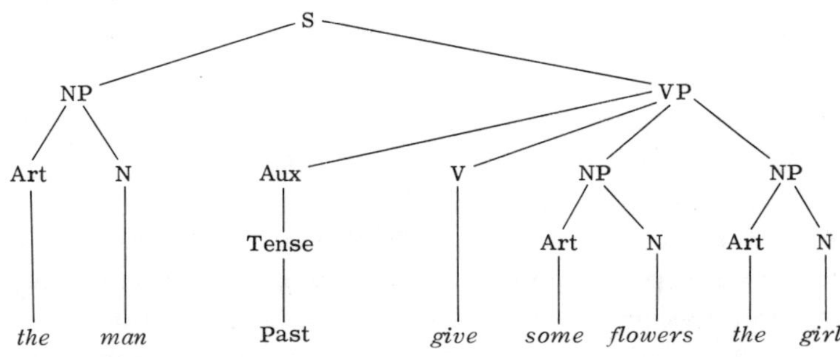

FIG. 5.5

first of which is a set of phrase-structure rules of the kind we
have already discussed. These generate strings of so-called preterminals and associated tree structures. A possible product of this
component of a transformational grammar might be as shown
in Fig. 5.4. The preterminal string, read from left to right, is as
follows:

ART N TENSE V ART N ART N.

A second part of the grammar, called the lexical component,
appends words or other lexical items beneath the preterminals
in the tree. After the work of this component is complete, the
tree might look somewhat as is shown in Fig. 5.5. This is now

the base structure of a sentence like "The man gave some flowers to the girl." Notice, however, that there are some words in the base structure, such as "Past," which do not occur in the sentence itself; "Past" must somehow be combined with "give" to yield "gave." This will be one of the functions of the transformational component of the grammar, as we shall see shortly. Notice also that the word "to" in the sentence does not occur anywhere in the base structure.

One single tree structure produced by the phrase-structure and lexical components can be the base structure for more than one sentence. One of the attractions of the transformational grammar is that it gives the same base structure to a whole family of sentences if they all mean the same thing and if they are grammatically related in some systematic way. The structure shown above underlies not only "The man gave some flowers to the girl" but also "The man gave the girl some flowers," "Some flowers were given to the girl by the man," "Some flowers were given the girl by the man," "The girl was given some flowers by the man," etc.

We do not intend to claim that the base structure we have exhibited is, in any ultimate sense, the correct base structure of all these sentences—that is a matter for debate; the point is that the correct base structure for any one of these sentences is presumably also the correct base structure for the rest. Furthermore, if two of these families of sentences are closely related in meaning, if one family contains the negations of the other, or if one contains statements and the other corresponding questions, then the relationship is usually transparent in the base structure. Notice that, in English, the sentence "The man did not give some flowers to the girl" differs from its positive counterpart not only in the presence of the word "not" but also in the introduction of an auxiliary "did" and in the fact that it is this auxiliary rather than the main verb "give" that is in the past tense. In other words, a straightforward change in the meaning of the sentence, as atomic a change as one could readily imagine, results in several changes in the sentence itself. In the base structure, however, the negative sentence differs from its positive counterpart only in the presence of the negative marker "not." One reason, then, for making a distinction between deep and surface structures is that there are fewer different kinds of deep structure so that they function as a kind of canonical form for sentences. If a program must take some action based on the meaning it obtains for a sentence, then there is much to be said for first transforming the sentence into a base structure so that the number of different kinds of operations that will have to be performed thenceforward will be reduced.

A second important advantage of deep structure is also related to the semantic interpretation of sentences. In elementary school grammar, children are sometimes taught that the subject of the sentence is the actor and the object is the person or thing upon whom the action described by the sentence is carried out, that the subject's role is essentially active whereas the object's is passive. It is reasonable to look for relationships of this kind in sentences; there must at least be various kinds of relations that words contract if it is to be possible to say that a sentence has any unity at all. But examination of a few sentences rapidly makes it clear that there is no more than a sporadic correspondence between the subject of the sentence and the actor or between the object and the patient. Consider the sentence "John received a blow on the head," in which John is undoubtedly the subject in spite of the fact that his role in the proceedings appears to have been passive. Or consider Chomsky's (1965) example of the two sentences "I persuaded John to leave" and "I expected John to leave." Only the verb is different and, at first glance, it may seem that they should receive the same grammatical analysis. But in the second sentence, John's leaving is the object because this is that I expected to happen, while in the first sentence, John's leaving is not what I persuaded; on the contrary it is John alone that I persuaded and the words "to leave" should presumably be given some other status in the sentence. If I say "I expected a specialist to examine John" I am saying the same as if I had said "I expected John to be examined by a specialist." But if I say "I persuaded a specialist to examine John" I am saying something very different from "I persuaded John to be examined by a specialist." The moral of the story is that notions such as subject and object, if they can be applied to surface structures at all, have little to do with the semantic interpretation of sentences. The relationships that are important for this interpretation are to be sought in the deep structure.

Deep structures are related to surface structures by the rules of the transformational component of the grammar. Each of these rules takes a complete tree structure as input and delivers a complete tree structure as output. The input to a rule is the output from the last rule that was applied so that there are in addition to deep and surface structures, a great many intermediate structures, which are, however, of no interest in their own right. A more or less complex set of conventions is established in each variant theory of transformational grammar for the order in which rules are to be applied; some rules are obligatory, so that they must be applied whenever the appropriate conditions are obtained, and others are optional so that two different sentences with the same base structure can be obtained, one by applying the rule, and one by omitting it. Transformational rules can change syntactic structures by moving part of the tree from one place to another, by making a copy of one part in another place, by adding and deleting elements, and so forth.

Form of Deep Structures

There is considerable difference of opinion about the form that deep structures should take. It is generally agreed that the base component should define a simple sentence which, according to some linguists, notably Chomsky, should be so simple as to allow only a finite number of different trees, and that the complexity of real sentences should be accounted for by embedding simple sentences inside one another. Thus, for example, the sentence "John saw a big bear" might come from a deep structure with a terminal string something like "John saw a bear (the bear was big)," in which the adjective which modifies the noun "bear" in the surface structure is represented by an embedded sentence. According to most generative grammarians, a simple sentence in the deep structure is broadly similar to a simple sentence in surface structure, with a subject, a predicate, and so forth. One school of generative grammarians, however, has recently popularized a different view of deep structure which seems especially interesting in the context of information retrieval.

Fillmore (1968) is the inventor of what has come to be known as case grammar. In his view, sentences in deep structure consist of a verb and a number of noun phrases, each of which is marked as being a certain case. The grammar allows for some set number of cases, say six, with names like "agent," "instrument," "location," and so forth. Each verb is permitted to "take" certain sets of cases that are specified for it in the lexicon. The connection between these cases and such things as subject, direct object, prepositional phrase, etc. in surface structure is relatively remote and complex. However, the scheme has several notable advantages of which the main one is that cases have a semantic coherence which is almost entirely lacking in surface relations. To take an example from Fillmore, one and the same event can be described by the sentences "John opened the door" and "The door opened." But "the door" appears in one as subject and in the other as object. It would be in the same case (object) in the deep structures of both sentences. The transformational rules are written in such a way that the deep object can become the surface subject only in the absence of a candidate with a higher claim to that position, such as an agent. Some writers have used the obviously appealing term "role" in place of "case" in discussing grammars of this kind (see, for example, Langendoen, 1970), and the analogy between these and the roles advocated for use in document description languages by some documentalists (for a discussion, see Lancaster, 1968b) is compelling.

Transformational Parsing

If a computer program is to be written that obtains deep structures for arbitrary sentences, then the sequence of events that we have described must presumably be reversed. A surface structure must be obtained for the given string, a set of rules applied to it whose effect is the inverse of that of the transformational component, and the resulting tree structure must be checked for acceptability against the phrase-structure rules of the base component. However, it is not obvious that the process is reversible, because, while the output of the transformational component is a tree structure, the input to the corresponding analysis procedure is not a tree structure but a list of words which would have occupied the bottommost nodes. An analysis procedure cannot, therefore, be constructed by simply reversing the steps involved in producing the sentence. This is not surprising—even with the much simpler formalism of phrase-structure grammar, analysis must be performed by much more devious strategies.

Techniques for obtaining deep structures for given strings of words, unlike those of phrase-structure analysis, are by no means well understood and the number of people actively pursuing the small number of lines of attack that have been proposed is remarkably small. Thus far, three such lines of attack have in fact emerged, and there are, as yet, no grounds on which to base an assessment of which of them will prove most productive.

Approaches Emphasizing
Rule Form

The first approach is followed by people who take the view that what is most important about a transformational grammar is the rules that it contains rather than, for example, the pairs of deep and surface structures that it establishes. For them, a parsing program is of interest only if it accepts as input a set of sentences to be analyzed on the one hand, and the phrase-structure, lexical, and transformational rules of a standard transformational grammar on the other. If the form of these rules is not suitable for analysis, then the program must have ways of changing their form. If it is necessary to provide different kinds of rules for the program, then the program is not, properly speaking, a transformational analyzer. The advocates of this approach, then, are linguistic purists, and, since our approach in this survey is preeminently practical, we have no reason to prefer their view above any others that might be taken. On the other hand, the programs that have been written by members of this school have been, from a fairly practical viewpoint, just as effective as those written by anybody else.

Transformational analyzers based on purist principles have been written by Petrick and by a group of researchers at the MITRE Corporation. The differences between the two programs are minor and need not concern us here. Both operate by first constructing one or more surface structures for the incoming sentences, carrying out on these a set of operations whose effect is the inverse of that of the transformational rules, verifying the one or more putative base structures obtained from this process against the rules of the base component, applying the rules of the transformational component of the original grammar to each of these putative base structures, and rejecting any base structure from which the sentence being analyzed cannot be obtained in this way. The last step, that in which the original transformational rules are applied to obtain the sentence being analyzed from the putative base structures derived from it, is necessary for two reasons. First, it can be shown that there is, in general, no way of writing a phrase-structure grammar which assigns to a set of strings exactly those structures that would be assigned to them by a transformational grammar. The best that can be done is to write a grammar that will never fail to assign the structure that the transformational grammar assigns but which may occasionally assign some additional structures that could not be obtained from the transformational grammar. Second, the effects of transformational rules are not, in general, reversible. In other words, it is not always possible to tell by examining a syntactic structure, whether a given rule must have been applied to produce it or not. Both possibilities must therefore be explored, and both may lead to what seems to be an acceptable base structure. It may, however, be the case that the original sentence is obtainable, using the original set of transformational rules, from only one of the alternatives.

The MITRE program did not, in fact, construct the phrase-structure rules of the surface grammar automatically from the rules of the transformational grammar, but the designers of the system subscribed to the view that this was a goal towards which they should strive. Petrick has achieved considerable success in his attempts to automate the production of this surface grammar, and if he has not been totally successful, a large part of the blame must be laid at the door of the transformational grammarians themselves. Whereas, in the pretransformational period of linguistics, it was often possible to show that linguists whose informal accounts of their activities looked very different were in fact using identical formal devices, in the transformational period it appears that each of the many subscribers to transformational grammar is, in fact, using a different formalism. It is no indictment of transformational grammar that it occurs in a bewildering number of varieties, each of which is constantly changing; this is, if anything, evidence only of the dynamism of the field. But it makes life difficult for a person with a purist turn of mind who, as a programmer, cannot bend quickly and easily with the wind.

Approaches Emphasizing
the Deep–Surface Distinction

Advocates of the other two approaches take the view that the distinction between deep and surface structure is the main insight that transformational grammarians have provided into the workings of ordinary language, and that the formalism for rules that they propose is of secondary interest. It matters little, they argue, what form the rules that we supply to the computer take or how much creative and essentially nonmechanical work we must do to produce them if they always produce the base structures we think right. The base structures they think right may in fact be dictated by an existing transformational grammar, but the steps prescribed by the transformational rules of that grammar for going from deep to surface structure are of no interest to them.

One of the nonpurist schools of transformational parsing exploits devices that were developed by computer scientists for use in programs intended to translate other programs from a standard programming language into the internal language of a particular computer. The vast majority of programs written today are in fact processed by such a compiler before they can be carried out by the machine. There is much interest at present in compilers that make central and explicit use of phrase-structure grammars to analyze the programs they translate. But a grammar is not itself a translation device and, in order to make it into one, each of its rules must be augmented by an extra clause specifying how the phrases it is used to construct are to be translated. These extra clauses are called, albeit misleadingly, the semantic part of the grammar. They consist of rules in their own right which accept inputs from the smaller phrases which go to make up the one being constructed and which produce outputs that will, in general, be used by other higher-level rules. The plan is straightforward: each phrase has a meaning which is derivable in a definite way from the meanings of the phrases that make it up.

When these notions are applied to the problem of parsing to obtain deep structures, they appear as follows: a phrase-structure grammar must be written which will probably generate something close to the surface structures assigned by the transformational grammar, though the structures it assigns are, in fact, not crucial. Whenever a new phrase is constructed with this grammar, an expression is associated with it which is, in this case, not a representation of the meaning of the phrase, but part of the description of the base structure of any sentence to which that phrase belongs. Again, the plan is clear: a surface phrase can be produced by a transformational grammar only as a result of certain conditions that obtained in the base structure; these are the conditions that are specified in the expression associated with the phrase. This approach was first taken by Kuno in his "Kernelizer." More recently it has been taken up again by Thorne *et al.* (1968), Bobrow and Fraser (1969), and Woods (1970). These last three groups call the methods they are developing those of the transition network parser, and, while the description they give of these methods is very different from ours, the underlying principles are the same.

The third approach is that of Colmerauer *et al.* (1970), Kaplan (1970), and Kay (1967). They aim to develop a scheme which will obtain the deep structures of sentences from the surface string of words without passing by the intermediary of the surface structure. The formalism they employ makes use of so-called general rewrite rules, where the objects being rewritten are not, as in the usual case, strings of simple symbols but strings of trees. The words in the sentence to be analyzed are treated as degenerate trees consisting of only one node. Each rule applied to some given sequence of trees and its output takes the form of another sequence, possibly combining some of the original trees into one, possibly reordering them, possibly introducing new material not in the original sentence, possibly deleting items, and so forth. The formalism is immensely powerful but, on the face of it, is nothing more than one of many ways of defining a general-purpose computing machine because, as Markov (1961) has shown, general rewriting rules over strings of simple symbols, leaving aside the complex operations for manipulating tree structures, are sufficient to specify any computation that can be done by any means whatever. In other words, if automatic syntactic analysis can be done at all, then it can certainly be done with rules of this kind; this is a matter of mathematical fact requiring no empirical verification.

What the proponents of this approach are concerned to demonstrate is not only that their methods can be made to work, but that they can be made to work in an efficient and theoretically revealing way. Their claim is not only that the necessary rules can be written according to their formalism, but also that these rules will be at least as perspicuous as those that any other formalism allows. Other parsing programs, such as those designed by Glasersfeld (1965), Sager (1967), Sakai (1962), and Schank and Tesler (1969), each have their own unique features and points of interest. But from the point of view of the level of generality we are forced to adopt in a survey of this kind, they will fall in one of the two classes of phrase-structure methods already described. Other schools of linguistics have contributed little to work on automatic analysis methods, largely for reasons we have already pointed out. Chomsky and his followers have been far more insistent on the use of well-defined formal systems in their activities, and it is therefore not surprising that the theories developed by this school have lent themselves more easily to computer applications. One possible exception is the stratificational grammar of Lamb (1966), which is in many ways the most eminently mechanizable of any linguistic theory we know. Stratificational grammar is nothing more or less than a wiring diagram for a machine which, set to work in one mode, will generate sentences and, in another, will recognize and assign structures to sentences. The components that are connected together in these diagrams are, to be sure, not standard components of electrical engineering. But it would be an entirely trivial matter to write a computer program that would simulate their operation and Reich (1968) has announced his intention to do this. However, as far as we know, no results are as yet available from this experiment. A remarkably similar, but independent, development is to be found in the machine-translation system of Hoppe, (1969).

Syntax in Information Retrieval

The foregoing gives a broad overview of current syntactic theories and of our knowledge of the computational techniques necessary to accompany them. We must now turn to the use made of syntactic information in information science, and the possible application of such syntactic theories to information retrieval. This means, referring to the three aspects of information science listed in Chapter 4, that we must examine first the reference made to syntax in the analysis of input documents or their surrogates, second the syntactic aspects of document description, and third the syntactic aspects of the indexing language itself. We are primarily concerned here with explicit syntax. As noted earlier, syntactic information may be used indirectly, for example, when complex index terms or subject headings are used. The term "steel beams," for instance, instead of the separate terms "steel" and "beams," avoids mismatches with texts on steel for beams through the implicit syntactic structure of the term. Coordinating separate terms, say, by links, on the other hand, represents an explicit use of syntax.

Whether syntactic information is of real value in information retrieval in general is perhaps the major debating point in the field. Experiments suggest some sort of trade-off. There are occasions when crassly false term coordinations can be successfully avoided by the use of syntax but there are also occasions when particular syntactic constructions preclude matches between really, of sufficiently, related structures. There is some evidence for the argument that syntax is helpful mainly in search situations where the prime objective is to retrieve only relevant documents, though minimizing the retrieval of nonrelevant documents is liable to mean that many relevant ones are missed as well. But in simple term coordination systems successful results may also be achieved without syntax because in practice term combinations are not matched by documents other than those having the appropriate underlying structure. Unfortunately it is difficult to reach any solid conclusions about syntax in indexing. Those believing in syntax can be criticized for not having demonstrated its value in serious experiments, while those who have apparently shown that it is of little value can be condemned for not using it in the right way. It is, however, of some interest to note that major experiments like those carried out by the SMART Project and the Comparative Systems Laboratory were negative and that similar conclusions have been reached by Lancaster (Comparative Systems Laboratory, 1968; Lancaster, 1968c; Salton, 1968a; Salton and Lesk, 1968). Indirect support is also given by tests comparing descriptors and subject indexing, in which descriptors gave better results (see Grinina and Sokolova, 1970; and Popova and Jakubson, 1969).

The most usual approach has been to make use of comparatively limited syntactic information and relatively simple structures. This may be merely the result of inadequate syntactic theories either for natural or indexing languages. If a sufficiently powerful theory were available, equivalences could be established between different expressions in analyzing input texts and in manipulating description texts. But it may alternatively be a consequence of the nature of information retrieval needs. If documents must be characterized in a fairly summary way, and allowance must be made for requests approaching topics from very different angles, descriptions must be designed for gross rather than refined matching. The experiments just mentioned in fact support this view.

This is perhaps the main reason for the fact that virtually no attempts have been made by information scientists to exploit current linguistic theories of syntax, either in providing procedures for analyzing input documents or in designing languages to describe them. A loose application of phrase-structure notions is generally discernible, but references to transformational grammar, for example, are nonexistent. It must, however, be recognized that the syntactic scene in linguistics is shifting enough to deter any information scientist from trying to pick up handy language-processing tools. Those working in syntax in documentation have either tried to develop their theories independently, like Farradane (1967; Farradane *et al.*, 1966), or have sought to apply symbolic logic, like Padučeva (1967, 1968). The former gain from starting with documentation needs but have a lot of work to do; the latter gain from taking over a well-developed discipline, but its relevance to information retrieval has to be demonstrated.

The final general point is that very little work has been done on automated syntactic analysis and description, though automated searching using descriptions with syntax may be done.

Input Text Syntax

Information about the syntactic features of an input document or surrogate text may be sought for two reasons: first, to provide indications of structural relations which will be represented in some way in the actual index description, and second, to permit the identification of significant items in the text which may be adopted as terms. For example, in the first case the presence of an adjective noun group in the text may be represented by a pair of terms having a main term-qualifying term relationship in the description. In the second we may seek to establish that a given text item is a noun because we are selecting nouns as content clues. A further distinction is between global and partial input parsing. The former implies a more or less complete analysis of the input text, though the resulting structural information may not be preserved, the latter a relatively limited search for particular types of structure.

The number of projects attempting anything like a full parsing of the input text for a document is very small. Among them are the SMART and SYNTOL projects, both of which use analysis to provide syntactic information later incorporated in descriptions.

Syntactic analysis and description routines provide one of the many document processing options investigated experimentally by Salton (1968a). The analysis procedure involves Kuno and Oettinger's Predictive Analyzer and a dictionary of criterion phrases represented by dependency trees. Each such tree represents a class of related input structures and is defined by a set of terms, or more accurately, of semantic word class names, with specified syntactic relations between them, the whole being sufficiently flexible to allow a variety of alternative natural language formulations. In analysis, sentences of the input document are parsed, and the resulting tree structure is examined to see whether it contains any criterion phrases. The recognition of criterion phrases in the sentence structure is not difficult, though it is not entirely trivial, because the description of a phrase may require one term to be dependent on another but allow the dependency to be indirect, so that a considerable amount of searching may be needed to determine whether the phrase is present.

This part of the SMART system clearly represents a major effort, and substantial provision is made for identifying the same structure in a whole range of different disguises. A major limitation of the method is the use of a dictionary. Identifying a criterion phrase in the system has the same logical status as assigning an indexing term taken from a previously constructed term dictionary if an appropriate entry word has been noted. The distinctive feature of Salton's process is that quite complex terms are allowed. One way to describe the procedure is to say that it identifies idioms. It is evident that reference even to a simple term dictionary may mean that information in a document is not picked up in indexing. This is very much more likely with a phrase dictionary since it has to attempt to deal with a far wider range of input expressions. It is therefore not surprising that the retrieval performance given by descriptions set up in this way was rather disappointing.

The SYNTOL project is a very ambitious one and, indeed, represents the major current project on automated syntactic indexing. But since the whole is complex, it will be considered in its entirety later.

Partial Parsing

Partial parsing of varying degrees of sophistication is represented by the work of Armitage and Lynch (1967, 1968), Borkowski *et al.* (1970), Clarke and Wall (1965), Earl (1970), Hillman (1968), and Weiss (1969b), as well as by the work of the Central Institute of Patent Information (Vasilievskij and Kravec, 1970).

The most interesting of these projects is Hillman's (1968; Hillman and Kasarda, 1969). The syntactic procedures form part of an integrated whole and have been specifically developed from a theory of the requirements of a retrieval system. In particular, Hillman argues that a document description should indicate what a document is about, that this is represented by referential noun phrases, and that these appear in sentences expressing logical relations or set inclusion. The object of Hillman's analysis procedure is therefore primarily to identify such document characteristics, or terms, and secondarily, to obtain information for weighting them by their status as arguments of one or more n-ary relations. This is done by reducing the sentences of the input text to their "canonical components" (underlying sentences expressing relations) and picking out the noun phrases referred to in them, with their relational qualifiers.

All the operations are relatively simple. The initial text processing assigns syntactic categories to words and picks out items like prepositional phrases, using a limited dictionary of function words and a small set of rules. The second phase reduces these strings to canonical components. This is done by looking for verb phrases, since these embody relations, and establishing their environments. The process involves an initial stage in which noun and verb phrases are identified, unamalgamated conjunctions being taken as component separators. Finally noun phrases are selected and their relations noted.

It should be emphasized that this procedure is applied to full document texts within a system designed for high-class treatment of a selected document collection. Salton's experiments were with abstracts, the analysis being very time consuming. Unfortunately, no real information is available about the performance of Hillman's system.

The system developed at the Central Institute for Patent Information involving English-Russian translation based on partial parsing, is an ambitious but somewhat specialized one. An overview is provided by Vasilievskij and Kravec (1970). (See also Gerasimova *et al.*, 1967; Giršberg and Šenderov, 1970; Kravec *et al.*, 1966; and the papers in *Experim.*, 1970.) The system is oriented to the particular properties of patents, since it is mainly concerned with the identification and processing of the long noun groups characteristic of patents. The input text analysis routines are designed to identify such groups; procedures for picking up idioms and for resolving ambiguities are included. This is followed by routines for breaking down the groups into segments and the establishment of patterns which are then matched against a pattern dictionary. Russian text is synthesized following this stage.

Work on partial parsing has also been carried out by Clarke and Wall (1965), continuing earlier researches reported in Baxendale (1962). This system is designed to obtain index terms or phrases from abstract texts, and the approach adopted resembles Hillman's in using a restricted dictionary to provide a surface parsing of sentences from which noun phrases can be extracted. It is, however, somewhat simpler, since the sophistication associated with Hillman's canonical components is absent.

The programs illustrate the advantages and disadvantages of partial as opposed to full parsing very well. The procedure divides sentences up into mutually compatible phrases without insisting that they be integrated into an overall structure. Thus the problem that causes the greatest difficulties to a complete analyzer like Robinson's PARSE program, namely that of uninformative multiple analyses, is largely avoided. The sentence "I saw the man in the park with the telescope" contains two prepositional phrases which Clarke and Wall's program would aim to identify, but it would not aim to establish which of the elements in the preceding sentence each of them modifies. The program itself is simple in that it consists of a set of rewriting rules like those provided for in the SYNTOL programming language, which are carried out deterministically so that only one analysis of the sentence is obtained. This is a reasonable approach because, though such a program may frequently obtain an incorrect structure, it would be faced with a worse dilemma if it found a multitude of solutions. In fact, actual tests showed a fairly high level of accuracy in phrase identification for Clarke and Wall's program, so it may be adequate as a means for selecting indexing items.

Further partial parsing experiments have been carried out by Earl (1970), though these were aimed at sentence extracting rather than indexing. Attempts to use the parser to establish significant forms of sentences were not successful, and it was subsequently exploited to obtain noun phrases. These were then used as clues to select sentences and, independently, in book indexing.

A more humble approach is represented by Armitage and Lynch's (1967, 1968; Armitage *et al.*, 1970) work on the computer-aided production of articulated subject indexes from document titles. Such indexes consist of headings and systematically organized modifying phrases, and the project is based on the assumption that these can be obtained by dividing titles at the points defined by prepositions and taking the resulting strings as headings and modifiers. The procedure is fairly successful but is limited in its objective and relies heavily on the content density of titles.

The lowest level of partial parsing, or minimal syntactic analysis, is to be found in the use of ad hoc syntactic clues like the presence of certain prepositions to guide the selection of terms. This is illustrated by Weiss's exploitation of "templates," or syntactic frames like, for example, "from ____ to ____," which may be filled out with certain sorts of content words—in this case, dates. He reports some successful but limited experiments in identifying bibliographic items like journals and dates. Similar work on a larger scale on the identification of case citations in legal literature through trigger expressions like "v." is reported by Borkowsky *et al.* (1970). The idea is also exploited for a role-incorporating descriptor system by Otradinskij and Kravčenko (1969) and Otradinskij and Vleduc (1970).

Finally, it is worth noticing that syntactic criteria may be exploited in a very refined way in the selection of terms; they can clearly be used to resolve syntactic ambiguities in input words, but they may also permit the resolution of semantic ambiguities. For example, Robison (1970) points out that different senses of the same word may be correlated with different accompanying prepositions. The exploitation of partial parsing for homonymy resolution in automatic descriptor indexing is a feature of Černjavskij's "Pusto–Nepusto" system (Černjavskij *et al.*, 1968, 1969; Laxuti *et al.*, 1967).

Statistical Syntax

Some analysis techniques rely on features of an input text which are at the limits of what is usually called syntax. These so-called statistical methods make no more use of the structure of the text than its division into sentences, content words cooccurring within a sentence being regarded as related. Salton's (1968a) statistical phrase procedure illustrates the idea. It depends on a prior dictionary of phrases, in fact of thesaurus group rather than word combinations, and the joint appearance of words from all the groups concerned in a sentence leads to assignment of the phrase name as an index term. Clearly the procedure is not very discriminating and experiments showed it did not do materially better than the (manual) thesaurus alone. Salton's comment is that the limited dictionary is more likely to be responsible for the not very striking performance obtained than false combinations. Further discussion of the procedure is to be found in Weiss (1969a).

Cooccurrence within sentences is also exploited by Artandi's Project Medico (Artandi 1967, 1969; Artandi and Wolf, 1969). In this case it is used to establish links between independent terms, rather than to obtain compound terms. Tests showed links were generally correctly established. Artandi considers the possibility of refining the procedure by using intrasentential word distances, but concludes that this is likely to be helpful only for abstracts, where author style is less variable.

Exploiting Syntactic Information

A wholehearted use of linguistic theories of syntax in information retrieval would be one in which the structural properties of document and request sentences obtained through syntactic analysis were retained for use in the matching process. The most straightforward way of doing this would be simply to store the result of the analysis process—the deep or surface structure of the sentence—as part of the document or request description. Such a simpleminded approach would probably not repay the cost of implementing it unless the grammar were of a very sophisticated kind. For the reasons noted earlier, the kind of superficial structures obtainable by phrase-structure analysis are immensely varied and semantically uninformative. But the deep structures obtained with a suitably chosen transformational grammar would have the effects (1) of reducing large numbers of sentence forms to a single canonical form, and (2) of exhibiting semantically revealing relations between them. The kind of deep structures generated by Fillmore's case grammar are obvious candidates for use in this way. Unfortunately far less is known about automatic analysis methods that are applicable to transformational rather than about that are those applicable to phrase-structure grammars, beyond the fact that the techniques are complicated and expensive. In fact, we know of no attempt to use the syntactic structures obtained from a fully automatic syntactic analysis of input texts directly as descriptions for retrieval. Salton preserves parts of the analysis only, and Armitage and Lynch merely transfer the input with its implicit structure. Our view is that this gap is unfortunate. Even if the requirements of document retrieval turn out to preclude the sort of descriptive treatment for documents that linguistics should provide, further experiments in this area would be of great interest.

Index Description Syntax

In contrast there are many examples of artificial languages for describing documents in which the syntactic structure of a descriptive unit is more or less explicit. In particular, the distinction between precoordinate and postcoordinate systems is, in large measure, a distinction between systems which rely heavily on syntax and systems in which its role is minimal. The way in which syntactic structure is indicated may also be close to natural language, some forms of indexing producing descriptions looking much like ordinary phrases.

One common approach is the use of term order as a substitute for directly indicated relations. Thus the construction of traditional subject headings normally involves the application of ordering principles, essentially so that more important terms are listed before less important ones. For example, if head terms are listed before modifying ones, "leather, shoe" does not mean the same as "shoe, leather." The rules for imposing an order on the component parts of a heading may be more or less strict; in the *British Technology Index*, for instance, Coates has applied carefully worked out rules including ones designed to distinguish, for what he calls ACTION and THING terms, headings referring to things characterized by a certain principle of action, and things serving a certain action. The term order in the first case is THING term, ACTION term, and in the second case the reverse (Coates, 1960; Sharp, 1965). In faceted indexing schemes the terms for different facets in a precoordinate entry are cited in some established preferred order of facets. This is a general prescription for classes of terms, so the order does not arise from individual entries, but while ordering could be arbitrary, it is generally intended to reflect overall, generally accepted conceptual dependencies. Thus, in Vickery's (1966) scheme for soil science, terms for sorts of soil precede those for constituents and properties.

More sophisticated languages call for a variety of explicit relational operators and possibly means of indicating nested structure. One example of such a language is that developed by Farradane (1967; Farradane *et al.*, 1966). This has nine relations, including appurtenance, association, and causation. The SYNTOL group have worked with similar general relations, the most recent tests involving three (Bely *et al.*, 1970). A more elaborate set is required in the system reported by Gladkij *et al.* (1962). Other approaches are discussed in Coyaud (1966) and Perreault (1967a) as well as in Sechser (1968) and Seménova (1969).

There is a conspicuous dearth of reported work on the automatic generation of structured index descriptions of any degree of complexity. This is not really surprising, since the difficulties involved are substantial. The major exception is the research of the SYNTOL group described below.

Postcoordinate Syntax

As noted, postcoordinate systems are distinguished by the fact that they make little appeal to syntactic devices. The ideal in postcoordinate indexing is the system in which a document description consists of an essentially unordered list of keywords. Each word in the description is on all fours with every other term, so that it becomes possible to profit from such techniques as Boolean search. But the manifest defects of such a simpleminded approach lead to the introduction not only of semantic devices like controlled terms and term classes but to that of syntactic devices as well. The result, as Lancaster (1968b) points out is to blur the boundary between precoordinate and postcoordinate systems. The devices adopted, namely links and roles, are somewhat minimal. Links bracket pairs or groups of terms together, while roles indicate the relational function of individual terms. Links do not indicate the character of the relationship between the grouped terms. But this is what roles are for. Bracketing, when applied thoroughly, is as strong a syntactic device as one can find, though in documentation practice it is not usually systematic. Role indication is a weak syntactic device; it effectively multiplies the number of terms in a vocabulary by allowing a given term to function in different ways, but the function is explicitly indicated and this implies a relationship with other terms.

Both devices are discussed by Lancaster (1968b) and have been investigated by Blagden (1966), Montague (1965), and Sinnett (1964) among others. Experiments with roles are reported by Lazarescu (1969) and their use is surveyed by Lancaster (1968c). Few attempts seem to have been made to assign role indicators automatically, but an example is Otradinskij's (Otradinskij and Kravčenko, 1969; Otradinskij and Vleduc, 1970) work, in which basic and aspect descriptors are assigned to documents through the occurrence of indicative phrases marked by trigger words in their texts. Some experiments in the automatic provision of links have been carried out, of which those described by Artandi (1969; Artandi and Wolf, 1969) are examples. A similar approach is described by Falkov and Alebastrova (1970). In general the value of both of these devices seems uncertain, though they may be helpful as precision aids in particular retrieval environments.

Syntax in Searching

It will be evident from the foregoing that there is not much to be said about the automatic exploitation of the syntactic features of indexing languages in searching. If descriptions do not contain any syntactic information, there is no reason to look for procedures for altering structures or relating one structure and another. The exception is the SYNTOL project, which contains rules for modulating relations, that is for performing elementary inferences with them. In logic, asserting that a relation is transitive implies a rule for modulating it, and though the SYNTOL rules differ from those of standard logic in detail, they are of the same kind.

There is, of course, no reason why syntactic index descriptions set up manually should not be manipulated automatically provided appropriate rules are supplied. Thus Farradane suggests that his rules of condensation, which are comparable with the SYNTOL modulation rules, could be applied automatically. But it is an empirical fact that this automatic processing does not usually happen, presumably because the effort of translating rules happily operated informally by humans into rigorous machine prescriptions is too great. The usual treatment of syntactic information in searching, if insufficient request document matches are obtained, is to abandon it.

The SYNTOL Project

The long-established SYNTOL Project directed by Gardin is one of the most interesting in the field. The recent book by Bely *et al.* (1970) together with earlier publications (Coyaud and Siot-Decauville, 1967; Cros *et al.*, 1964; Gardin, 1965) gives a detailed picture of the philosophy and progress of a group conspicuous for its adherence to the belief that elaborate high-quality indexing is essential for retrieval and for its attempts to achieve this automatically. Bely and co-workers describe the current state of work on automated analysis and indexing, recent experiments being much more successful than the earlier ones described by Coyaud and Siot-Decauville. In the first experiments, Coyaud and Siot-Decauville attempted to extract syntactic information for forming structured descriptions without going through a detailed analysis of the input. The procedure relied on the occurrence of relational clue words and checks to see whether the clues plus flanking items conformed to an acceptable message type linking terms of certain semantic classes in a specified syntactic way. The conclusion drawn from these tests was that the authors were wrong to dismiss full-scale syntactic analysis as unnecessary, because the identification of relations, as opposed to terms, was frequently incorrect. The recent experiments do incorporate syntactic analysis of a fairly determined kind, though the approach does not depend on a systematic linguistic model and is far from providing the level of analysis theoretical linguists would expect.

This is primarily because the treatment of input texts is intended to provide descriptions of a certain sort for retrieval, and if these can be obtained without a costly full analysis, so much the better. In fact the group cheerfully mixes theoretical and empirical attitudes. The members combine the view that optimal index descriptions must have a certain form with a willingness to make use of any information and processes which appear to work to obtain them. At the same time, the project workers have consistently held that adequate indexing depends on human effort at some point. For example, while the actual treatment of individual texts may be automatic, it requires a range of tools such as elaborately organized thesauri, and it is difficult to imagine that these could be set up automatically.

The distinctive features of the SYNTOL approach are (1) the relation between an indexing description and its source document, and (2) the form of the description. A description is not intended to be a drastic summary or radical simplification of its input text but rather a means of exhibiting its essential character more clearly, though some simplification is usual. It should, however be noted that the group typically works with abstracts as input, and their approach might well not be suited to full texts. The distinctive feature of the index language is the use of syntagms, or pairs of index terms linked by a basic relation. Since the same term may appear as an argument in different syntagms, a description may consist of a single structured expression (a directed graph), or perhaps of several expressions representing different themes. The actual number of relations has varied, recent tests exploiting only three; more were advocated earlier. But the SYNTOL workers do not maintain that any set of relations is necessarily correct, only that some set of basic logical relations for generating syntagms is required. As noted earlier, rules are provided in the language for relating some different structures to one another.

The tests reported by Bely and co-workers were carried out with 1000 abstracts. The complexity of the whole indexing process is well illustrated by the fact that analysis depends on a dictionary containing 7000 words, each elaborately characterized by information covering morphological features and grammatical functions (with 57 syntactic categories), word group formation, and polysemy resolution, with attendant rules. The formation of descriptions after partial parsing, depending on 750 rules, necessitates a thesaurus of 3000 descriptors for the subject area, grouped to form 13 trees, as well as procedures for converting the parsed material to syntagms depending on the recognition of any of several hundred clue words and tests of the associated text against syntactic and possibly semantic schemas.

The analysis procedure has two functions: (1) to identify and disambiguate both individual words and word groups constituting entries to the thesaurus, and (2) to pick up the predominantly syntactic information required to form syntagms. The authors' judgement on the experimental output of the analysis phase is that the recognition of groups is very good and that the resolution of polysemy is creditable, considering their wish to avoid global parsing. The error rate is around 10%. The empirical approach adopted is well illustrated by the fact that group identification depends on mixed criteria including word distance, the absence of subordinating conjunctions or verbs, and so on. It is interesting to find that polysemy resolution works better when only grammatical information is involved than when reference is made to thesaurus relations for the index terms concerned.

The quality of the output from the second indexing stage is perhaps best judged from an example. The abstract text *"Chez dix singes stimulés par électrochoc cortical direct et chez un malade la procaine intraveineuse a protégé de l'épilepsie pendant une demi-heure; la xylocaine a un effet moindre"* gave syntagms involving descriptors and associative relations (A) or consecutive relations (C) as follows: PROCAINE C CRISE, PROCAINE C EPILEPSIE, PROCAINE

A PROTECTION, PROTECTION A EPILEPSIE, DIRECT A
CORTEX, ELECTROCHOC A CORTEX, ELECTROCHOC A
STIMULATION, STIMULATION A ETRE, XYLOCAINE A —.
Some isolated descriptors were also obtained. The interesting point
about the results is that the semantic check on potential syntagms
leads to far more incorrect than correct rejections. The results
are evaluated by comparison with human indexing, though some
details of the comparison are regrettably unclear. However, the
figures given show that while the success rate for syntagms and
isolates after the semantic checking was 73 and 40%, respectively,
the success rate before this predominantly mistaken action was
97 and 80%, which indeed looks encouraging.

In considering the work as a whole three questions must be asked:

1. Is all this apparatus necessary? The answer, given the previous
experiments, is presumably, yes. It is of course provided for a
specific language and subject matter, so the amount of work
involved in adopting this approach has to be repeated for different
languages and subject areas.

2. Since only three very general relations are permitted, are they
worth the effort? The answer here presumably depends on that
to question:

3. Does this form of indexing work in retrieval?

Unfortunately no answer is provided for this question. Given the
care evident in the SYNTOL group's research, the results of proper
experiments can be expected to be of great interest, though unfortunately it does not seem that they can be expected soon.

Syntax in Information Retrieval: Conclusion

It is difficult, when considering syntax in information retrieval,
to avoid a feeling of puzzlement. Many apparently convincing arguments for its use have been advanced, and many apparently sensible
syntactic procedures have been proposed. But insofar as systematic

comparative experiments have been carried out, they show that syntactic information contributes little to retrieval performance and may even detract from it. Some relevant findings are reported in Grinina and Sokolova (1970), Melton (1966), Popova and Jakubson (1969), Salton (1968a), and Western Reserve University (Comparative Systems Laboratory, 1968). It may be that all the experiments to date have been inadequate. Other possible explanations are (1) that retrieval needs are not properly understood; (2) that the value of the syntactic component of an index description is affected by other system components: it may either be that the correct relationships between different components have not been established, or that other components are defective; and (3) that essentially inadequate or inappropriate methods of handling syntax have been adopted. We are reluctant to consider the possible fourth explanation, namely that an indexing language cannot materially contribute to a good retrieval performance.

It is more interesting to accept the third explanation, and we thus conclude with some speculation on untried approaches to syntax. For example, it is intriguing to imagine a system in which document descriptions using links and roles would be obtained automatically from deep structures produced by an advanced transformational analysis technique. This would be a difficult enterprise, but there is no doubt that it would blend theories and methods of interest in both linguistics and information science, and the results could hardly fail to be instructive.

6

SEMANTICS

Semantics in Natural Language

There is no need for us to emphasize either the fact that meaning is the crucial feature of language or the fact that it is the most intractable problem of linguistics. Semantics, the study of meaning, has a long and eminently respectable history as an activity for philosophers, logicians, grammarians, philologists and linguists, but unfortunately the obviousness of meaning in words and discourse is matched by its eel-like slipperiness when the philosopher or linguist tries to catch it. The area is a battlefield in which the current generation of language theorists struggles, under a banner labelled "deep structure," with its protean foe, surrounded by the abandoned banners of its predecessors, banners with strange devices like the Saussurean triangle, and slogans like "Don't ask for the meaning, ask for the use."

Semantics is an important part of linguistics because the main concern of the field is with explicating the relationship between words and sentences on the one hand and meanings and referents on the other. How is the meaning extracted from a piece of discourse and how can a discourse be constructed so that it will convey a particular meaning? In modern formal linguistics, a language is defined as a set of strings of symbols—the sentences of the language—a set of objects called semantic interpretations corresponding to the set of expressible meanings, and a mapping of the former into the latter. In other words, a language is a set of pairs such that one member of each pair is a sentence and the other is a meaning. The principal problem that this kind of formal linguistics faces is that of specifying the boundaries of this set of pairs, given that it is clearly infinite in size.

There is an important distinction between the broad linguistic question—that of explaining how meaning is obtained from or injected into a text—and the formal question of characterizing the set of sentence-meaning pairs. To answer the first question it appears that one must have a detailed understanding of what a meaning is and what its properties are. To answer the second it is necessary, at least in principle, only to be able to discern when a given expression has more than one meaning and when a number of expressions have meanings in common. For the second question, just enough information is required to set up some kind of formal counterpart for each. What is not clear is how much needs to be understood of the fundamental nature of meaning for the purely formal requirements to be met.

Semantic Notation

Most linguistic theorists, formal or informal, have agreed that the first problem in semantics is to establish some kind of alphabet, or notation, that can be used to represent meanings unambiguously. This is necessary because the number of expressible meanings is presumably infinite, so that it is not possible to give a simple name to each. A meaning must, therefore, be represented by an expression in some notation and the primitive symbols of this notation will turn out to be a set of elementary building blocks with which any meaning whatsoever can be represented. These semantic primitives appear as "thesaurus heads," "semantic markers," "concept numbers," and in many other guises. The overwhelmingly difficult problem is that of identifying them. How shall we know a semantic primitive when we see one? What would it be like to see one anyway?

Behind these questions lies an even more profound one that has perplexed philosophers for centuries. If a language must be invented in which there will be an expression to represent every possible meaning, and if everyday sentences are expressions, but in another language, then what is to be gained by substituting one for the other? The problems of ordinary language are surely great enough without insisting that we add the problems of a new notation to them. This is not the place to argue this point. We shall be content to list some desirable qualities that a notation based on semantic primitives might have, leaving aside the question of whether a notation that would have all these qualities could actually be constructed.

First, the notion of a semantic notation rests on the assumption that meanings can be distinguished from one another and that each will be represented by a different expression. In other words, the expressions will be unambiguous.

Second, the semantic notation will have as simple and as perspicuous a syntax as possible so that relations between different meanings will be apparent from corresponding relations between the expressions that represent them. If one is an assertion and another a detail of that assertion, or if one entails or contradicts another, this will be revealed by operations that could be carried out on the expressions. The same is not true of sentences in an ordinary language which may mean the same but look very different or mean unrelated things while looking almost alike.

Third, it is to be hoped that the total number of semantic primitives would be very much smaller than the number of words in the vocabulary of an ordinary language. This would entail that the practical problems of processing them in a computer would be different and possibly less severe.

There are some linguists who, with Lyons (1968), attempt to avoid the problems associated with a notation based on semantic primitives by dismissing the notion altogether. They point out that a word or sentence may be meaningful without there necessarily being any indentifiable object which is its meaning. If I say that this sentence entails or contradicts in virtue of its meaning, I am arguing backwards. If the sentence is meaningful at all, it is in part in virtue of the entailment I noted, and not the other way about. Words and sentences contract relations with other words and sentences and the total set of relations that a linguistic entity contracts *is* that entity's meaning. The only semantic primitives are the relations themselves, and it is usually assumed that there will not be more than a handful of these.

Semantic Component of a Transformational Grammar

At present, there are several different views of what the semantic component of a transformational grammar should look like. It is agreed that the semantic component should contain a set of primitives, and there is general agreement on the kinds of questions for which this part of the theory should provide answers. There is less agreement on the form of the expressions that will be formed with the primitives and on the ways in which this component of the theory will interact with the others.

The early transformational theory of Chomsky (1957) had little to say on semantic questions. The first attempt to provide a formal semantic component for transformational grammar was proposed by Katz and Fodor (1963) and integrated into a new version of the theory as a whole by Chomsky (1965). It provides for two kinds of semantic primitives, called markers and distinguishers, respectively. Each item in the lexicon of a language is provided with one or more sets of markers and distinguishers depending on the number of different meanings that it has. The markers correspond to fairly broad intuitive notions and carry the main burden of classifying meanings. Broadly speaking, two meanings are more similar the more markers they have in common. Distinguishers are necessary to represent aspects of the meaning of an item that are too idiosyncratic to be captured in a general classification. The primary meaning of the word "red" will doubtless contain a marker for "color" in its representation, but it must also contain a distinguisher "red" because there is nothing more general that can be used to distinguish this color from all others.

This version of transformational semantics provides a semantic interpretation for every node in the deep structure of a sentence. The interpretations for the nodes corresponding to individual words are obtained from the lexicon and those for the remaining nodes are derived by applying projection rules to these. The notion is intuitively satisfying: the meaning of a phrase is derived from the meanings of the words and phrases that make it up until a meaning is obtained for the sentence as a whole. Notice that these operations apply to the deep structure of a sentence only. It is a stipulation of the theory that sentences may have the same deep structure only if they have the same meaning and one of the claims made for deep structure is that it provides a basis on which to define projection rules in the simplest possible manner.

As we have said, the semantic interpretations of transformational theory do not aim to capture everything that might be said about the meaning of a sentence. What is important is that there should be one of them to represent every possible meaning; they act as names for rather than complete descriptions of meanings. Furthermore, we have said that two or more sentences can share a deep structure only if they also share a meaning. Clearly, the most appealing way to fulfill these requirements would be to conflate the notions of deep structure and semantic interpretation. This is just what the advocates of generative semantics propose to do. For them, the deep structure of a sentence has much in common with an expression in the predicate calculus with constants which are semantic primitives. Clearly, the burden put on the transformational component in a grammar of this type is much greater because there is less similarity between deep and surface structures than was previously proposed, and because there must be provision for combining sets of semantic primitives to form words. Because of this extra burden on the transformational component, advocates of generative semantics are sometimes referred to as transformationalists.

Those transformational grammarians that are not transformationalists are referred to as lexicalists. They claim that the major burden should be on the lexicon and that there should be a distinction between deep structures and semantic interpretations. They base their view on the belief that much of the information associated with a word is entirely idiosyncratic and therefore inappropriate for representation in general grammatical rules. Some of the members of this school, notably Jackendoff (1968), no longer believe that the process of semantic interpretation can be applied to deep structure alone but that it must also take into account surface structure and possibly also intermediate structures. The arguments for this position are too detailed to go into here; suffice it to say that they have to do with the importance of word order in surface structure for the representation of quantifiers and negation.

Semantic Aspects of Information Retrieval

In Chapter 4 we distinguished three aspects of the documentation process. Thus we now have to examine the semantic component of:

1. methods of identifying meaningful units in the input document or surrogate text;
2. the derivation of document descriptions from these;
3. the construction and use of classifications and other forms of index language organization.

More particularly, we shall concentrate on automatic techniques for doing any or all of these and will therefore have a subsidiary theme, namely, the comparison between automatic and manual indexing and their respective performance in retrieval. The general state of retrieval experimentation was considered in Chapter 2, so only tests relevant to specific points and the conclusions which can reasonably be drawn from these tests when taken together will be examined here. In fact, although many of the experiments which have been done are comparatively limited, the evidence supporting some important points is sufficient for them to be taken seriously; thus, the general trend of the experiments we shall be discussing is to show that relatively simple indexing techniques can be as effective as more complex ones, and that automatic methods of providing simple index descriptions are as effective as manual ones.

This area has been authoritatively surveyed by Salton (1970a), and we are happy to be in a position to cannibalize his paper. Salton's own very substantial investigations support both of these conclusions (Salton, 1966–1969; Salton and Lesk, 1968), but his results are corroborated by a variety of experiments carried out by other projects. Comparisons can only be made at a high level, and every allowance must be made for such facts as variable depth of indexing, the difficulty of substantially improving on the low to middling performance typical even of sensible systems, and so on. But the conclusion that simple indexing methods can compete with complex ones is supported by the major Cranfield and Western Reserve University projects (Cleverdon *et al.,* 1966; Comparative Systems Laboratory, 1968), and smaller experiments like those carried out by Shaw and Rothman (1968), for instance, and must therefore be treated with respect, however surprising and unwelcome it may be.

Remarks about the comparative effectiveness of manual and automatic indexing must be made with caution, since in many experiments manual and automatic indexing differ not merely in whether humans or machines are used to provide descriptions but also in the actual form of description. For example automatically extracted keywords may be compared with manually generated subject headings. This is legitimate as far as retrieval performance as a whole is concerned, but strict comparisons should be confined, for example, to automatically and manually selected keywords or automatic and manual keyword classifications, as in Salton and Lesk (1968).

It must also be admitted that these conclusions can be stated only somewhat tentatively, for two reasons. One is that comparatively few solid experiments have been carried out, and they do not always match. For example Cleverdon found simple keywords worked as well as a manual thesaurus; but for the same collection, Salton found a revised thesaurus worked better. The second problem is that the real optimal performance for a given collection is not readily determined, and while experience will suggest some sort of base line or average performance, it is difficult, assuming gross changes like switching from titles to full text or from simple to interactive searching are excluded, to make radical improvements on this; and how near any improvements are to reaching the optimum, is also unclear.

We have already noticed the difficulty of separating the semantic and syntactic aspects of an indexing language, a difficulty which is compounded by the very loose use of the word "term," and to a lesser extent, of "subject." We shall be content to make a thoroughly arbitrary distinction based on relative complexity: we shall use *term* for single words or short strings, like adjective–noun combinations, whose syntactic structure is not made explicit, and *subject* for more elaborate items, whether or not the structure is made explicit. Thus, "aerodynamic" and "boundary layer" are terms, and "aerodynamic effects of explosions" and "boundary layer flow around cylinders" are subjects. A subject is generally a whole descriptive unit, while a term may be a whole unit, or merely a component of one. Subject specifications as wholes may not be elements in a classification, their constituent terms only participating; but in other cases, like the UDC, entire subjects are classified.

In general it is difficult to separate term and subject classification, and the two will be considered together here, though the emphasis will be on the treatment of terms.

Semantic Input Analysis

Automatic abstracting and indexing was first advocated in the late 1950s, notably by Luhn (see Schultz, 1968a). The work on this and automatic classification done up to 1964 was surveyed by Stevens (1965), and is well represented by the participants in the symposium on statistical association methods (Stevens *et al.*, 1965; see also Agraev *et al.*, 1963; Purto, 1961). This work is summarized in Borko (1967a) and has been more recently surveyed by Batty (1969), Karasev (1970), and Salton (1968a, 1970a). There is clearly no need to consider this early work in detail here, but some reference to it must be made because most of the basic ideas were put forward then, notably by Baxendale (1958, 1962), Doyle (1961, 1962), Edmundson and Wyllys (1961), Maron (1961), Maron and Kuhns (1960), Needham (1963), Stiles (1961), and Swanson (1960, 1962), and most of the characteristic problems were encountered in the early experiments. The approaches to classification adopted are illustrated by Baker (1965), Borko (1965), Doyle (1965), Giuliano and Jones (Jones *et al.*, 1967), Needham and Sparck Jones (1964), and Spiegel and Bennett (1965).

Quite apart from their general assumptions about the value of statistical information derived from the occurrences and cooccurrences of signs, the early workers emphasized the importance of the actual words used in a text and of collection determined relations between words; noticed the importance of index vocabulary features like collection frequency; adopted a tolerant attitude to usual distinctions like that between analysis and description; suggested that statistical techniques could be used to pick up different linguistics facts, for example through first- and second-order associations or exclusive and overlapping classes; and grappled with the difficulties of defining association measures and classification criteria, not to mention grouping algorithms, and of distinguishing significant and nonsignificant associations or good and bad classifications.

There has been no substantial intellectual advance in this area in recent years, the major experiments serving to test the original ideas in more detail or on a larger scale. The main feature of the more recent work, as Salton (1970a) points out, has been the direct testing of automatic indexing systems in retrieval as opposed to the earlier emphasis on feasibility and evaluation by comparisons between automatically and manually derived document descriptions. Actual retrieval tests are of course preferable, and the experiments done since 1965 have brought out two important points (Sparck Jones, 1970, 1971). One is that automatic methods should not be treated simply as (economically desirable) ways of obtaining the same or same types of indexing descriptions as manual techniques. Tests quite often show that very different descriptions may lead to the same retrieval performance. The other point is that the purpose for which index descriptions are required must be borne in mind when, for example, independently developed statistical techniques are considered for automatic term extraction and classification. The encouraging feature of the results obtained in these experiments is that automatic indexing methods may well be competitive with manual. Simple automatic title processing is now widely practiced and is accepted as satisfactory for limited purposes, but automatic indexing in general is still regarded as suspect in many quarters, and the recent experimental results are therefore welcome.

Derivative and Assignment Indexing

In her survey, Stevens (1965) distinguishes derivative and assignment indexing: the former includes simple KWIC indexing, with various supplementary devices to remedy its more obvious defects on the one hand, and techniques taken over from automatic abstracting on the other. The latter includes methods of allocating descriptors to documents on the basis of extracted information, where the extraction process itself does not provide descriptors directly. Automatic term classification and the construction of term networks are treated separately, though they can be related to both derivative and assignment indexing, as they are formed from extracted words, but assign either class labels and hence the other terms in a class indirectly to documents containing individual class members, or assign proximately connected terms directly. The function of automatic classifications and associative semiclassifications is the same whether the information is exploited at the time of indexing or of searching, though the effects of modifying document descriptions at the time of indexing, or requests at the time of searching, may be quite different, for example. Stevens regards both association maps primarily intended to aid searchers, and also probabilistic indexing, as outside the main area of indexing though they can be related to it.

Stevens notes that the boundary between these forms of automatic document processing is not clear and that specific devices originally suggested in one context have been taken over for other purposes. This is evident in the adoption for indexing purposes of techniques originally proposed for automatic abstracting (see, for example, Baxendale, 1962). For the present, the distinction between derivative and assignment indexing is a subsidiary one, since it represents the difference between using the extracted information directly and replacing it in some way in the second stage of processing when document descriptions are set up. At the same time, the subsequent intention must influence the selection of input information to some extent, though to what extent is difficult to determine.

Whether assignment indexing involves human intervention, primarily in constructing the descriptor list, is more important. In experiments like those described by Stevens and Urban (1965), computer procedures are used to identify the textual correlates of manually assigned descriptors for a sample of documents, so that for new documents, text items are correctly used as entry words for descriptor assignment. In the usual approaches to automatic term classification, descriptors are classes of extracted words, so that the appearance of a word in a document text leads to the assignment not of a completely independent index term but of a set of terms including itself.

In general, however, the same devices are used to extract information from the input text automatically, whether or not this information is subsequently adopted to form a description or leads to the assignment of other descriptors. Thus, if we want to obtain items which will either be treated as terms or replaced by terms from a dictionary, we may extract single words, word pairs or n-tuples from our document or surrogate text, taking account in selecting them of their absolute or relative frequency of cooccurrence, tendency to cooccur and positional proximity, and perhaps their syntactic class and role.

Extraction Procedures

In considering procedures for extracting items, which we shall for convenience refer to as words, though they may in fact be word strings, from an input document or surrogate text, we can distinguish those procedures which rely on grammatical analysis of the text from those concerned to identify key items by statistical means. Interest in the former is usually, but not necessarily, correlated with the subsequent use of complex descriptive units, being designed to identify not merely significant words but relations between them. It in any case involves full or partial parsing, and so was considered in Chapter 5. It is sufficient here to refer to the work of Hillman (1968; Hillman and Kasarda, 1969), where syntactic procedures are used to select noun phrases for future use as terms. Partial parsing for selecting noun phrases is also advocated by Earl (1970), the SMART Project (Salton, 1968a), where syntactic analysis is used to identify text phrases representing various types of dependency structure for use as descriptive units, and the SYNTOL group (Bely *et al.*, 1970), where analysis is used to identify future terms and relations between them, which will be reformulated in the index description. These procedures are all automatic, and those of the SMART and SYNTOL projects are also of interest here in making some use of semantic message types or templates, that is, checks to see whether words in the text having specific syntactic relations also fall in semantic categories between which the syntactic connection is appropriate. Further SMART studies of this idea are reported by Weiss (1969b), where specific text words and formats are taken as indicators of the semantic category membership of associated words. Similar principles underlie Robison's (1970) study of prepositions as triggers for disambiguating words, and work by Borkowski *et al.* (1970) on the use of text expressions as clues to legal citations.

The possibility of selecting words by text locations, say, in headings or the initial and final sentences in paragraphs, was recognized by early workers on automatic extraction (see Stevens, 1965), but this idea has not been extensively pursued, chiefly because working with full texts is so demanding. This is a pity, since the linguistic consequences for views of discourse structure could be of interest.

Our main concern in this chapter is with word extraction by nonsyntactic, and predominantly statistical, means. The syntactic procedures just mentioned are typically applied to abstracts or even full texts, and syntactic methods may be also applied to titles (see Armitage *et al.*, 1970). Statistical extraction techniques naturally require a sufficient amount of text per document. Simple nonsyntactic, nonstatistical processes are widely used for titles in particular, but also abstracts. Even these simple keyword extraction techniques present problems, both in the selection of information and its subsequent utilization in indexing, and if the extracted items are used more or less directly as descriptive terms, some problems remain unsolved.

KWIC indexes are conspicuous examples of the straightforward use of keywords. They are now well established as devices which are remarkably effective within their limits, and they are widely employed. *Chemical Titles* is a well-known example. The original work in this area was analyzed by Stevens (1965), and surveys of a variety of examples appear in Adams (1965), and more especially Fischer (1966). More specific studies include those by Adams (1967), Brodie (1970), Chonez (1968), Mextiev and Kuznecova (1969), and Rosenberg and Blocher (1968). It is possible to regard a KWIC index as a postcoordinate retrieval device, though it is not very convenient to manipulate as such, and in general, comparisons between KWIC and other indexes have to be made with caution, since they may not be intended for use in the same way. It is difficult to compare a KWIC index with another form of description without throwing away its characteristic format and treating it just as a keyword system, though KWIC indexes may be compared among themselves for general user handiness; and over-all comparisons of KWIC indexes with others as search tools are legitimate. At the same time, the basic KWIC index is deliberately unassuming, and it is improper to condemn it for defects it does not attempt to avoid. The main difficulty about a KWIC index is that it relies on the value of the text being permuted, and hence, usually, on the status of a document title as a surrogate. Fortunately, title words tend to match their document vocabulary. Stevens, for example, reports a variety of tests designed to show that there is a substantial overlap between the main words in the title of a document and terms assigned by indexers using the whole document, average correlation being around 50% (Stevens, 1965).

In the present context, KWIC indexing is relevant because it exhibits some characteristic problems of keyword extraction in a simple and clear way. Further problems arise when statistical information is used for extracting, or when statistical information about extracted words is exploited for indexing. If we consider forming an index from titles, assuming these are acceptable surrogates, we encounter difficulties associated on the one hand with the elimination of useless words, and on the other with the treatment of selected ones. The use of a stop list to eliminate syntactic

operators is straightforward, but words that are sometimes informative and sometimes not, such as "analysis" in most contexts,
are more difficult to weed out. Selected and hopefully useful words
may be ambiguous, and it is difficult to make provision for separating senses. They may alternatively have related forms and also
synonyms, and it is equally difficult to bring these together. In
short, extracted words are at the same time not specific enough
and too specific. Of course, dealing with such problems is part
of the indexing process proper; it is simply that, in providing an
initial interpretation of a document by extracting words, the subsequent stage is made harder than is usual in manual indexing,
where greater control is typically exercised in the provision of the
interpretation itself. One object of the KWIC format is indeed to
avoid difficulties like keyword ambiguity, but in substantial listings
they still make themselves felt.

Simple extracting of keywords from abstracts, with function
words eliminated by a stop list, is illustrated by Salton (1968a).
In some cases reference is made to a dictionary of acceptable content words, as by Artandi (1969). Clearly, checking input words by
dictionary lookup means that the automatic extraction of keywords
is a fairly minimal business.

Statistical Extraction

In considering statistical techniques for extracting words we can
usefully start with a comparison with citation indexing. The general
assumption behind the extraction of words on a statistical basis,
whether these are to serve as entry words to a dictionary or as
terms, is that conspicuous words are significant content indicators.
It is not necessary to make any more concerted attempt to discover
what a document is about, because a document wears its heart
on its sleeve, and any nontrivial word that occurs sufficiently frequently must be a valid content indicator, or it would not be used
so often. Looking only at the surface of a document, it is clear

that prominent physical features reflect important features of its content, so we need not examine the latter directly.

Citation indexing can be regarded as a further step in the use of indirect content clues. The content of a document is approached not through the words it contains, but through other documents. Bibliographic details are also indirect clues, mostly of a different kind, and there is indeed a whole range of such facts about a document which may serve as search keys, or access points, or both (Cooper, 1970; Vickery, 1968). Citation indexing is subject to the same problem as keyword indexing, namely that indirect clues are relatively opaque: a specific citation may not in fact have much to do with the prime topic of a document, any more than an individual word. The whole hypothesis on which this kind of approach to document characterization depends, however, is that there is a correlation, and that in general enough information about documents is obtained in this way to characterize them for retrieval purposes. This point about citations was made by Kessler (1963, 1965a); and citations have been exploited both by Project TIP (Mathews, 1967), and notably, the *Science Citation Index.*

Statistical extraction techniques are both required and justified by long sources. For full texts in particular, some selection of the words extracted is necessary, and the obvious way of being selective is by retaining only frequent words. How selective we are depends largely on how exhaustive we wish our document characterization to be. This is not a question that is easy to answer, because the consequences of changes in exhaustivity are not simply predictable. But since it concerns actual descriptions rather than their input information, it will be considered later. In general, we can expect the extraction process to reduce document or surrogate length, because the whole object of the enterprise is to summarize.

The exploitation of statistical criteria in indexing is derived from earlier work on automatic abstracting, chiefly by Luhn (see Schultz, 1968a). The first experiments acted as a confirmation of Zipf's law and raised the complementary problems of eliminating both frequent and nonfrequent noise words. The former are primarily syntactic operators, which are usually removed by a stop list during text processing, rather than by cutting off the upper end of the ranked word list. The main difficulty is sorting sheep from goats among the remainder (see, for instance, Damerau, 1965). Most frequent nontrivial words are good content indicators, but not all; and equally, most infrequent words are bad content indicators, but not always. In other words, topics of no distinctive interest are sometimes referred to repeatedly in the same terms, and others of interest are referred to repeatedly, but in different terms.

In the last resort, both the upper and lower cutoffs are arbitrary, the general view being that the fine details don't matter too much. Defects of the initial information may be remedied by the subsequent indexing stage. Thus omitted words, for example, may be brought in again by thesaurus associations. Furthermore, these defects will often not affect overall retrieval performance at all. On the whole, the conclusion to be drawn from any large-scale experiments, like the Medlars ones, for instance, is that while the effect of bad information extraction on individual documents or requests may be large, the average effect is small (Lancaster, 1968a).

A more interesting question in this area concerns the choice of frequency criteria for ranking text word types, and in particular whether absolute or relative frequencies should be exploited. Should words be selected for a document because they occur frequently in it, or only if they occur in it with greater frequency than their frequency for the collection as a whole? The latter represents a more sophisticated interpretation of a distinctive property of a document and is related to the earlier point about the distinction between indexing as a means of characterizing a document in itself and as a means of distinguishing a document from the others in the collection. A word which occurs frequently in a document and also in the collection may truly reflect a topic of interest in the document but does little to identify its distinctive features. There is, however, clearly a limit to the extent to which it pays to concentrate on what makes one document different from another, since retrieval is mainly concerned with whether a document topic matches a request.

This point, like most of the others in this area, was canvassed in the early literature, as indicated by Stevens (1965). Relative frequency was first effectively publicized by Edmundson and Wyllys (1961). Different formulae have more recently been studied by Carroll and Roelloffs (1969), Curtice and Jones (1967, 1969), Damerau (1965), Dennis (1965), Stone (1967), and Stone and Rubinoff (1968). Relative frequencies are clearly more tedious to work with than simple ones, and selection by simple frequency may be good enough.

A rather different use of frequency information is not to provide a base for selection, but to allow future index term weighting; this will be considered in the next section.

Statistical Extraction: Conclusion

The detailed conclusions to be drawn from the experiments with statistical methods to date are not clear, since full enough comparative information based on tests using differently extracted keyword lists for retrieval is lacking. But overall there is little doubt that frequency based techniques can give helpful lists of words. Some experiments have been carried out on an impressively large scale, for example, by Cagan (1970), Curtice and Jones (1967), Dennis (1965), Giuliano and Jones (1966), and Stone (1967); frequency extraction is also exploited in an operating system at A. D. Little (Curtice and Jones, 1969). Equally, several interesting points arise from the work reported. Thus, Cagan (1970) argues that very rare words may be valuable in some circumstances, like drug names in medical literature; Carroll and DeBruyn (1970) emphasize that frequency computations are influenced by whether given words or word stems are counted; Curtice and Jones (1967) consider word frequency in relation to cooccurring words over the collection, where Cagan exploits the same idea, but within documents; and in the A. D. Little system, Curtice and Jones also take word usage statistics into account.

The statistical approach to extracting information about documents, forming descriptions, and organizing the descriptive vocabulary, is the most distinctive contribution of computers to document retrieval, for, while it is in principle possible to do the necessary operations by hand, it is unacceptably tedious. The fact that computers are unable to recognize the meaning of a piece of discourse in any ordinary sense, while they are much better at counting than humans, has, moreover, led some workers to reappraise the kind of information we should seek to extract from documents for effective retrieval. The overall conclusion as to the value of statistical extraction techniques is, however, necessarily a relative one, for while much depends on the adequacy of the initial information about a document supplied to the indexing process, much also depends on the subsequent use of it in forming descriptions and manipulating them in retrieval.

The final point to consider is whether extraction is confined to single words or longer strings. The suggestion is that pairs in particular are more useful, because more complete or precise, than single words. Nonstatistical approaches to the extraction of strings or phrases typically depend on some form of input parsing. Salton's so-called "statistical phrase" procedure is nonsyntactic, involving a dictionary check for acceptable pairs of words appearing within an abstract text (Salton, 1968a). The statistical extraction of word-tuples was early studied by Oswald (see Borko, 1967a), more recent advocates of pairs being Curtice and Jones (1969), exploiting the findings of Giuliano and Jones (1966). The problem here is that phrases as wholes may have a low frequency. More generally, a decision is required as to whether the words in a tuple must be juxtaposed in the source text, or merely be sufficiently close, according to some criterion. The use of word strings may come close to the use of links, as discussed in Chapter 5, and the extraction of word groups indeed refers to the question of implicit versus explicit syntax raised earlier.

Looking at the extraction phase as a whole, it is evident that as far as semantics is concerned there is little direct relationship between documentation and linguistics. The most direct connection between automatic extraction and current linguistics is in syntax. Very little can be said about the "standard" manual techniques because they are formally opaque. The statistical extraction procedures described here are concerned with features of discourse which are elementary and are currently not of interest to linguists, though they are connected with the challenging and barely touched topic of large scale discourse structure. From the linguistic point of view the statistical procedures used in documentation are relatively undiscriminating, and it is an open question whether more refined methods would be noticeably more productive.

Semantic Indexing Procedures

As noted earlier, in considering document descriptions we are concerned with the semantic character both of descriptive units as wholes and of their components. But since complex units involve syntax, these were considered in Chapter 5, and we shall concentrate here on the relation between index terms and input document words, and with the character of the terms themselves. More particularly we shall be concerned with automatic methods of providing terms for documents and then with automatic procedures for setting up the term vocabulary itself.

There are various ways of obtaining index terms, given initial extracted words. The main possibilities are:

1. the more or less direct use of the extracted items as keywords;
2. methods involving some check on the acceptability of the extracted items;

3. procedures where the extracted items are treated as entry words and are replaced by accepted terms, which may coincide in sign;

4. the substitution of descriptors of a different logical type.

Given approaches may be borderline between (1) and (2), or (2) and (3); and similarly, if concept names become somewhat arbitrary under (3), they may resemble numerical labels used for extracted word classes ostensively defining concepts, under (4). (It must be emphasized that the logical status of extracted items changes once they are used for indexing.) The headings also cover a variety of alternatives. For instance, checks under (2) may exploit statistical criteria, so only words occurring infrequently in a collection are retained; alternatively, extracting may involve dictionary lookup.

An important distinction is between term-based and class-based indexing, according to whether the terms indexing a document are backed up by classificatory references. Thus any of (1) to (4) may be related to the use of a classification in indexing or searching. For example, under (1) and (2), given words may be supplemented by additional words provided by statistical association techniques; terms under (3) are frequently class names; and classes of extracted words may be used as descriptors under (4). Reference must also be made to the earlier distinction between derivative and assignment indexing, as one which applies to all of (1)–(4). Superficially (1) and (2) represent derivative indexing, and (3) and (4) assignment, but, for example, additional words may be assigned under (1), and classes used under (4) may be derived. More generally, the distinction is between the source of items indexing documents, that is, whether they are ultimately derived from the collection or set up independently, rather than between index terms derived from a document text and external ones, and this cuts across (1)–(4). In the following discussion we shall be concerned first with derivative and assignment procedures not making explicit reference to a classification, and then with classification dependent approaches. Some remarks on descriptions as wholes follow. The semantic aspects of setting up index descriptions automatically, since syntax is excluded here, are fairly straightforward.

Keyword Normalization

It is possible to adopt extracted words as they stand as terms, but, given the normalizing purpose of indexing, it is more usual to impose some standardization. The most obvious move is to conflate singular and plural forms of the same word, and the next is to reduce all the variant forms of a word to a single normal form. Various approaches may be adopted, using either a dictionary of form groups or, more ambitiously, suffix-stripping routines, with or without a stem as well as a suffix dictionary. For the latter see, for instance, Lovins (1968) and Salton (1968a). Comparisons between the use of keywords as they come, plural-suppressed terms, and more extensive suffix-stripped terms, or stems, have been made by both the Cranfield and SMART Projects (Cleverdon *et al.,* 1966; Keen, 1967b; Salton 1968a, 1970a). In all cases, significant performance improvements are noticeable with the latter, even when done automatically, so some semantic anomalies appear. (Outside documentation, considerable effort has been devoted to automatic suffix-stripping, originally in connection with machine translation. See, for example, Resnikoff and Dolby, 1965, 1966.)

Further control may be imposed by explicit reference to a prior dictionary, whether this is manually set up or automatically derived from a collection sample or entire collection. In derivative indexing the function of such a dictionary is mainly to eliminate useless content words given by the initial word-extraction procedure or, more generally, to define words which are acceptable as terms.

Term Assignment

A more serious use of a dictionary is to provide a controlled term vocabulary for assignment indexing when the distinction between entry words and index terms is explicitly maintained. This is presented as the normal procedure in coordinate indexing by Lancaster (1968b), for instance, and appears in the literature in many guises, and automatic lookup procedures for replacing extracted text words by controlled vocabulary or thesaurus terms have an obvious attraction.

Such procedures may vary in complexity, mainly according to the sophistication and degree of organization of the indexing vocabulary, though the type of information initially extracted also affects the process. The automatic assignment project of the CETIS group for Euratom represents a more ambitious approach, the volume of material handled making automatic assignment highly desirable (Fangmeyer and Lustig, 1969, 1970). A variety of relations linking text words or words and descriptors are considered, covering morphological variation, notational equivalence, compositional relations between the words in a complex expression, glossary relations within the Euratom Thesaurus, and statistical connections between words and descriptors established from previous indexing. Chains of related items are allowed, so indexing consists of picking a subset of the available chains linking words and descriptors according to various criteria; these include, for instance, the number of components of a complex present, the strength of statistical association, and so on, assignment possibilities being defined by Boolean combinations of criteria. The strength of the criteria affects indexing depth. Initial tests comparing automatic and manual assignment (Fangmeyer and Lustig, 1969) show that the former is as good as the latter, differences being no greater than manual indexer variation. Further retrieval tests (Fangmeyer and Lustig, 1970) showed that a middling level of assignment appeared to provide a competitive level of performance with manual.

A number of interesting projects in the U.S.S.R. are also concerned with assignment indexing. These include the "Pusto–Nepusto" system of Černjavskij and his colleagues (Černjavskij et al., 1967, 1969; Laxuti et al., 1967; Pevzner, 1969), and that developed by Šenderov and his colleagues for patents (Gerasimova *et al.*, 1967; Giršberg and Šenderov 1970; Kravec *et al.*, 1966). These incidentally incorporate a translation component, from English to Russian. As part of the indexing procedure the former includes procedures for homonymy resolution, and the latter procedures for checking the validity of descriptor assignment; a term is assigned if its frequency for the document is greater than would be predicted, pronominal references being included in the calculations for this purpose.

Indexing for Substitution and Expansion

In any of the foregoing, the modification or replacement of extracted keywords is aimed at normalizing the descriptive vocabulary; the effect is to treat one starting word as substitutable for another, where this is marked by the appearance of a single index term in the description. In searching, the range of substitutions may be further extended if classificatory relations among the terms in the indexing language are given. Classificatory index languages are of interest, however, because they allow other possibilities in the provision of the semantic units of a document description. This is clearly seen in indexing techniques using statistical associations, or where a statistical classification of extracted keywords is available. In these cases related terms may be added to an initial keyword list to expand a document (or request) specification. This is an obvious use of association lists, and with a classification the members of a class may also be used in this way instead of being regarded as alternatives.

The word "expansion" is used loosely to refer to providing either alternative terms for matching or more terms to match, but the difference is illustrated by the two different reformulations of a request consisting of A and B, given that C and also D are related to B. We replace "$A \wedge B$" by "$A \wedge (B \vee C \vee D)$" if we are interested in substitution, while addition gives us "$A \wedge B \wedge C \wedge D$." The importance of the second approach is that it provides longer specifications, and hence allows matches on more items, a desideratum of coordinate indexing. Substitution may allow one match as opposed to none, but document or request expansion by addition may allow three matches instead of one; and since in coordinate systems matches on more items may be correlated with improved retrieval performance, optimal modes of enlarging specifications are of interest.

Addition changes the exhaustivity of a specification, making it more exhaustive: a reduction in the exhaustivity of a request is a familiar search strategy (Lancaster, 1968a). Expansion by addition may be regarded as a one–many mapping of entry words onto index terms, in contrast to the many–one mapping of normalization, and as such be related to familiar thesaurus-using practice. But workers on statistical techniques have taken the idea much further, largely because the linguistic relations between statistically related keywords are more varied: with a thesaurus or classification primarily confined to synonymic and generic relations, an interest in substitution is more natural than one in addition.

Expansion by addition has been investigated in particular by Lesk (1969), Sparck Jones and Barber (1971), and Vaswani and Cameron (1970). All three projects considered enlarging both document and request specifications; Sparck Jones and Barber also considered requests only, and Vaswani and Cameron documents only. Expanding requests via associations is also typical of the Arthur D. Little project (Giuliano and Jones, 1966). Though the process, as Lesk points out, is quite different from the regular use of a classification, comparisons were made with a manual thesaurus classification by Lesk and with automatic classifications by the others. It was less good than Lesk's manual thesaurus but competitive with automatic classifications. There were considerable differences of detail between the projects, accounting for variations in results. In all cases, however, some improvement in retrieval performance over the initial keyword lists was obtained.

The results of these experiments were probably influenced by differences in the length or exhaustivity of the initial keyword lists as well as in the degree of enlargement and hence exhaustivity of the final lists. The remaining points to be made about the formation of index descriptions concern such aspects of descriptions as wholes. We earlier distinguished units of description, like subject headings, and components of these like individual terms. An entire description could consist of several units, linked or independent, representing one or more topics. In SYNTOL, for example, the units represented by syntagms may or may not be connected by common terms. In cases where units are relatively simple, as in the typical postcoordinate system, it is alternatively reasonable to regard the entire list of terms for a document as a single unit, though the member terms are not explicitly connected on indexing. They are connected in searching, and hence the number of terms available influences retrieval performance.

With a closed indexing vocabulary the consequences of variations in the number of terms assigned to a document are clearly exhibited and are well known: the more terms assigned, that is, the more any individual term is used, the greater the chance of unhelpful matches, that is, the less discriminating a term is. The same holds for extracted keywords in a relatively homogeneous collection. Increasing the number of terms also increases the possibility of false coordinations. The need to control marginal indexing is recognized, but to maintain discrimination care must be taken over the assignment even of more obviously appropriate descriptors. These points are discussed by Lancaster (1968b), for instance. Lancaster distinguishes the exhaustivity of indexing descriptions from the specificity of indexing languages; but in extractive indexing the connection is close, and it is possible then to relate term specificity explicitly to term collection frequency rather than term meaning (Giuliano and Jones, 1966).

The problem of description length has been approached from the point of view of document length by, for example, the SMART Project (Salton and Lesk, 1968), and also Caras (1967), variations in description length reflecting the length of the source text for the document. The overall retrieval consequences of using titles as opposed to full texts were considered earlier. We can naturally expect titles, abstracts, and full texts to yield, for instance, progressively longer extracted keyword lists. But while there is a general correlation, titles in particular being unlikely to yield long and complex descriptions, when abstracts, and even more, full texts are used, conscious variation in amount of detail in descriptions is possible. The choice of a level of exhaustivity in indexing is a recognized policy decision for manual systems, and the consequences of different levels have been studied systematically by the Cranfield project (Cleverdon *et al.*, 1966). The tests showed that performance is normally distributed, indexing in great depth leading to the excessive use of descriptors and the introduction of noise being as pernicious as brief and inadequate indexing. In automatic systems using keywords ranked by document frequency, the problem takes the form of choosing a cutoff point dividing indexing from nonindexing terms. The advantage of the expansion techniques discussed earlier is that they allow changes in exhaustivity after indexing.

Term Weighting

The other point about descriptions as wholes, mainly relevant to coordinate indexing, is the use of term weights, indicating the relative importance of the terms in a description. These may be assigned manually, or automatically using either text location—terms derived from headings being more heavily weighted, say—or text frequency. Weighting may be relatively simple, using only a few grades, or more sophisticated, as when frequencies are used to calculate weights. Request weighting, including marking terms as obligatory, will be considered later.

Some studies of the effects of manual weighting have been made, for example, by the Cranfield project (Cleverdon *et al.*, 1966). Automatic location based weighting, emphasizing title terms, has been considered by Salton (1968a). Automatic frequency based weighting of a simple kind has been examined by, for instance, Artandi and Wolf (1969). In these tests terms were assigned to three grades by relative frequency, good agreement with manual weighting being obtained. Artandi and Wolf note that the most heavily weighted words derived from full text tend to be the same as words derived from abstracts, a conclusion bearing on the question of choosing source documents. The SMART Project has carried out a variety of experiments with automatically computed weights derived from frequencies, showing that weighted terms lead to a noticeable improvement in retrieval performance compared with unweighted ones (Salton, 1968a, 1970a; Salton and Lesk, 1968). Salton comments on the fact that sophisticated matching coefficients permit better use of the information contained in weights. A rather different approach is adopted by Cagan (1970), term weighting depending on statistical associations: term pair linkages are defined via cooccurring terms, and the terms for a document are ordered by the value of their linkages with the other terms. This has the effect of favoring rare terms. Clearly, whether weighting is valuable depends largely on the character of the source text and the size of the description. Weighting barely applies to title-derived descriptions, though the SMART Project has found weighting effective with abstracts, and it is probably not useful for descriptions containing less than a half a dozen terms, whatever their source.

Further possibilities are available with classifications, especially keyword classifications; for example, descriptors or class names may be weighted according to the number of source text items leading to them; or, with expanded descriptions of the kind discussed above, initial keywords can be weighted more than added ones. Such ideas are discussed, for example, by Sparck Jones (1971), and experiments attended with some success on these lines have been carried out by Sparck Jones and Barber (1971) and Vaswani and Cameron (1970). Alternatively, with expansion via associations, terms may be weighted by connection strength (Giuliano and Jones, 1966).

Index Languages

The character of the indexing language used in a retrieval system has sometimes been regarded as the most important problem of documentation, though providing adequate descriptions has also been treated as a major problem. One of the outcomes of systematic retrieval tests over the last decade has been the suggestion that the effects of the indexing language on system performance may be less significant than was supposed and perhaps less important than other factors. This suggestion is supported by experimental findings that quite different languages give a similar performance (see, for example, Aitchison *et al.*, 1970; Cleverdon *et al.*, 1966; Comparative Systems Laboratory, 1968; Salton and Lesk, 1968). The conclusion drawn from the Western Reserve University experiments in particular is that the language used may be much less important than such system features as the handling of questions and searching and, indeed, may be a relatively unimportant system component (Comparative Systems Laboratory, 1968).

It must be admitted that even though more serious recent experiments tend to agree on this point, they have still been fairly limited. In particular, large variations in the implementation of a certain type of language, and hence use of a given form of description, occur, with noticeable effects on system performance. This is seen, for instance, in the results for different versions of the same type of thesaurus for one collection obtained by the Cranfield and SMART Projects respectively (Keen, 1967c). It must also be emphasized that these results are mainly for sets of one-off searches divorced from user inspection, and do not, for example, cover such library service points as the utility of a language organization as a guide to user query formulation. More generally, particular types of language may be highly suited to specific documentation requirements. Further, the typical level of system performance obtained in such tests appears somewhat uninspired and encourages the belief that when the behavior of documentation systems is better understood, the right language will enable one to hit the jackpot.

So the nature of indexing languages retains its fascination as a research topic.

Dictionary, Thesaurus, Classification

In considering index languages we have to look at their functions both as normalizing and elaborating devices, or, to present the contrast from the conventional user's point of view, as nomenclatures and displays. We thus have to look at the choice of index terms for the language, and their organization. The former gives us the indexing vocabulary, and we can refer to any indicated set of relations between the terms in the vocabulary as a classification. As noted earlier, the vocabulary may consist essentially of derived keywords, or of independently provided terms or subject headings constituting a controlled vocabulary; a classification may be applied to either.

The controlled vocabulary is a familiar article in documentation, representing one interpretation of the word "thesaurus," a thesaurus being regarded merely as an authority list of terms. It provides for assignment indexing in which the distinction between entry words and index terms is maintained. This approach is treated as standard in coordinate indexing by Lancaster (1968b), for instance, and appears in the literature in many guises. In general, in such vocabularies, there is a larger list of entry words and a smaller list of terms, with a many–one mapping between them indicated by "see" references. The mapping brings together groups of semantically related different words, typically mapping synonyms or near-synonyms onto one representative term, or more specific words onto generic terms. The mapping relationship may also cover the mapping of variant word forms onto a single item, or of words onto the null term. One–many mapping may of course also occur. The provision of a full enough entry vocabulary is emphasized by Lancaster, though in practice in manual indexing it is often assumed that indexers will make the necessary translation without such explicit assistance. For automatic assignment a sufficient entry vocabulary is mandatory.

The difference between such a vocabulary and one exihibiting classificatory relations is exemplified by the distinction between "see" and "see also" references, the former linking a word with a term and the latter one term with another. It is more fully seen in the difference between term references defined by "use" and "use for" on the one hand, and those defined by "broad term," "narrow term," and "related term" on the other. Every degree of classification is possible from the minimal to the most elaborate. Of course whether the classificatory relations are clearly exhibited in a schedule, or are merely implicit in a listing with cross-references is logically immaterial, though visual displays are regarded as desirable in manual systems. As noted earlier, with automatic procedures depending on extracted keywords, the boundary between entry words and index terms may appear fluid: a class of keywords may be regarded as a mapping of several entry words onto a concept, or as a set of related terms. The distinction depends on the use made of the structure concerned, the same classification being usable in the two ways. Linguistic differences tend to underlie the relation between entry words and terms on the one hand, and between terms on the other, the former reflecting synonymy and the latter collocational relocations, say; but in statistical classifications, for example, this correspondence tends to be blurred. For convenience we shall speak of a simple controlled vocabulary as a *dictionary*, of such a dictionary with some relations indicated as a *thesaurus*, and of a vocabulary with a more elaborate structure as a *classification*.

There are many extant examples of each of these, predominantly manually constructed and intended for manual or at most semiautomatic, that is, mechanized search use. The spread of the postcoordinate approach to documentation has led to the appearance of large numbers of dictionaries and thesauri in particular, variously referred to as keyword, term and descriptor lists, or thesauri. These are primarily intended for particular document collections or subject areas, and include such conspicuous major examples as the *Thesaurus of Engineering and Scientific Terms* (Project LEX, 1967; see also Heald, 1967; Heald *et al.*, 1966), the *ASTIA Thesaurus* (ASTIA, 1962), the *Euratom Thesaurus* (Euratom, 1966), and the *NASA Thesaurus* (NASA, 1967). Other examples are illustrated in "Thesauri" (1966). Alongside the continuing global classifications like the UDC (recently surveyed by Mills, 1970) there are many specialized term classifications of all sorts, random examples being Broxis's classification for the fine arts (Broxis, 1966) and Moys's classification for law (Moys, 1968). All the major languages present substantial organizational and administrative problems due to their size and the need for continual updating, reflecting not only changing ideas, but changes in the linguistic usage of the words taken as term names.

Vocabulary Formation

The ordinary view is that the choice of terms for an indexing vocabulary is of prime importance, though their retrieval effectiveness may be materially improved by classification. Vocabularies like those underlying the major classifications are intended to have universal coverage, but more usually a vocabulary is intended to consist of terms able to characterize an actual or potential set of documents in a subject area in a comprehensive and nonredundant way. There is a substantial premium, since ordinary vocabularies are used by human indexers and searchers, on term names being transparent and unambiguous, the result generally being the use of ordinary language words with the appropriate special senses, though in some languages they may be used in a more artificial way as defined concept labels. Thus from the linguistic point of view the main feature of the typical term vocabulary is that it is ad hoc; it is oriented to a particular subject area, and individual term names represent specific or extended meanings of their ordinary language counterparts.

(Any code representing terms does not concern us here. Numerical or other notations like the familiar decimal ones, however valuable, are essentially secondary. Access to them is via words, either term or subject names, or entry words. It is these words which are important, and we shall concentrate on them.)

Manual vocabulary construction and maintenance is a topic on which there are many publications (see, for example, the references in Gaster, 1967). Vocabulary organization is typically seen as involving solutions to a variety of problems including identifying subjects or concepts to be covered, choosing a suitable level of detail for individual terms and headings, providing a set of descriptors without gaps and duplicates, and so on. With systems of the Universal Character type like the Western Reserve University Semantic Code (Melton, 1962), there is the further problem of sorting out the basic concepts which are used in combination for terms.

The difficulties encountered in vocabulary construction increase with the degree of control imposed. In general, derivative vocabularies, whether consisting of keywords or classes, are subject to less linguistic control, though more attention may be paid to their statistical properties, largely because relevant information is more easily obtained. For instance, whether terms would occur very frequently or very rarely may be apparent, allowing decisions as to their potential usefulness. The distinctive feature of derivative vocabularies is their collection orientation,, and this has consequences for the indexing vocabulary. For example, very general terms are regarded as unhelpful, primarily because they are likely to be heavily used and hence undiscriminating. With a collection based vocabulary highly technical words may occur frequently and so be regarded as unhelpful, though it is unlikely such a decision would have been made a priori on regular linguistic grounds.

Vocabulary Requirements

The idea that in constructing a vocabulary problems have to be solved implies a view of the requirements an indexing vocabulary should satisfy if it is to be effective as an indexing vocabulary, where these requirements in turn rest on assumptions about the objectives of vocabularies. The requirements are of interest in throwing light on the linguistic character of an indexing vocabulary.

The requirements an indexing vocabulary should satisfy have been more recently discussed by Lancaster (1968b), Lesk (1968), and Salton (1968a). Some requirements should be met by indexing vocabularies of any kind, whether these consist of independently set up term lists, or are derivative, consisting either of keywords or class-based descriptors. These requirements are related mainly to the distributional properties of the entire vocabulary, and are concerned with, for example, avoiding terms with uninformatively high collection frequencies, and so on. Another requirement made by Salton is that index terms should have a comparable distribution, or matching potential. The formation of descriptor dictionaries has been extensively studied in the U.S.S.R., and similar points are to be found in the many publications describing research or working practice in this area. See, for example, *Aspects* (1970b), Černjavskij (1969), Černyj (1968), Gerasimova *et al.* (1967), Gorobcov (1969), Goroxov (1969), Leont'eva and Margaritov (1968), Morozov and Šemakin (1969), Pavličenko and Raznikova (1970), Pokras (1969a), Šemakin (1969), Šneiderman (1969), Vaxabov (1970a), and Vaxabov *et al.* (1969).

Such requirements are not merely applicable to vocabularies, but can be satisfied even if purely statistical procedures are used for forming a vocabulary. Requirements are sometimes couched in a form more suited to manual dictionary and thesaurus construction. An example is the desirability of avoiding vague and ambiguous terms. This is naturally important if the terms are to be assigned manually to documents, and is primarily a remark about term names, the choice of term names having consequences for indexing. The complementary requirement is that of avoiding overlapping terms. These criteria nevertheless, except when they refer to terminology, apply to derivative vocabularies; avoiding wild variations in term specificity, for instance, is Salton's criterion, and statistical classifications may be designed to provide nonoverlapping, or exclusive classes.

The effects on retrieval of the distributional properties of an indexing vocabulary have been particularly studied by workers on automatic indexing, since the problems concerned are most clearly manifested in derivative indexing vocabulary. They are especially noticeable when a set of extracted words is used directly as an indexing vocabulary. But the properties of these same words influence the behavior of descriptors representing word classes. For instance, if two frequent words appear in the same class, this will lead to an even more frequent class description (Vaxabov, 1970a).

This is an area in which not very much has been done, though it is of importance. For though guidelines for manual dictionary construction are frequently provided, it is difficult to obtain a clear picture of the consequences of choice of vocabulary or to change an existing system. Some studies connected with automatic indexing and classification have been carried out, for example, by Sparck Jones (1971). It is clearly possible, with extracted keywords, to remove words with a large collection frequency as not particularly useful. A more subtle possibility is to weight terms by collection frequency, so that in searching a match on a collection a rare term counts for more than a match on a frequent one. In this case index terms have values for documents not based on the individual documents themselves. This has advantages with specialized collections where frequent terms are in no sense linguistically vague and are likely to be encountered in requests. Successful experiments on these lines are reported by Sparck Jones and Barber (1971). Some theoretical discussions of these questions, which also bear on the earlier points about description exhaustivity, are to be found, for example, in Avramescu (1969), Kozačkov (1969a), Wall (1964), and Zunde and Slamecka (1967).

Overall rules for vocabulary construction cannot be expected, though general experience suggests that terms which are or can be expected to be frequent for a vocabulary should be avoided. Whether terms or descriptors should be exclusive, on the other hand, is an example of a requirement for which there is insufficient empirical support.

Automatic Dictionary Formation

Setting up a dictionary automatically other than by derivative techniques presents severe and probably insoluble difficulties, at least as far as the choice of the index terms themselves goes. The relation between index terms and entry words is also important, and some work has been done on establishing correlations automatically between terms from an independently established list of index terms and text items justifying their assignment to documents. This is clearly relevant to automatic indexing since once the relation between text items and term is established, the latter can be assigned automatically.

Early experiments on these lines, like those by Maron (1961), are discussed in Stevens (1965). The most notable work in this area is perhaps that carried out by Williams (1965, 1968), though the general pattern of experiments in this area is the same, the chief differences being in the criteria used to establish word–term relationships. For test purposes a collection already indexed in some way is divided into two parts: a teaching and a test sample. Coefficients correlating the assigned index terms with text words of the sample are computed, permitting the selection of discriminating words for the terms. The test sample is then used to check the validity of the word–term relationships obtained through a comparison between manually and automatically assigned terms. Other experiments are reported by Stevens and Urban (1965), and statistical associations between words and terms from the Euratom thesaurus are exploited by Fangmeyer and Lustig (1969, 1970).

The automatic construction of derivative vocabularies comprises procedures associated with simple extracted keyword lists and those used for forming entry word classifications defining terms. The character of the former will be apparent from the discussion of vocabulary requirements, since it involves the deletion of useless words and the like. The most rudimentary form of classification represented by the conflation of variant word forms can be obtained automatically by exactly the techniques considered earlier under the derivation of descriptions from input document information. More interesting are techniques for grouping different words to cover semantic rather than morphological relations. These are essentially statistical, and since the same or similar methods are used to organize term vocabularies they are more conveniently considered later.

Index Language Classification

The nature of index language classifications is too large a subject for us to attempt to cover all its aspects, even in the most elementary way. Library classification has a long and respectable history, and has an interesting background involving taxonomies, encyclopedias, dictionaries, and universal or international languages. The importance of subject and term relationships in information retrieval is generally accepted, and whole ranges of relations and structures have been canvased. It is indeed extremely difficult to analyze indexing classifications because they exist in such an alarming variety of forms. It is possible to find every organizational feature in some system or another, and often several in the same system. Some indication of the bewildering variety appears in Coyaud (1966), and a random illustration of the complexity is provided by Aitchison and Day's "thesaurofacet" (1969). We cannot hope to give anything like an adequate list of examples here and so will do no more than point at sources of further information like de Grolier (1962), Mills (1970), 'Thesauri' (1966), and the volumes in the Rutgers series (Artandi, 1964–1966).

Some general remarks can be made. For example, we have already made an informal distinction between systematic and nonsystematic classifications, the former represented by enumerative schemes like the UDC, and the latter by cross-references in thesauri like the *NASA Thesaurus* (NASA, 1967). Essentially the contrast is between complete and partial classification, the former constituting an attempt to organize all the subjects or terms in a vocabulary, the latter merely an attempt to indicate more salient relationships. Another comparison is between one- and many-level classifications. Further differences are between univocal and multivocal classifications, or between exclusive and overlapping term classes, and between unidimensional and multidimensional classifications depending on one or more than one analytic relation respectively. Both of these are mentioned by Coyaud (1966), citing Gardin. A difference of attitude to classification is also apparent separating those concerned with the more traditional precoordinate subject classification ("analytico-synthetic" classification in Lancaster, 1968b), which is set up manually, and those concerned with a classification of terms for postcoordinate use, which may be set up automatically. The former tend to be more elaborate than the latter. The popularity of postcoordinate systems has, however, stimulated a relaxed and hospitable approach to classification. The result is a variegated range of intermediate or combination languages intended to mitigate the respective defects of the precoordinate and postcoordinate approaches, and of over- and underclassification. Further stimuli have been the growth of special-purpose systems, and the spread of automation.

There is a substantial literature on the principles and practice of library classification, though this is chiefly concerned with precoordinate classifications, whether of the older enumerative or newer faceted types. See, for example, de Grolier (1970), Mills (1970), Perreault (1967a), Sharp (1965), and Soergel (1969). But there is also a large literature on the construction of thesauri, Gillum (1964), Heald *et al.* (1966), Mandersloot *et al.* (1970), Neville (1970), Soergel (1969), and Wall (1969) being random examples. (Many of the references cited earlier in connection with dictionary construction are also relevant: see, for instance Černyj, 1968; Pavličenko and Raznikova, 1970; and also Gaster, 1967.)

Points arising from the classification literature relevant to our main interests include the following. First, though it is generally stated that these classifications are based on certain principles, these may not in practice be adhered to consistently. As Sharp (1965) notes, the dependence of the UDC on the genus–species relationship is somewhat mythical. A second complementary point is that apparently quite different classifications may be substantively equivalent. For example, as Sharp (1965) shows, though it is generally recognized that some subjects are extremely difficult to specify in enumerative terms, and that faceted classifications are more flexible, the same subject characterizations can in principle be generated by both enumerative and faceted classifications. This sort of thing suggests that we are far from having any real understanding of the desirable features of retrieval classifications and that experiments like those associated with automatic classification should be encouraged. Proper experiments comparing the retrieval performance of different classifications in an informative way are rare: in most cases the languages concerned differ so completely that it is impossible to ascribe performance features to particular classificatory properties. Examples are the tests reported by Popova and Jakubson (1969). More systematic tests have, however, been carried out by, for instance, the Cranfield project (Cleverdon *et al.*, 1966). Suggestions as to criteria for comparing classifications in themselves have been put forward by Ovčinnikov (1969) and Pokras (1969b), for instance, but the value of such comparisons depends on the validity of the underlying assumptions as to the desirable properties of classifications, and this may not be established. These difficulties are another reason for encouraging work on automatic classification, where alternative classifications and corresponding descriptions are more easily generated, allowing better comparisons.

A rather different point is that the connection between older forms of subject classification and linguistics is somewhat remote. Such classifications clearly exhibit the ambiguity of indexing classifications, namely, whether they have to do with words or concepts.

On the whole, the theory is that they are conceptual classifications, so that their relationship with vocabulary classifications, which are widely thought of as belonging to the lexicons of natural language grammars, is obscure. Library classifications are nevertheless of potential interest to linguists since they involve a large variety of relations, suggesting that a lexical classification may have to be much more complex than has generally been supposed. The final point is that these classifications are universally constructed by hand, and it is quite unclear how they could be generated automatically. The use of computers to assist in the formation and maintenance of classifications, particularly thesauri, has been suggested in recent years, for example by Gotlieb and Kumar (1968), Hersey and Hammond (1967), Rolling (1970), and Stone (1967). But while computers may be extremely useful in this case, the essential organization of the vocabulary is manual.

Term classifications associated with postcoordinate systems are more interesting, in part because they have a closer relation to linguistics, and in part because serious attempts have been made to construct them automatically.

Automatic Term Classifications

We have already noted that term classifications may have different functions according to whether they are used in indexing and searching as sources of substitute or additional terms, and also that they may have various properties, like consisting of exclusive or overlapping classes. But the detailed picture of automatic term classification is fairly confused, since it is difficult to sort out classification objectives and characteristics in the reported work. There are good reasons for this. First, all the approaches to automatic classification rely on about the same type of information about terms, namely distributional information, and different processes may be applied even to the same information, or classifications for different purposes derived from it. Second, essentially similar statistical techniques are involved, and the same procedure may in fact be adopted to derive classifications from different information, or for different purposes. Third, classifications for the same purpose may be derived from different information, or by different procedures. In general, the needs which a classification of this kind should satisfy are not at all well defined, and experiments in this area are mainly concerned with trying to determine the real requirements to be satisfied, and their consequences for the choice of input information and a grouping procedure.

The problems encountered in automatic term classification are, of course, those of retrieval classification in general. It is merely that the need to define every stage rigorously, to permit automatic operations, focuses attention on them in a way not typical of manual classification. In particular, the fact that word meanings are not directly accessible to the computer means that the grounds and processes of classification have to be viewed afresh. The underlying difficulty is that the ultimate objective of retrieval classification, namely to select relevant documents, cannot be stated in any form which leads directly to a specific choice of input information and grouping technique.

We have to work instead with beliefs that certain approaches to indexing and searching will lead to this result, and that for these purposes we should seek classifications with particular characteristics. Thus we may conclude that a classification (for a certain collection in a certain user environment) should have a specific linguistic character, a specific matching character, and a specific formal character. For example, we may decide that we are interested in providing for restricted term substitution. This may then lead us to ask for classes of synonyms which do not retrieve too many documents (or there is a noise danger), and which, by class overlap, allow for different term senses. More generally, automatic term classification can be examined for feasibility and effectiveness in retrieval. We are also interested here in the semantic characteristics of statistical term classifications.

The essential feature of statistically based term classifications is the identification of distributional relations between terms, the relation between a pair of terms depending primarily on their respective occurrences, and their cooccurrences with one another—either direct or indirect via cooccurrences with common other terms—over the documents in a collection. The set of statistical associations between the terms in an indexing vocabulary thus defined can be exploited in various ways: as an associative network, or semantic map (primarily intended for human users, perhaps in interactive searching); as an associative semiclassification, where each term is supported with a list of associated terms; or as a classification proper, where sets of associated terms are separated out. Further organization of these initial classes is possible. The important feature of the classification proper is that information which is merely implicit in the map or lists is made explicit and productive; to obtain it, the computation of term pair associations is followed by the identification of groups of associated terms. The result may of course cover only some, or all, of the terms in the vocabulary.

The computational procedures adopted to generate a term structure, that is, map, series of lists, or set of classes, are typically as follows. The input data consists of an array giving the incidence of terms in documents. This array is then processed to give a matrix of associations between terms (otherwise referred to as a connection, correlation, resemblance, or similarity matrix). The contents of the array may then be suitably manipulated to supply a network or lists, or used as input to the group-finding procedures. Dealing with large vocabularies, especially if the procedures involved are at all sophisticated, presents nonnegligible computing problems, though one important aspect of work in this area over the past decade has been the growing freedom from petty computing cares. More powerful machines, and a better understanding of data structures have both contributed.

The main problems involved in automatic classification are on the one hand that of determining the linguistic base for term associations, and on the other those of providing suitable formal definitions of association between a pair of terms, and association among a class of terms. An important subsidiary difficulty appears in the provision of economical algorithms, especially for finding groups.

Classification Base

Deciding on the base for a term structure involves arguments like the following. Such structures have been suggested as devices for providing term substitutes. It is therefore natural to think that association should be defined in such a way that, if possible, synonymous or nearly synonymous terms come out strongly associated—specialized subject synonymy rather than general language synonymy being allowed. Although computers cannot recognize sameness of meaning directly, they can recognize sameness of contextual behavior, which is just what we expect synonyms to exhibit. For example, if a and b each occur sufficiently often with c and d, this suggests that a and b are close in meaning. This is, after all, the classic linguistic distributional hypothesis. The term lists for the documents in a collection constitute a set of contexts, and these relationships can therefore be established by inspecting the document occurrence patterns of terms.

The idea that statistical procedures should be used to identify such term relations is a natural consequence of the originally widespread belief that the object of automatic procedures was to generate classifications like manual ones, with less effort. But it is evident that for effective retrieval we need not confine ourselves to synonyms or near synonyms. We can perfectly well use the relations between words which tend to cooccur. If a and c tend to appear in the same documents, this suggests that they are effective substitutes in the formal sense, that is, alternative means of retrieving documents on the same topic. Collocational relations between words may thus be of value in retrieval, in allowing approaches to the same topic from different angles, rather than to the same concept via different expressions of it. If document descriptions are to be enlarged with extra terms, collocational relations are even more sensible.

Both approaches were early canvassed (see, for example, Doyle 1962; Giuliano, 1965; Stiles, 1961), and experiments with both have continued since. Formally, the choice does not present problems, since indirect associations can be obtained simply by recycling the computation of associations, the initial first-order association matrix being taken as input data for a further calculation of association coefficients. The computational effort involved in using second-order associations is greater, and most work in this area has been based on first-order associations only. The latter have been exploited by, for example, Dennis (1965), workers at Arthur D. Little (Curtice and Jones, 1969; Jones *et al.*, 1968); the SMART Project (Lesk, 1969), Sparck Jones (1971), Sparck Jones and Jackson (1970), Stone (1967), and Tague (1966). Second-order associations have been used by Cagan (1970) and by Vaswani and Cameron (1970). Explicit comparisons between the two have been made by Jones *et al.* (1968), and, on a small scale, by Tague (1966). The conclusions drawn from these two investigations are that the two bases do not give a significantly different retrieval performance, and also that second-order associations do not link synonymous terms, presumably because the initial information supplied for terms is not sufficiently full or discriminating.

Classification Procedures

The formal problems of the whole area are severe, especially where classification is concerned. In principle we should be able to call on a well-organized set of mathematical methods, supported by a theoretical understanding of associative grouping. At the same time, the choice of formal procedures has to be related to retrieval circumstances and needs. But though the measurement of association is well developed, there is not much in the way of classification theory available. Equally, a sufficiently precise specification of the required structure to guide the choice of an associative procedure generally cannot be provided. Experiments in this area have therefore tended to involve a great deal of groping in the dark, theoretically unsatisfactory procedures being adopted in an ad hoc manner on the basis of largely unjustified assumptions, and being inadequately tested.

Automatic classification in general is, however, currently an area of active research, and though most of the effort is devoted to taxonomic methods not obviously suited to term classification, gains for documentation can be expected. Representative publications in this area include Ball (1965), Bonner (1964), Cole (1969), Good (1965), Jardine (1970), Jardine and Sibson (1968, 1971), Lance and Williams (1967a, b), Lerman (1970), MacNaughton-Smith (1965), and Sokal and Sneath (1963). An informal discussion of retrieval classification in the context of classification in general is to be found in Sparck Jones (1970). See also Kurbakov (1969) and Šreider (1968). Further, as mentioned earlier, there is a growing understanding of the operation of retrieval systems, so we can hope for a better formulation of the problems to be dealt with by mathematical techniques.

Term Associations

Some theoretical discussions of association coefficients in the context of information science are to be found, notably in papers from Arthur D. Little (Giuliano, 1965; Jones and Curtice, 1967; Jones *et al.*, 1968; see also, for example, Ivanova and Moskovič, 1967; Kuhns, 1965; Lustig, 1968). The problems of choosing a unit of cooccurrence, which can be expected to have an effect on associations, are recognized, though in practice alternatives may not be available. So are those of distinguishing significant from nonsignificant associations (Lesk, 1969; Vaswani and Cameron, 1970). Apart from the basic information about term occurrences, measures may exploit such facts as collection size and term collection frequency.

Within-document frequencies or weights may also be used, as by Lesk (1969), though usually only information about the presence of a term in a document is available. Unfortunately, little has been done to compare retrieval performance for different measures in a comprehensive way, though, for example, Jones and Curtice (1967) comment on the linguistic characteristics of association lists derived with different measures. There are some grounds for thinking that any straightforward normalized measures will give a comparable performance. It is also evident that though term relationships selected by statistical associations may differ from those picked out manually, and indeed may appear odd on inspection, they may be as effective for retrieval. This point is made by, for instance, Jones and Curtice (1967), Lesk (1969), and Sparck Jones (1971).

Term Structures

Theoretical discussions of the choice of different term structures, particularly classifications, and systematic comparisons between them, are less common, presumably because more variables are involved and this makes experimental effort greater. A general defect of work on automatic vocabulary organization is that it tends to be based on unexamined, or inadequately justified, assumptions about the use of such structures in retrieval, and hence the form they should take. An example is Dattola and Murray (1967). In earlier work in particular the assumption that an automatic classification should look and behave like a manual one was widespread. The character of association lists has, however, been considered by Jones and Curtice (1967), and the properties of class definitions and their retrieval implications are considered by Sparck Jones (1971).

Not very much has been done on full-blown term classification for retrieval. The two most favored approaches, treating the association matrix as a graph, are to define a class as a connected component subgraph, or as a maximal complete subgraph (or clique), and as the latter may lead to heavily overlapping classes, a further amalgamation stage may be gone through. But there is not sufficient evidence that either of these forms of class is especially suited to documentation. Other definitions, including that of a clump (Needham, 1963), have been studied by Sparck Jones and Jackson (Jackson 1969; Sparck Jones and Jackson, 1967, 1970), and further approaches are described by Vaswani and Cameron (1970). Even more than with associations, little has been done to compare different techniques systematically. However, in so far as any conclusions can be drawn from them, these are similar to those for associations, namely that sets of related terms derived by quite straightforward techniques may be effective in retrieval.

Experiments with Automatic Term Structures

The work done in this area as a whole over the last ten years falls naturally into two phases. The first phase was mainly concerned with justifying the distributional approach as a whole and with investigating its feasibility. It is summarized by Stevens (1965) comprehensively and is represented by the papers in Stevens *et al.* (1965). The experiments and supporting theoretical work were concerned with identifying correlation measures and grouping procedures apparently suited to documentation needs, and with showing that these gave plausible results. There was little direct testing of term structures in retrieval, as opposed to surface comparisons between manual and automatic structures. On the whole, the approach seemed to be promising, but the problems of the next stage appeared daunting. These are the difficulties of working on a large scale, of performing retrieval tests in general, and of distinguishing the effects of different structures or their uses on retrieval performance from those of other system components. Some of the earlier enthusiasts were apparently frightened off, though two groups—at Cambridge, England, and Arthur D. Little—have continued long-term projects.

Since 1965 this line of research has been pursued more systematically, and with more reference to actual retrieval testing. Thus, experiments on a usefully large scale have been carried out by Cagan (1970), Jones *et al.* (1967), Stone (1967), and Vaswani and Cameron (1970). Actual retrieval experiments of a nonnegligible order have been performed by Cagan (1970), Dattola and Murray (1967), Curtice and Jones (1969), the SMART Project (Lesk, 1969; Salton and Lesk, 1968); Sparck Jones (Sparck Jones, 1971; Sparck Jones and Jackson, 1970); and Vaswani and Cameron (1970), those by Sparck Jones and by Vaswani and Cameron, in particular, covering several alternatives.

Studies of the different forms of structure have been mainly concerned with lists on the one hand, and classifications proper on the other. Thus lists have been investigated by Cagan (1970), Arthur D. Little (Curtice and Jones, 1969; Giuliano and Jones, 1966; Jones and Curtice, 1967; Jones *et al.*, 1968); the SMART Project (Lesk, 1969; Salton and Lesk, 1968), Rubinoff and Stone (1967), Stone (1967), Tague (1966, 1967), and Vaswani and Cameron (1970), while classifications have been examined by Augustson and Minker (1970), Dale and Dale (1965), Dattola and Murray (1967), Gotlieb and Kumar (1968), Hillman (Hillman, 1968; Hillman and Kasarda, 1969), Sparck Jones (Sparck Jones, 1971; Sparck Jones and Barber, 1971; Sparck Jones and Jackson, 1970), and Vaswani and Cameron (1970). Maps, though advocated by Curtice (1966) and Dennis (1965), following Doyle (1961), have not been much studied, though in interactive retrieval statistical associations may be exploited in a manner reminiscent of both lists and maps (and also classes). Interactive retrieval is an area of recent growth, and the exploitation of statistical associations in search formulation has been pursued by, for example, Curtice and Jones (1969) and Hillman and Kasarda (1969). The use of statistical associations for assisting thesaurus building is advocated by Abraham (1964), Augustson and Minker (1970), and Jones *et al.* (1968). It is worth noticing that experiments with statistical associations have included both ones using more or less as-extracted keywords, and ones involving independent controlled term vocabularies: thus Gotlieb and Kumar (1968) have studied statistical relations between LC subject headings, and Jones *et al.* (1968) worked with *NASA Thesaurus* terms.

The long series of experiments carried out at Arthur D. Little under Giuliano and Jones (Curtice and Jones, 1967, 1969; Jones and Curtice, 1967; Jones *et al.*, 1967; Jones *et al.*, 1968), at the National Physical Laboratory by Vaswani and Cameron (1970), and by Sparck Jones and colleagues (Jackson, 1969, Needham and Sparck Jones, 1964, Sparck Jones, 1969; 1971; Sparck Jones and Barber, 1971; Sparck Jones and Jackson, 1967, 1970) may be picked out, since taken together they have provided a substantial amount of information about statistical association techniques. Work at Arthur D. Little has been concentrated on association lists: a variety of measures have been examined, large matrices computed, and different retrieval techniques tested. The other two projects have investigated classifications of different types in a series of controlled experiments designed to show up the effects of changes in the parameters of a classification-using retrieval procedure; these include the choice of the input term vocabulary, association measure, class definition, method of characterizing documents and requests, and so on. The defect of these experiments is their small scale. Vaswani and Cameron's experiments were less exhaustive, but on a larger scale. All these projects have found some advantages in associations, and have noticed the importance of such factors as the distributional properties of descriptions and vocabularies, though detailed procedures and results have varied and few direct comparisons on specific points are possible.

Value of Automatic Term Structures

From the retrieval viewpoint two questions present themselves:

1. Does the use of automatically obtained term associations lead

to a better retrieval performance than that obtained for simple coordinated terms?

2. Is it competitive with that given by a manual thesaurus or classification?

The conclusions to be drawn from experiments to date, inadequate though they are, do have much in common and do support a hopeful view of the potentialities of automatic term structures. Thus, experiments like those by the SMART Project (Lesk, 1969; Salton and Lesk, 1968) and by Sparck Jones (Sparck Jones, 1971; Sparck Jones and Barber, 1971; Sparck Jones and Jackson, 1970) show that substantial improvements in performance over un-structured vocabularies can be achieved, and that the differences between automatic and manual vocabulary structures are not great. In particular, it seems fairly clear from these results, and from those of Vaswani and Cameron (1970), that if statistical associations are used as a means of providing additional rather than substitute terms for searching, which may be done in various ways, this is helpful. It also seems to be the case that only strong associations are of use.

An increasing amount of attention has been focused on automatic document clustering. (See, for example, Chien and Preparata, 1968; Dattola, 1969; Doyle and Blankenship, 1966; Ivie, 1966; Litofsky, 1969; Preparata and Chien, 1967; Prywes and Litofsky, 1970; Rocchio, 1966; Salton, 1968b.) It is mentioned here partly because the same grouping procedures may be used as for terms, but also because it represents a complementary form of statistical proces-sing, and may use the same initial incidence information about terms and documents as term processing, though citation connec-tions have also been exploited (Balcarová and Königova, 1968; Ivie, 1966; Preparata and Chien, 1967).

From the linguistic viewpoint, the interesting aspect of statistical associations is the character of the derived lists or classes, compared with those typical of manually organized vocabularies. In general, as noted, words brought together by statistical criteria are linked by very varied semantic relations, and sets of manually associated words are not usually dependent on single or well-defined meaning relationships. Further, many of the relationships are highly local, that is, collection specific.

Semantics in Searching

The structure of the indexing language is primarily designed to promote effective searching and retrieval, and some ways in which the relations among terms may be exploited for this purpose will be clear by now. Many of the points about document descriptions apply equally to the treatment of requests: random examples are description expansion and term weighting. Other features of descriptions are more narrowly associated with the formulation of requests. The expression of a request as a Boolean function is an obvious example. Another is the marking of some request terms as obligatory.

Searching strategies may be divided into two: those which reduce a request specification so that, say, matches on only two terms out of three are required; and those which generalize by replacing one term by a less restricted one. This is where the relational structure of the language is clearly exploited. The replacement of a narrower by a broader term is typical of the many classifications with a specific–general term ordering, but the same effect may also be achieved in an unordered associative system if further links between terms are utilized to enlarge the set of alternative terms allowed to substitute for the initial terms. Further choices of strategy, primarily concerned with the properties of request-document matches but indirectly reflecting the characteristics of requests, have to do with output scoring: matching with ranking is an example.

Discussion of these questions are to be found in Giuliano and Jones (1966), Lancaster (1968b), and Salton (1968a); and various approaches to searching are suggested by, for instance, Mulvihill and Brenner (1968), Rublev and Ivaniuškin (1969), and Ullmann (1969).

Improvements in computing facilities have made iterative searching more attractive, whether the user is simply required to evaluate successive outputs for automatic request reformulation, or is invited to participate in the process of setting up a request, on-line. Associative techniques lend themselves to the latter: see, for example, Curtice and Jones (1969). This area has been extensively explored by the SMART Project, striking improvements in performance being obtained (Brauen, 1969; Ide, 1969; Rocchio, 1966; Salton, 1968b, 1969b).

Automatic Classification in Linguistics

The impact of all of this on the main stream of linguistics is not discernible, and the impact on linguistics of any kind has been slight. However, a few experiments have been performed in which text based statistical associations have been exploited to obtain semantic characterizations of words (for an overview, see Needham, 1967). Thus, following the line of argument concerning synonyms mentioned earlier, Lewis *et al.* (1967) report on a study intended to see whether synonymous word pairs can be distinguished from nonsynonymous pairs by their patterns of cooccurrence with other words. Their tests were designed to see how well carefully developed measures could discriminate synonymous and nonsynonymous pairs, compared with human judgments. The results, using words taken from document titles, were quite successful.

A series of experiments of a related kind, involving attempts to find semantic classes of words using restricted contextual properties, were carried out by Harper (1965), Needham and Kay (Needham, 1967), and Sparck Jones (1967). The tests depended on the selection of a syntactic relation like that holding between a verb and its subject, or between a noun and its modifying adjectives. One term in the relation was treated as a property of the other and used to characterize it. Grouping identified sets of words with common contextual properties, and the results exhibited a measure of intuitive coherence which speaks well for the whole approach. Similar experiments by Saikevič in finding semantic fields are reported by Ivanova (1969).

Earlier experiments by Sparck Jones (1964) were concerned with the automatic generation of classes of similar words, like those in Roget's *Thesaurus of English Words and Phrases*. The classification procedure was applied to word senses represented by sets of synonyms or "rows" defined by text substitution. These rows were analogous to the most closely related words appearing within a Roget class. A pair of word senses is likely to be more similar the more words there are that express both of them, and sets of rows may be similarly related. This is based on the assumption, not always, but usually, correct, that though a single word may have different senses these are likely to be closely related to one another; their rows are therefore related. The rows were grouped automatically on the basis of their common words, giving very plausible thesaurus classes.

It is difficult to know what criteria to apply to experiments of this kind. The techniques used were new, and while the classes had the kind of coherence one expects of a section in a regular thesaurus, a plausible appearance is no guarantee of linguistic truth; the same holds for the other investigations. The problem is that lexical relations are properly tested by being part of the information utilized by a grammar. But theoretical linguistics has had, for example, no place for a thesaurus except, possibly, as a source of semantic markers in a scheme like that proposed by Katz and Fodor (1963). Until very recently, the structure of the lexicon has been a matter of relatively little interest to linguists, and they have as yet found little of substance to say about it. This situation can be expected to change, at least if the lexicalist school of generative grammarians is not defeated by the transformationalists. Today, the interest is primarily in semantic problems and, more specifically, those associated with characterizing word meaning.

Semantics in Information Retrieval: Conclusion

In attempting an overall conclusion on semantics, we have less reason to feel puzzled than we had with syntax. Nevertheless, the experiments which have been carried out suggest that great refinement in document analysis and description and the use of elaborate term structures may be less valuable in retrieval than has been supposed. Information scientists may not be justified in concentrating on concepts as opposed to words, or on hypothetical conceptual relations as opposed to actual verbal collocations. It is to be regretted that the experiments carried out in this area do not cover the desired range or provide us with enough detail. But the findings for syntax that simple postcoordinated descriptors work as well as precoordinated subject headings, are paralleled by the semantic results obtained by such investigations as those of the Cranfield and SMART Projects (Cleverdon *et al.*, 1966; Salton, 1966–1969), which show that a comparatively simple vocabulary organization supporting simple keywords may be as good as more elaborate approaches.

7

FACT RETRIEVAL

Fact Retrieval and Document Retrieval

We said, at the outset, that we would regard the phrase "document retrieval" as synonymous with "information retrieval." Less cavalier use of the terminology might have led us to exclude the present chapter from our report on the grounds that it belongs to information science but not to documentation. But that would have been an unfortunate decision because fact retrieval, which is the function of a question-answering system, is at the center of some of the most speculative research that is being done in computational linguistics and artificial intelligence, and work in this area shows more of the shape of things to come than anything else we could look at. Whether or not fact retrieval should be regarded as a proper part of documentation, there is little doubt that it is from this direction that many of the new ideas introduced into documentation over the next few years will come.

The document retrieval system responds to a user's request for information, not by supplying the desired information itself, but by providing documents, or the descriptions of documents, in which there is some hope of finding the information. A fact retrieval system, on the other hand, aims to answer questions directly. For this reason, such systems are also frequently referred to as question-answering systems. The difference is not one of principle because, clearly, a document retrieval system is nothing more than a fact retrieval system restricted to operate on facts about documents. The main difference between the two types of retrieval comes from the fact that a useful fact retrieval system cannot rely on finding a ready-made answer to more than a very small proportion of the requests it receives in the file of data available to it. Instead, it must be capable of finding facts in that file on the basis of which to infer a correct answer to the question. Suppose, for example, that the file of facts contains the information that the Mona Lisa is in the Louvre and that the Louvre is in Paris. If we now ask whether the Mona Lisa is in Paris, we should expect the system to be able to answer "yes," even though it does not have the information we are asking for in just the form in which we cast it.

As we have said, a document retrieval system can be viewed as a special kind of fact retrieval system, and it is possible to imagine one with this ability to make inferences. But, whereas this ability is a luxury in a program to retrieve documents, it appears that a program designed to retrieve facts would be almost useless without it. The reader who doubts this is urged to think of a number of simple questions that might be answered by referring to a standard encyclopedia and then to see for how many of these he can find a sentence in the encyclopedia that is a direct answer.

The paradigm example of a fact retrieval system contains a number of electric typewriters, or television sets associated with typewriter keyboards, through which a person can communicate directly with a central computer. Information to be entered into the system's file of facts is typed on one of the keyboards in some agreed language, ideally the language of everyday conversation.

Requests for information are also typed on the keyboards in the same language,* and the computer responds through the typewriter, or by displaying messages on the television screen. Before accepting a new piece of information, or before answering a question, the computer may have questions of its own to put to the user in order to clarify his request. Thus, for example, if the question or the new piece of information is expressed in an ambiguous sentence, or if it contains referring terms whose references must be known to make sense of it, then the machine may ask for this additional information.

Fact retrieval systems currently under development vary in the kinds of language in which they are prepared to communicate and also in the restrictions that are placed on the kinds of data they can accommodate. Most workers are agreed that the ideal system would communicate in ordinary language and place no restrictions on the data. But, in view of the magnitude of the problem and the scarcity of resources for this kind of work, some have decided to provide access to the system only through the medium of a special language which is either artificial or is a severely restricted subset of a language like English. This is a reasonable strategy if one assumes that information storage and retrieval together with inference–making techniques can be developed independently of techniques to process the data of ordinary language. In the final analysis, this will doubtless prove to be an insecure position, but it is nevertheless one from which to begin work on interesting problems in a way which will not prove entirely fruitless.

The utility of a fully fledged question-answering system is easy to grasp, and there is little doubt that innumerable practical applications would be found for a system of this kind if the knowledge necessary to build one were at hand. But at least as much, and possibly more, of the driving force for work of this kind comes from another direction. A fact retrieval, or question-answering, system could not be said to be completely successful unless it were

---

*Otherwise the computer must do translation. In a sense, sophisticated fact retrieval is translation.

able to answer questions of every imaginable sort, including questions of opinion, emotion, and the like. Furthermore, it would have to be able to cope with the kinds of very imprecise questions that human beings are wont to ask, to engage in long and sometimes complex conversations in order to clarify a user's request, but to abandon these conversations when they became too tedious and, instead, to go in search of the best answer that could be found, given the poor information available on what was actually required. This is to say that the intellectual capabilities of the machine would have to be precisely those of a human being. In other words, the fact retrieval system would be a model of human psychology, and the best and most complete model imaginable. Logic does not guarantee that, if a machine of this kind could, in fact, be built, it would say anything about the way the human mind works. But, in view of the immense complexity of the tasks involved, it is implausible that they could be performed so convincingly in a manner totally unrelated to the human one. The argument that such a machine was a valid psychological model would be immensely compelling. It is for this reason that work on fact retrieval systems is usually said to belong to the discipline of artificial intelligence, and hence to psychology.

Early Systems

Shapiro (1971) sees the deductive capabilities of a question-answering program as its most important feature, and, on this basis, he distinguishes three categories of program. Members of the first category are characterized by the fact that such deductions as are made are made as data is entered into the system. Programs in the second category contain a fixed set of executive routines that can be invoked at suitable points in the course of answering a question to make inferences. Members of the third category are capable of making inferences on the basis of rules that are pre sented to them in the form of ordinary facts. Typically, these will be facts that are stated with the use of quantifiers, as in "All men are mortal": this fact can be used whenever there is need to establish the fact that a particular man is mortal.

An early example of the first kind of program is SAD SAM designed by Lindsay (1963). SAD SAM is an acronym standing for "Sentence Appraiser and Diagrammer and a Semantic Analyzing Machine." Its vocabulary was limited to the approximately 850 words of basic English, and Kuno and Oettinger's predictive syntactic analyzer for English was used to obtain structures for the input sentences. The semantic component of the system first translated each incoming sentence into a set of triplets consisting of the names of a pair of people and the name of the relationship in which they stood. The triplets were then used in the construction of a fact file consisting simply of a set of family trees with a place for everybody so far introduced to the system. Each person had a record in the file giving the name of his or her husband or wife, offspring, etc.

SAD SAM contained no mechanisms for following out a scheme of inference, but it is nevertheless possible to ascribe some logical capability to it because it was able to answer questions otherwise than by repeating a sentence originally offered to it as data. If the program were told that John was Mary's son and, possibly on some quite different occasion, that Jane was Mary's daughter, then the family tree stored by the machine would be adjusted to reflect these facts. If it were then asked if John was Jane's brother, it would be able to answer correctly because the necessary fact was directly available in the tree. It is just as though a sentence such as "John and Jane are siblings" had been entered explicitly.

Another program that belongs to this class is LISP-A proposed by Sandewall (1968). This is an extension of the LISP programming system of McCarthy *et al.* (1963). The programmer is allowed to define a special class of functions each of which applies to arguments of certain specified types. He might, for example, define a function of this type called *father* which applies to all people. The definition of the function consists of a rule enabling it to determine, for each person, who that person's father is. When the function is first defined, it is applied to all people and, where possible, an explicit record is made of that information. When a new person is introduced to the system, the function is automatically applied. In an interactive system, these functions could doubtlessly be designed so as to ask the user for necessary information when the information required for a deduction is not at hand.

The important thing about both SAD SAM and LISP-A is that the decision as to what propositions might be needed to answer questions is made before the questions are posed. The programs store their data in a rigidly prescribed format which provides slots for certain kinds of information, and they endeavor to fill vacant slots as soon as possible.

By far the largest category of fact retrieval programs that have been written thus far perform the deductive processes of which they are capable, as required, to answer particular questions. To this category belong BASEBALL (Green *et al.*, 1963), DEACON (Craig *et al.*, 1966), Woods's program that answers questions based on the Official Airline Guide (Woods, 1967, 1968), Kellogg's Natural Language Compiler (Kellogg, 1968) and the RAND Corporation's Relational Data File (Levien and Maron, 1965, 1969) with its associated INFEREX language for specifying inference schemes and retrieval requests. These systems share the property of compiling requests into sequences of program steps that are then executed using the file of facts as data. A program step can be of arbitrary complexity and can involve calls to subroutines provided as part of the overall system. If a step fails to find the sentence it is looking for, then a subsequent step can look for other sentences from which the truth or falsity of the desired sentence could be inferred. If, for example, the question is "Is Harold Ann's uncle?" the first move would presumably be to look for the internal representation of the sentences "Harold is Ann's uncle" and "Harold is not Ann's uncle" in the file. If one of these is found, it can be used immediately as the answer to the question. Failing this, a search might be instituted for a sentence of the form "x is Ann's father" or "x is Ann's mother." If this is successful, then the name that fills the

position of the x could then be inserted in a sentence of the form
"Harold is x's brother," "Harold is x's sister," "x is Harold's brother,"
or "x is Harold's sister."

BASEBALL was one of the most ambitious of the early fact retrieval systems. Once again, the language in which it was possible to
communicate with the system was a severely restricted subset of
English allowing no conjunctions, comparatives, or superlatives.
As the name of the program implies, it was intended to answer the
questions about games of baseball. The file of facts consisted of
a list of baseball games arranged in a hierarchical structure. The
record for each game contained the names of the two teams involved and the scores they obtained. The largest divisions of the
file corresponded to months, the next largest to towns, and the
games themselves were to be found on the third level of the structure. The program was able to perform a simple phrase-structure
analysis of questions and to resolve certain simple kinds of ambiguity. It was, for example, able to decide, at least in some cases,
whether the word "Boston" was to be taken as the name of a place
where a game was played or the name of a team that took part.
The program was provided with some simple arithmetic capabilities to enable it to answer such questions as "How many games
did the Red Sox play in August?"

Another program in this general category is SIR (Raphael, 1968)
which goes further than those already mentioned in supplying a
generally applicable internal format for data storage and in exploiting logical properties of the relations it establishes between items.
SIR is not restricted to one internal data structure and notions
like "parent" and "baseball game" are not built into it. The particular
version of the system described by Raphael accommodates the following relations between data items:

  (i)   set membership;
 (ii)   set inclusion;
(iii)   equivalence (x and y name the same object);
 (iv)   ownership;
  (v)   ownership by each member of a class;

    (vi) part–whole;
   (vii) part of each member of a class;
  (viii) right–left;
    (ix) immediately to right–left.

No claim is made for the comprehensiveness of this set, but it is nevertheless clear that it covers a large number of subject areas to which one could imagine a fact retrieval system being applied. But more important than this is the fact that new relations can be added or old ones replaced without disturbing the overall structure of the system.

Each relation in the SIR system is accompanied by a statement of logical properties that it has which enable it to be used in the making of certain simple kinds of inference. In particular, each relation is marked for symmetry, transitivity, and reflexivity. So, for example, the relation "right-of" is transitive so that if b is to the right of a and c is to the right of b, the machine can correctly infer that c is to the right of a. On the other hand, the relation "right-of" is not reflexive so that, if b is to the right of a, it cannot be concluded that a is to the right of b. In the case of equivalence, such an inference would have been valid. The important point is that SIR can accommodate a variety of different sets of relations, but those properties of them that come from logic and are not apt to vary are built into the system.

The salient feature of data retrieval, as opposed to fully fledged fact retrieval, is that it is well known, both to the constructor of the system and to the person who will use it, just what kinds of objects are represented in the system and by what kinds of property each one is indexed. By this definition, SAD SAM and BASEBALL are data retrieval systems, for all that they are also fact retrieval systems. In SAD SAM, the only kinds of entity the system knows about are people, and the properties that it ascribes to a person are precisely the names of that person's husband or wife and the names of their offspring. It is true that, at any given moment, there may be certain people for whom the system does not have information in all categories; the important thing is that these are the only categories available and no other kinds of information can be stored. Exactly the same is true of the question-answering system designed by Woods (1967, 1968) for the kind of data that the official airline guide provides. The items in the file are flights and airports, and the properties of these entities are precisely those that the airline guide furnishes, the most important ones being arrival and departure times. But fact retrieval systems will be of real value, both practically and as psychological models, only when these restrictions on the kinds of data they can manipulate are removed.

Semantic Networks

More recent work has therefore concentrated on systems capable of accommodating much more amorphous kinds of data. The systems proposed by Shapiro and Woodmansee (1969) and Kay and Su (1970) are much less restrictive than those described above. In both of these systems, the fact file consists of a directed graph, that is, of a collection of labeled items joined together to form a network by labeled connectors. It is simplistic to think of such a structure in terms of a two-dimensional diagram in which the items are represented by points, or nodes, and the connections by labeled lines. An item in the file can represent anything that can be the referent of an ordinary word or phrase. And the lines between them can be of as many kinds as there are names of relations in the dictionary or grammar.

Neglecting certain matters relating principally to time and tense, the sentence "Brutus killed Caesar" might be represented in such a system somewhat as shown in Fig. 7.1. The lower-case letters at the nodes can be thought of as representing the addresses in the physical archive where the node is stored. They serve here mainly to make it easier to talk about the diagram. Node a represents the class of individuals each member of which is named "Brutus." Node c represents one of the members of that class and b represents a proposition assigning the individual c to the class a. Node b is

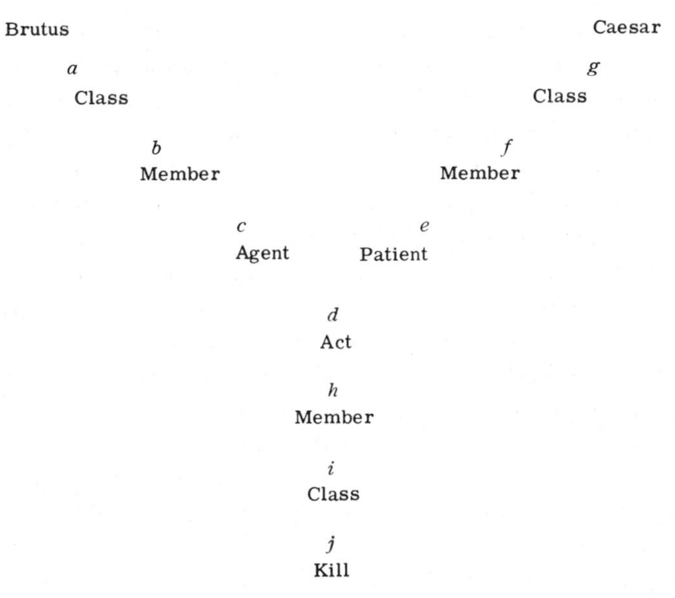

FIG. 7.1

introduced, instead of relating *a* and *c* directly, in order to accommodate facts stated in sentences like "John did not believe that Brutus was the person that killed Caesar." What John did not believe was presumably *b*. Node *g* represents the class, and *f* the proposition that relates them. Node *j* represents the class of events each member of which is a killing, *h* a member of that class, and *i* the proposition that relates them. The proposition that *c* participated in the event *h* as agent and *e* as patient is represented by node *d*. The event *h* is represented separately from the proposition *d* because of the difference in interpretation between sentences like "Brutus killed Caesar and Cassius saw it happen" and "Brutus killed Caesar but Cassius did not believe it had happened." What Cassius is asserted to have seen in the first sentence is the event *h;* what he is asserted to disbelieve in the second is the proposition *d*.

Notice that relatively few of the nodes in the network—only *a*, *g*, and *j* in the example—are associated with words in the dictionary.

Other special kinds of nodes are necessary to accommodate negation and facts involving quantifiers in their statement.

An effective fact retrieval system must make some provision for
propositions involving words like "all" and "some," which correspond to the quantifiers of propositional logic, for it is on the
proper use of such propositions that the system's ability to make
inferences rests. Consider the sentence "Everyone likes food." It
is possible to imagine a fact retrieval program which, on receiving
this sentence, searches its store of knowledge for every node representing a person and appends to it a new proposition to the effect
that that person likes food. It would also have to be on the lookout
for any subsequent sentences about hitherto unknown persons,
to create a new proposition about their like of food.

This strategy is not only exceedingly clumsy but also psychologi-
cally implausible. A sentence containing a word like "all" or a plural
noun used generically would set off a long and complicated process
resulting in the addition of untold numbers of new nodes and
connections. A sentence like "Dogs love people" would be enough
to bring a system that knew more than a very few dogs or people
to its knees, because it would presumably cause a new proposition
to be set up for every pair consisting of a dog and a person.

Words like "some," which correspond to the existential quantifier
in logic, present even more severe problems. To store the fact expressed in "Mary loves someone" presumably requires an arrow to
be added to the diagram pointing to the person that Mary loves.
But we are not told who Mary loves. We are not even told whether
the one she loves is someone the system already knows about. The
only solution is presumably to create a node to represent this
unnamed person and to be prepared to make all arrows that end
at this node point elsewhere if we later discover who the person
is. But this new node represents the bound variable of propositional
logic and, if it can be used to solve the present problem, it can
presumably be used elsewhere.

The attempt to represent the quantifiers of the predicate calculus
directly in a network structure of the kind we are discussing leads
to an important difficulty, arising from the fact that the order

in which quantifiers appear in a formal logical expression or in a sentence of ordinary language is crucial for its proper understanding. In many, perhaps most, dialects of English, the sentence "Everyone loves someone" and "Someone is loved by everyone" are most readily interpreted as having two different meanings. The first means that, for every person that you care to name, it would be possible to find at least one other person whom that person loves. The second sentence has the much less plausible interpretation that there is one single person whom everybody loves. In the notation of the predicate calculus, the distinction is approximately that between

$$(\forall x)(\exists y)(\text{Loves}(x, y)) \quad \text{and} \quad (\exists y)(\forall x)(\text{Loves}(x, y)).$$

In these examples, we have left out the fact that the lovers, x and y, refer only to people because this brings up other issues that are not important for the present discussion.

One way to represent the proposition expressed by "Everyone loves someone" in a storage network might be as shown in Fig. 7.2. The proposition as a whole is represented by the node c. The fact that this is a proposition containing quantifiers is indicated by the fact that there are three arrows leading from this node labeled "quantifier," "binding," and "matrix," pointing respectively to nodes representing the universal quantifier, the variable bound by that quantifier, and the remaining information in the proposition. The remainder, represented by node d, also represents a proposition involving a quantifier, in this case the existential quantifier. This quantifier binds the variable y at node g and the remainder of the proposition is represented by the node f. The quantifier-free part of the logical expression, which can be read approximately as x loves y," is represented by f. The remainder of the diagram is similar in all essentials to that for "Brutus killed Caesar." The diagram for "Someone is loved by everyone" would be the same as that for "Someone loves everyone" except the quantifier arrow from node c would point to node b, and the quantifier arrow from the node d would point to node a.

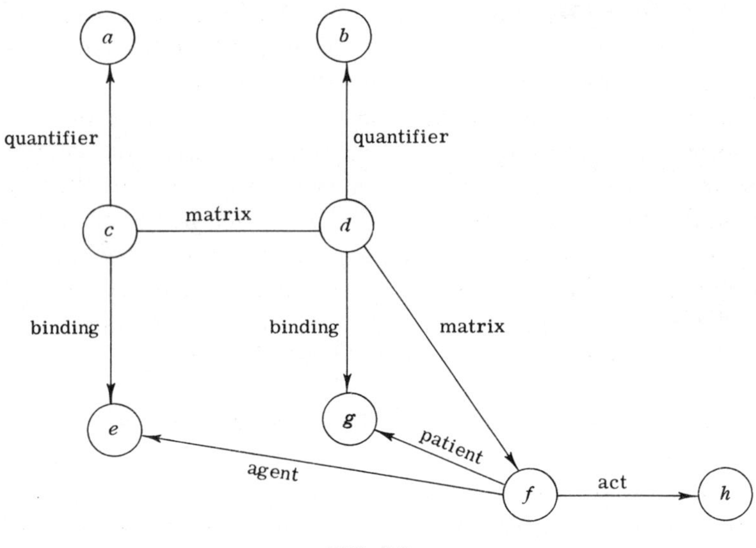

FIG. 7.2

Any number of other devices can be imagined for representing
quantifiers in a network structure. One possibility which is not
open is the one used in standard logical notation, because the network exists in a space in which there is no such thing as left-to-right
ordering. Making a careful choice among the possible methods
of representing quantifiers is important because the logical flexibil-
ity and overall deductive capacity of the system rest squarely on
their proper handling. It is not always easy to recognize what quantifiers underlie a sentence in ordinary language: there is, for
example, no reliable way of distinguishing plural nouns used
generically; but, to the extent that this can be done, the resulting
system attains a power altogether greater than any of those previously discussed can claim. This is because the system does not
distinguish facts which are potential rules of inference from other
facts that it receives and, indeed, it does not need to recognize
potential rules until the need to use them arises.

The second important point about the fact retrieval systems proposed by Kay and Su (1970) and Shapiro and Woodmansee (1969)

is that the choice of the relations that can be established between items in the file, while it is not an integral part of the computer programs themselves, is based on a principle which is intended to ensure the general applicability of those relations. Generally speaking, the items in the file are to be thought of as corresponding to the records of words. But an important departure from this principle has already been made when quantifiers and the variables they bind are introduced into the file and represented in the same way in referring terms. The ontological status of propositions is not straightforward, but if quantifiers and variables can be admitted, then surely so can they. We have shown examples of the way in which a relation, such as membership in a set, can be decomposed into a pair of more elementary relations and an item representing a proposition. The reasons for doing this are straightforward. A text that asserts that all men are mortal is apt also to refer to this proposition in other sentences, such as, for example, the sentence "This proposition asserts that all men are mortal." This provides grounds for decomposing the set membership, or the set inclusion relation, or both, and introducing a new proposition which will be the object of the verb "assert" in this sentence. But where does this process end? Is it not always possible to construct sentences that refer to any of the relations, however elementary, implied in some other sentence. The answer appears to be "no." There is at least some reason to believe that a small set of relations can be obtained from linguistic theory into which all others can be decomposed but which cannot, themselves, be used as references. One place to look for labels for these relations is among the names of cases in a grammar of the kind proposed by Fillmore (see Chapter 5).

Let us now consider briefly how inferences are made in the systems we have been considering. Suppose that the system has been told

(1)   Adam is Charles's parent;

(2)   Bill is Adam's brother;

(3)   If a is b's parent and c is a's brother, then c is b's uncle.

Suppose, now, that the following question is posed:

(4)   Who is Charles's uncle?

The system first searches for a sentence of the form

(5) x is Charles's uncle,

but fails. This search is conducted by following appropriate pointers leading from the nodes representing "Charles" and "uncle" and constructing a list of the propositions on each path. If the required proposition is in the file, it must be in the intersection of these two lists. If it is not, the next step is to construct a pair of new propositions, namely:

(6) x is y's uncle;

(7) x is Charles's z.

where x, y, and z are to be understood as variables which, in the network, will be bound by some quantifier. Both of these propositions are more general because they contain more variables, each of which has a variety of potential values. A search is now conducted for propositions in the file that have one of these forms. This is successful in both cases because (6) has the same form as the consequent of the implication (3), and (7) has the same form as (1). But (1) tells us who Charles's parent is and not who is his uncle, and it is therefore set aside. It is possible that it would be taken up later in the hope of establishing that a person's parent was also his uncle, a hope which would prove forlorn. Making suitable replacements in the antecedent of (3), on the other hand, we obtain

(8) a is Charles's parent and x is a's brother.

This will now serve as a replacement for the original question. What it says is that we are now interested in finding someone who is the brother of Charles's parent. Further, a replacement for a in (8) can be found because the first part of (8) has the same form as (1). This yields

(9)   Adam is Charles' parent and x is Adam's brother.

If a replacement can be found for x in the second part of this proposition, it will provide the required answer. Such a replacement can in fact be found in (2), and we thus obtain the answer "Bill."

The fundamental operations involved in this process are

   (i)   searching for propositions which have the same form as a given one, where having the same form means simply that one can be derived from the other by replacement of variables;

  (ii)   establishing the antecedent of an implication as a new question when the consequent has the same form as a current question;

(iii)   generalization of a question by replacing constants with variables.

The success of the scheme, which is far from proven, rests on being able to find sentences of a given form very rapidly, and it is precisely for this purpose that the network was designed. All sentences involving a given constant can be found by following links that emanate from the corresponding node, and an efficient algorithm exists for finding intersections of lists of propositions constructed in this way.

Theorem Proving and Fact Retrieval

The imagination of a number of people interested in fact retrieval has been caught by the analogy between this problem and the one of constructing computer programs to prove theorems in mathematics. A branch of mathematics has a set of axioms which are assumed to be true and a set of theorems that have been shown to be true in the past. When we attempt to prove a new theorem, we ask a question that can only be answered by reference to this existing body of facts. If it is difficult to prove or disprove a proposition in mathematics, it is usually because the chain of inference that must be constructed is long, and the axioms and existing theorems that must be used are not obvious. This is exactly the case with a question-answering system. The facts that are put into the system's file have the status of so-called nonlogical axioms, that is, propositions that are true not for purely logical reasons, but because of observations that have been made in the world or simply because they are assumed to be true. But this difference does not change the nature of the problem that has to be solved. The main difference between fact retrieval and theorem proving is one of scale. Finding answers to questions about ordinary objects and events usually requires relatively short chains of inference to be constructed on the basis of facts chosen from a prodigious inventory of nonlogical axioms. The proof of a nontrivial theorem typically requires much longer chains of inference to be constructed on the basis of a much smaller inventory of already known facts.

A theorem in logic is said to be valid if, whatever the terms in it are taken to refer to, it turns out to be true. In other words, the theorem is said to be valid if it is satisfied by every possible model. It is clearly impossible to test any proposition against all possible models, and it is for this reason that proof procedures are necessary. A more productive approach, and the one adopted in most automatic systems, is based on a method first proposed by Herbrand (1930), sometimes called the Semantic-Tableau method, in conjunction with the so-called Resolution Principle of Robinson (1965a, 1965b). According to the Herbrand proof procedure, an attempt is made to find a model which satisfies the negation of the potential theorem. Since, for any given proposition, every model satisfies either the proposition or its negation, but not both, then finding a model for the negation of a proposition is sufficient to dismiss the proposition. On the other hand, and this is the main point, if the attempt to find a model for the negation of a proposition leads to a contradiction, then the proposition can be accepted as a theorem.

Consider once again the proposition

Everybody loves somebody.

This can be paraphrased as "No matter who you consider, it will be possible to find at least one person that that person loves." In other words, there is a function whose range and domain is the set of people and which yields, for any person, a person whom he loves. Symbolically, we may write

$$(\forall x)(\text{Loves}(x, f(x))),$$

where f is the function that carries a person onto another person whom he loves. All variables bound by the existential quantifier can be replaced by so-called Skolem functions in this way. As a result, the only variables remaining in the expression will be bound by the universal quantifier. This being so, the quantifier itself can be deleted, so that we have

$$(\text{Loves}(x, f(x))),$$

where the free variable x is assumed to be bound by the universal quantifier. The fact that x appears as an argument of f indicates that the existential quantifier occurred to the right of the universal quantifier. The sentence "Somebody loves everybody" would translate as

$$\text{Loves}(g, x),$$

where g is a Skolem function of no arguments, indicating that the corresponding existential quantifier appears to the left of the universal quantifier that translates as x. In general, an expression of the form

$$(\forall w)(\exists x)(\forall y)(\exists z)P(w, x, y, z)$$

translates as

$$P(w, f(w), y, g(w, y)).$$

The principal reason for replacing the standard notation of the predicate calculus by one which uses free variables and Skolem functions is that the latter can be treated as expressions of sentential logic. In other words, the formal operations that can be performed on them are greatly simplified.

Robinson's Resolution Principle is a single rule of transformation that can be proved to be sufficient for any deduction. It is

$$((a \wedge b) \vee (\sim a \wedge c)) = b \vee c.$$

Let us now return to an example used previously. Suppose that the system has been told

(1)   Adam is Charles's parent;

(2)   Bill is Adam's brother;

(3)   If a is b's parent and c is a's brother, then c is b's uncle

and suppose that it represents these as

(4)   Parent(Adam, Charles);

(5)   Brother(Bill, Adam);

(6)   Parent(a, b) $\wedge$ Brother(c, a) $\Rightarrow$ Uncle(c, b).

For the resolution principle to be used, all expressions must be in conjunctive normal form, so that (6) must be converted to

(7) $\sim$Parent(a, b) $\vee$ $\sim$Brother(c, a) $\vee$ Uncle(c, b).

The question is

(8)   Who is Charles's uncle?

Corresponding to this, we create the proposition

(9)   Uncle(x, Charles).

If we can show this proposition to be true, it must be by finding a replacement for x, and that replacement will constitute an answer to the question.

Recall that the proof procedure will take the form of attempting to derive a contradiction by assuming the negation of the proposition to be proved. Accordingly, we posit the proposition

(10) $\sim$Uncle(x, Charles).

Substituting x for c and Charles for b in (7) yields

(11)   ~Parent(a, Charles) $\vee$ ~Brother(x, a) $\vee$ Uncle(x, Charles).

We can now apply resolution to (10) and (11) and obtain

(12)   ~Parent(a, Charles) $\vee$ ~Brother(x, a).

Replacing a by Adam, we obtain

(13)   ~Parent(Adam, Charles) $\vee$ ~Brother(x, Adam).

Resolution now applies to (4) and (13) and yields

(14)   ~Brother(x, Adam).

The next step is to replace x by Bill, recalling that the replacement made for x is to constitute an answer to the question. We now have

(15)   ~Brother(Bill, Adam),

which contradicts (5), thereby establishing the validity of (9) and verifying that "Bill" is a correct answer to the initial question.

The most notable attempt to use resolution proof procedures as the basis of a question answering system is that of the artificial intelligence group at Stanford Research Institute (see Green, 1969; Raphael, 1968). The method is clearly powerful, though it has yet to deliver a proof of a really interesting theorem, and it has a reassuring sense of theoretical solidity. However, it does not touch the main points at issue in the design of fact retrieval systems. The outstanding problem here is that of identifying propositions in the file that are relevant to answering the question posed. Various methods of identifying probably relevant propositions have been proposed, such as the so-called set of support strategy. Most of these, however, are relatively powerless in the face of the great number of nonlogical axioms that would have to be stored by a useful system. We know of no attempt to combine a semantic network of the kind proposed by Shapiro and others with a resolution theorem prover. Such a combination would require artistry to construct, but there is reason to believe that the performance of the resulting system would be better, though doubtless not sufficiently better, than existing programs.

The day of the machine that could pass itself off as a human being, entering into lively conversations and sensing the motives that lay behind its interlocutor's questions, is not yet in sight. The attempt to construct programs that prove worthwhile theorems has led to interesting, but by no means wholly successful results. The notion of looking upon fact retrieval as a special case of theorem proving is ingenious, but it does not open up any really new possibilities. There is little doubt that the processes that people use in seeking the answers to questions partake of little of the nature of a theorem proving machine. But, if our aims are purely practical, need we be concerned about whether the methods we adopt have anything in common with the strategies people use? Apparently so, for the utility of a question-answering system lies, at least in part, in how natural it is to use. A person can be trained to use a formal computer language and to accommodate himself to the conventions of a particular computer system, and systems that require such accommodation can be of undoubted utility. But the only kinds of restriction that significantly simplify the basic problems are invariably of a kind that makes the result more like a document retrieval than a fact retrieval system. The utility of an interactive document retrieval system, or even an interactive library catalog goes without question, but to claim that such a device provides fact retrieval in the sense in which we have been using the term is to debase the terminological currency unnecessarily.

8

CONCLUSION

We began this survey with two questions: since linguistics and information science are both concerned with the product of linguistic behavior, namely discourse, we may ask, first, what linguistics can or should be able to offer information science, and second, what information science can offer linguistics. We have in fact concentrated mainly on the role of linguistic theory in information science, and we have also been primarily interested in the documentation subarea of information science. Our conclusions will therefore refer chiefly to the contribution of linguistics to documentation; but we have hopefully covered enough ground in the survey to attempt some more broadly based ones as well.

We looked first at the current state of documentation and linguistics in general. In both cases we found that considerable progress has been made in some areas over the last decade, but that there are large gaps, unfortunately just where one might seek to make a connection between linguistics and documentation. We still know too little about the linguistic requirements of information retrieval;

and in linguistics not much has been done to provide the models of the semantic and larger organizational features of discourse which would apparently be most useful to documentalists. In Chapter 4 we sought to isolate the linguistically important components of information retrieval systems for more detailed examination. Specifically, we have the natural language of the input document texts, and the more or less artificial language of the description texts characterizing the documents. A retrieval system thus involves linguistic operations on the input texts designed to collect the information needed to generate descriptions, and to generate these descriptions; and it involves linguistic operations on the description texts themselves during retrieval. The former may be broadly referred to as a translation procedure, and the latter as an inference procedure. Document retrieval is thus related to other branches of information processing, like fact retrieval (or question answering), which have the same general properties. We can also reformulate our initial question to ask what linguistics can offer documentalists, first in handling the natural input language, and second in designing and using the information language. In Chapters 5 and 6 we examined these two linguistic components from the syntactic and semantic points of view respectively. In general the treatment of syntax in documentation, in the input or in the information language, is elementary, though greater sophistication appears in fact retrieval systems. That of semantics is more interesting, and the recognition of contextual semantic relationships, whether statistically identified or not, is in particular a feature of work in documentation from which linguists might learn something.

Our initial hypothesis was that the information scientist or documentalist would be assisted in his attempts to devise linguistic processing procedures for retrieval if he could exploit the findings of linguists. It is not unreasonable to suppose that while his use of linguistic theory will be influenced by his specific purpose, he needs a substantial general linguistic apparatus. For example, while only some information may be selected from an input document text for further processing, the correct identification of this information may require a parser capable of handling the perfectly ordinary sentence structures occurring in the text: a general syntactic theory of the kind which interests linguists is presupposed, even though the information it supplies is exploited for a particular purpose. The assumption this whole survey has been intended to examine, in other words, is that the data and objectives of information retrieval do not imply nongeneral, purpose-oriented linguistic theories which are qualitatively different from those that concern ordinary linguists. Further, if it is believed that information scientists need general linguistic theories which they have not themselves developed, it follows that they should be encouraged to take advantage of the apparently greater progress made by professional linguists, though it is likely that a crunch will come when the attempt is made to marry general theory and specific need in the most productive way. It is unfortunately true that much linguistic discussion is not presented in a form likely to attract information scientists, but the presumption is that, with effort, useful trees could be hacked from the wood.

The most striking fact to emerge from the literature, however, is the difficulty of marrying linguistic techniques and retrieval objectives. The difficulty is indeed so great as to cast doubt on the assertion that general linguistic theories are prerequisites for effective information processing and retrieval. As noted, linguistically very crude procedures seem to work quite well in retrieval, and it is in practice not obvious how more sophisticated ones should be used. For example, while a good deal of information about collocational meaning relations may be extracted from text, it may be far from clear how it should be exploited to provide answers to a simple request. But the point where it is most difficult to connect linguistics and documentation is in the role of syntax. There is no doubt that, quite apart from its currently important status in linguistic research, syntax matters in natural language. It is nevertheless uncertain what its role in information retrieval should be: the evidence as to the extent to which syntactic information in either input or description texts should be exploited is slight and difficult to interpret. It may be the case, as some experiments seem to show, that syntactic information contributes little or nothing to effective retrieval; or it may be that the ways in which this information has been provided and used have been mistaken. Our view is that the range of possibilities in handling syntactic information in both input and description texts is sufficiently wide to justify much further investigation.

Nevertheless, the tempting general conclusion to draw from experience to date is that for the special purpose of document retrieval general linguistic theories are not required. Since comparatively simple approaches like those involving statistically extracted key words, simply coordinated, seem to work as well as ones relying on richer linguistic information, we may conclude that document retrieval systems are necessarily crude. Abbreviated document descriptions are presumed, and ill-designed requests are probable or even certain. Some simplicity in the characterization of information is therefore inevitable, and it is unlikely that performance for poor requests can be much improved by sophisticated simplicity. This is, however, a somewhat negative line to take. It is more productive to maintain that the difficulty of relating linguistics and information retrieval comes from the fact that linguistic theories are still far from adequate, and that the design of good information retrieval systems is not at all understood. We may then hope that even if simplicity is all that is linguistically needed, it had better be sophisticated simplicity; we should surely be able to do better in providing document summaries than mere keyword lists, and we may legitimately believe that linguistics should help us here.

It will not be an easy task to relate linguistics and documentation more effectively. In particular, the onus is on the documentalist to provide a proper specification of what he needs to satisfy his retrieval objectives, and this in turn requires an adequate specification of his objectives. It is not enough for him to say that he wants to retrieve the right documents, and that he will be happy with anything that will help him to do this: this is unhelpfully tautological.

A more detailed specification of the tolerances of request formulation and request-document matching is required. But though some progress towards an understanding of the many factors involved in an information retrieval system and their interrelationships has been made, documentalists are still far from being able to provide such a specification. We do not, however, doubt that this specification or some approximation to it could be provided. In our view, saying that it cannot because users are too various and idiosyncratic is sheer defeatism. At least experiments to date have not suggested that the answer to the question "Why can't we do better than we do?" is that it is impossible. The fact that they have not suggested any other answers either constitutes our real challenge. Retrieval performance in general is pretty poor; but since we can usually see a difference between relevant and nonrelevant documents, surely we should be able to find ways of characterizing documents and searching which do separate the sheep from the goats.

If we thus continue to look for linguistic assistance, we may yet ask whether we can expect linguistics to help us with the artificial language of description texts as well as with the natural one of input texts. It may be that this distinction is an unnecessary one, in that with a better understanding of both retrieval and natural language we can work effectively with natural language as description language. In principle the two need not differ. In question-answering systems, for example, if we can devise programs to pursue inferences as we do, there may be no call for a formalized information language, as opposed to a more convenient notation. On the other hand, if some artificial information language does turn out to be necessary, it can be maintained that its character and use are not topics on which linguistics as currently understood can have anything to say. After all, formal logic has an independent status. To some extent this is a matter of the way "linguistics" is interpreted. It must also be admitted that the information languages we have surveyed, and documentary languages in particular, are not, by comparison with natural language, especially sophisticated. They generally do not allow fine semantic distinctions, complex syntactic structures, and subtle inference procedures. Their relationship to natural language is therefore not striking. Whether linguistics should have anything to say about the more effective information languages that are desirable is unclear; it depends in part on the form which the needs of information retrieval impose on them, and in part on what are viewed as the concerns of linguistics. A good case can be made for assuming that there will be a range of information retrieval situations, and hence information languages, so there is no natural division between contexts in which linguistics is relevant and those in which it is not. If we consider the whole gamut of information processing and retrieval activities including translation, abstracting, and question answering, as well as document retrieval, the assumption that we will in some cases be concerned with information languages which are qualitatively different from natural language becomes difficult to sustain.

These are not very definite conclusions. It would have been nice if we could have produced a neat list of the points supported by the literature, and a following list of the recommendations for the future they would imply. But we feel that such lists would be tendentious or meretricious. We hope that our readers will be able to draw detailed conclusions relevant to their own interests from the survey itself. The only conclusion we wish to present is a general one: namely, that it is evident that too little is known about either linguistics or information science to justify dogmatic assertions about the relation between them. This conclusion immediately leads to one recommendation: go and find out more about them.

REFERENCES*

Abraham, C. T. Techniques for Thesaurus Organization and Evaluation. *Parameters of Information Science, Proceedings of the ADI,* 1964, **Vol. 1,** 485–498.

Adams, W. M. *A Comparison of Some Machine-Produced Indexes.* Institute of Geophysics, University of Hawaii, 1965.

Adams, W. M. Relationship of Keywords in Titles to References Cited. *American Documentation,* 1967, **18,** 26–32.

Agraev, V. A., Borodin, V. V., and Glebskij, Ju. V. (Certain Methods of Automatic Reviewing). Učenye Zapiski Gor'kovskogo Gosudarstvennogo Universiteta im. N.I. Lobačevskogo, 66, Serija-Filologia, Prikladnaja Lingvistika i Metodika, Gor'kij, 1963.

Aitchison, J. The Thesaurofacet: A Multi-purpose Retrieval Language Tool. *Journal of Documentation,* 1970, **26,** 187–203.

Aitchison, J., and Day, P. (Eds.) *Thesaurofacet: A Thesaurus and Facetted Classification for Engineering and Related Subjects.* English Electric Co., Whetstone, Leicester, 1969.

*Titles in parentheses are English translations of the titles of publications in other languages. *A.J.* references appended to Russian sources refer to English abstracts of the articles in question as found in *Abstract Journal: Informatics,* a monthly publication of the Institute of Scientific Information of the Academy of Sciences of the U.S.S.R., Moscow.

Aitchison, T. M., Hall, A. M., Lavelle, K. H., and Tracy, J. M. *Comparative Evaluation of Index Languages, Part II: Results.* Project Inspec, Institute of Electrical Engineers, London, 1970.

All-Union Conference on Information Retrieval Systems and Automatic Processing of Scientific and Technical Information, 3rd, Moscow, 1967, Transactions; Edited Machine Translation of Selected Articles. Translation Division, Foreign Technology Division, Wright-Patterson Air Force Base, Ohio, 1969; MTD-MT-24-130-69; AD 697 687.

Altmann, B. A Natural Language Storage and Retrieval (ABC) Method: Its Rationale, Operation and Further Development Program. *Journal of Chemical Documentation,* 1966, **6,** 154–157.

Altmann, B. A Multiple Testing of the Natural Language Storage and Retrieval ABC Method: Preliminary Analysis of Test Results. *American Documentation,* 1967, **18,** 33–45.

Altmann, B., and Reissler, W. A. Theory, Testing and Mechanization of the ABC Retrieval System. *American Documentation,* 1969, **20,** 6–15.

Annual Review of Information Science and Technology: See Cuadra (1966–1970).

Armitage, J. E., and Lynch, M. F. Articulation in the Generation of Subject Indexes by Computer. *Journal of Chemical Documentation,* 1967, **7,** 170–178.

Armitage, J. E., and Lynch, M. F. Some Structural Characteristics of Articulated Subject Indexes. *Information Storage and Retrieval,* 1968, **4,** 101–111.

Armitage, J. R., Lynch, M. F., Petrie, J. H., and Belton, M. Experimental Use of a Program for Computer-Aided Subject-Index Production. *Information Storage and Retrieval,* 1970, **6,** 79–87.

Artandi, S. (Ed.) *Systems for the Intellectual Organization of Information:* Vol. 1, J. Mills, *The Universal Decimal Classifiaction,* 1964; Vol. 2, J. C. Gardin, *SYNTOL,* 1965; Vol. 3, J. Metcalfe, *Alphabetical Subject Indication of Information,* 1965; Vol. 4, S. R. Ranganathan, *The Colon Classification,* 1965; Vol. 5, B. C. Vickery, *Facetted Classification Schemes,* 1966; Vol. 6, H. Selye, *Symbolic Shorthand System,* 1966; Vol. 7, J. C. Costello, *Coordinate Indexing,* 1966. Graduate School of Library Service, Rutgers, The State University, New Brunswick, New Jersey. 1964–1966.

Artandi, S. Automatic Indexing of Drug Information. *Levels of Interaction between Man and Information, Proceedings of the ADI,* 1967, **4,** 148–151.

Artandi, S. Computer Indexing of Medical Articles. *Journal of Documentation,* 1969, **25,** 214–223.

Artandi, S., and Wolf, E. H. The Effectiveness of Automatically-Generated Weights and Links. *American Documentation,* 1969, **20,** 198–202.

(Aspects of the Development of a Mechanized IR System for the Central Reference Information Collection in Chemistry and the Chemical Industry)), A Series of Papers. Moscow: N-i In-t Texno-Econ. Issled., ca. 1970.

(Aspects of the Development of a Mechanized IR System for the Central Reference Information Collection in Chemistry and the Chemical Industry), Moscow: N-i In-t Texno-Econ. Issled., 1970. (a)
21 Issue: (Description of Domestic and Foreign IR Systems), 1970. *(A.J. 70.7.123)*

(Aspects of the Development of a Mechanized IR System for the Central Reference Information Collection in Chemistry and the Chemical Industry). Moscow: N-i In-t Texno-Econ. Issled., 1970. (b)
22 Issue: (A Statistical Analysis and Quantitative Characterisation of Elements in a Thesaurus System), 1970. *(A.J.* 70.7.110)

ASTIA, *Thesaurus of ASTIA Descriptors.* (2nd ed.) Armed Services Technical Information Agency, Arlington Hall Station, Arlington, Virginia, 1962.

Atherton, P. (Ed.) *Classification Research: Proceedings of the Second International Study Conference.* Copenhagen: Munksgaard, 1965.

Augustson, J. G., and Minker, J. Deriving Term Relations for a Corpus by Graph Theoretical Techniques. *Journal of the ASIS,* 1970, **21,** 101–111.

Austin, C. J. *MEDLARS 1963–1967.* U.S. Department of Health, Education and Welfare, Public Health Service, Washington, D.C., 1968.

Avram, H. D. *The MARC Pilot Project.* Final Report. Information Systems Office, Library of Congress, Washington, D.C., 1968.

Avram, H. D., Knapp, J. F., and Rather, L. J. *The MARC II Format: A Communications Format for Bibliographic Data,* Information Systems Office, Library of Congress, Washington, D.C., 1968.

Avramescu, A. (Evaluation of IR Systems Efficiency). In *International Forum on Informatics.* Moscow: VINITI, 1969. *(A.J.* 70.3.138)

Bach, E. *An Introduction to Transformational Grammars.* New York: Holt, 1964.

Baker, F. B. Latent Class Analysis as an Association Model for Information Retrieval. In Stevens, Heilprin and Giuliano (Eds.), *Statistical Association Methods for Mechanized Documentation.* Washington, D.C.: National Bureau of Standards, 1965.

Balcarová, O., and Königová, M. (Statistical Processing of Citations in Mathematical Linguistics Literature). *Metodika a Technika Informaci,* 1968, **10, 5,** 40–47. *(A.J.* 69.6.41)

Ball, G. H. Data Analysis in the Social Sciences. *Proceedings of the 1965 FJCC, AFIPS Conference Proceedings,* 1965, **27** (Pt. 1), 533–559.

Bar-Hillel, Y. Some Theoretical Aspects of the Mechanization of Literature Searching. Hebrew University, Jerusalem, 1960. (See also Theoretical Aspects of the Mechanization of Literature Searching. In Y. Bar-Hillel (Ed.), *Language and Information.* Reading, Massachusetts: Addison-Wesley, 1964).

Bar-Hillel, Y. Is Information Reteieval Approaching a Crisis? *American Documentation,* 1963, **14,** 95–98. Reprinted in Y. Bar-Hillel (Ed.), *Language and Information.* Reading, Massachusetts: Addison-Wesley, 1964.

Barhydt, G. C. The Effectiveness of Non-User Relevance Assessments. *Journal of Documentation,* 1967, **23,** 146–149.

Batty, C. D. The Automatic Generation of Index Languages. *Journal of Documentation,* 1969, **25,** 142–151.

Baxendale, P. B. Machine-made Index for Technical Literature—An Experiment. *I.B.M. Journal of Research and Development,* 1958, **2,** 354–361.

Baxendale, P. B. An Empirical Model for Computer Indexing. In *Machine Indexing: Progress and Problems.* Washington, D.C.: American University, 1962.

Bely, N., Borillo, A., Virbel, J., and Siot-Decauville, N. *Procédures d'Analyse Sémantique Appliquées à la Documentation Scientifique.* Paris: Gauthier-Villars, 1970.

Bennett, J. C. On-line Access to Information: NSF as an Aid to the Indexer/Cataloguer, *American Documentation,* 1969, **20,** 213–220.

Bernštejn, E. S., Laxuti, D. G., and Černjavskij, V. S. (Certain Problems of Construction of Information Retrieval Systems). *Naučno-Texničeskaja Informacija,* 1963, **No. 1,** 31–39.

Berul, L. *Information Storage and Retrieval: A State of the Art Report.* Auerbach Corporation, Philadelphia, 1965.

Blagden, J. B. How Much Noise in a Role-Free and Link-Free Coordinate Indexing System. *Journal of Documentation,* 1966, **22,** 203–209.

Bloomfield, L. *Language.* New York: Holt, 1933

Bobrow, D. G., and Fraser, B., An Augmented State Transition Network. In Norton and Walker (Eds.), *Proceedings of the International Joint Conference on Artificial Intelligence.* Bedford, Massachusetts: Mitre Corporation, 1969. pp. 557–567.

Bonner, R. E. On Some Clustering Techniques. *I.B.M. Journal of Research and Development,* 1964, **8,** 22–32.

Borko, H. Studies on the Reliability and Validity of Factor-Analytically Derived Classification Categories. In Stevens, Heilprin, and Giuliano (Eds.), *Statistical Association Methods for Mechanized Documentation.* Washington, D.C.: National Bureau of Standards, 1965.

Borko, H. (Ed.) *Automated Language Processing.* New York: Wiley, 1967.(a)

Borko, H. Indexing and Classification. In Borko (Ed.), *Automated Language Processing.* New York: Wiley, 1967.(b)

Borko, H. Interactive Document Storage and Retrieval Systems—Design Concepts. In Samuelson (Ed.), *Mechanized Information Storage, Retrieval and Dissemination.* Amsterdam: North-Holland, 1968. pp. 591–599.

Borkowski, C., *et al.* Structure and Effectiveness of 'The Citation Identifier': An Operational Computer Program for Automatic Identification of Case Citations in Legal Literature. *Journal of the ASIS,* 1970, **21,** 8–15.

Bottle, R. T. Title Indexes as Alerting Services in the Chemical and Life Sciences. *Journal of the ASIS,* 1970, **21,** 16–21.

Brauen, T. L. *Document Vector Modification in On-line Information Retrieval Systems, Information Storage and Retrieval.* Report No. ISR-17. Department of Computer Science, Cornell University, 1969.

Brodie, N. E. Evaluation of a KWIC Index for Library Literature. *Journal of the ASIS,* 1970, **21,** 22–28.

Brookes, B. C. The Measures of Information Retrieval Effectiveness Proposed by Swets. *Journal of Documentation,* 1968, **24,** 41–54. (a)

Brookes, B. C. The Derivation and Application of the Bradford-Zipf Distribution. *Journal of Documentation,* 1968, **24,** 247–265. (b)

Brookes, B. C. The Complete Bradford-Zipf Bibliograph. *Journal of Documentation,* 1969, **25,** 58–60.

Brownson, H. L. Evaluation of Document Searching Systems and Procedure. *Journal of Documentation,* 1965, **21,** 261–266.

Broxis, P. F. Facetted Classifications and the Fine Arts. *Journal of Documentation,* 1966, **22,** 40–54.

Bud'ko, N. S., Kudin, N. I., and Goroxov, S. A. (The Automated Retrieval System Setka 3 for Sources of Scientific and Technical Information in Radioelectronics). *Naučno-Texničeskaja Informacija,* 1966, **10,** 26–35.

Burnaugh, H. The BOLD (Bibliographic On-Line Display) System. In Schecter (Ed.), *Information Retrieval: A Critical View.* Washington, D.C.: Thompson, 1967. pp. 53–66.

Cagan, C. A Highly Associative Document Retrieval System. *Journal of the ASIS,* 1970, **21,** 330–337.

Caless, T. W., and Kirk, D. B. An Application of UDC to Machine Searching. *Journal of Documentation,* 1967, **23,** 208–215.

Caras, G. J. Comparison of Document Abstracts as Sources of Index Terms for Derivative Indexing by Computer. *Levels of Interaction between Man and Information, Proceedings of the ADI,* 1967, **4,** 157–161.

Carroll, J. M., and DeBruyn, J. G. On the Importance of Root-Stem Truncation in Word-Frequency Analysis. *Journal of the ASIS,* 1970, **21,** 368–369.

Carroll, J. M., and Roelloffs, R. Computer Selection of Keywords Using Word Frequency. *American Documentation,* 1969, **20,** 227–233.

Černjavskij, V. S. The Logic of Descriptor Retrieval Systems. In *All-Union Conference on Information Retrieval Systems and Automatic Processing of Scientific and Technical Information.* (Transl.), Wright-Patterson Air Force Base, Ohio, 1969.

Černjavskij, V. S., and Laxuti, D. G. (Concerning the Problem of Search System Evaluation. *Naučno-Texničeskaja Informacija,* Ser. 2, 1970, **1,** 24–34. (*A.J.* 70.8.141).

Černjavskij, V. S., Laxuti, D. G., and Bernštejn, E. S. (Automatic Descriptor Retrieval Systems with Fixed Coupling of Descriptors). *Trudy Sympozium SEV,* 1966, 329.

Černjavskij, V. S., Laxuti, D. G., and Fedrov, E. B. On the Automatic Construction of Automatic Indexing Algorithms for 'Empty-Nonempty' Type Systems. *Naučno-Texničeskaja Informacija,* Ser. 2, 1969, **10,** 24–28. (*A.J.* 70.3.162).

Černjavskij, V. S., Laxuti, D. G., and Lesskis, G. A. (Automatic Indexing of Homonyms). *Vsesojuznaja Konferencija po Informacionno-Poiskovym Sistemam i Avtomati-zirovannoj Obrabotke Naučno-Texničeskoj Informacii,* 3rd, Moscow, 1967, 106.

Černyj, A. I. (General Methodology of Thesaurus Construction). *Naučno-Texničeskaja Informacija,* 1968, **5,** 9–32.

Chapin, P. G. and Norton, L. M. *A Procedure for Morphological Analysis.* MTP-101. MITRE Corporation, Bedford, Massachusetts, 1968.

Chien, R. T., and Preparata, F. P. Search Strategy and File Organization in Computerized Retrieval Systems with Mass Memory. In Samuelson (Ed.), *Mechanized Information Storage, Retrieval and Dissemination.* Amsterdam: North-Holland, 1968. pp. 108–121.

Chomsky, N. *Syntactic Structures.* Janua Linguarum, Ser. Minor 4. The Hague: Mouton, 1957.

Chomsky, N. *Aspects of the Theory of Syntax.* Cambridge, Massachusetts: MIT Press, 1965.

Chonez, N. Permuted Title or Key-phrase Indexes and the Limiting of Documentalist Work Needs, *Information Storage and Retrieval,* 1968, **4,** 161–166.

Clarke, D. C., and Wall, R. E. An Economical Program for Limited Parsing of English. *Proceedings of the 1965 FJCC, AFIPS Conference Proceedings,* 1965, **27** (Pt. 1), 307–316.

Classification Research Group. *Classification and Information Control: Papers Representing the Work of the CRG from 1960 to 1968.* London: The Library Association, 1969.

Cleverdon, C. W. The Cranfield Tests on Index Language Devices. *Aslib Proceedings,* 1967, **19,** 173–194.

Cleverdon, C. W. Evaluation Tests of Information Retrieval Systems. *Journal of Documentation,* 1970, **26,** 55–67.

Cleverdon, C. W., Mills, J., and Keen, E. M. *Factors Determining the Performance of Indexing Systems.* Vol. 1, Design, Parts 1 and 2; Vol. 2, Test Results (Cleverdon and Keen). Aslib Cranfield Project, Cranfield Institute of Technology, 1966.

Coates, E. J. *Subject Catalogues: Headings and Structure.* London: The Library Association, 1960.

Coates, E. J. Switching Languages for Indexing. *Journal of Documentation,* 1970, **26,** 102–110.

Cole, A. J. (Ed.) *Numerical Taxonomy.* New York: Academic Press, 1969.

Colmerauer, A., Kittredge, R., and Stewart, G. *(Preliminary results.) Résultats préliminaires* Projet de Traduction Automatique, Université de Montréal, 1970.

Comparative Systems Laboratory. *An Inquiry into Testing of Information Retrieval Systems.* Final Report, Part I, Objectives, Methodology, Design, and Controls; Part II, Analysis of Results; Part III, CSL Related Studies. Center for Documentation and Communication Research, Case Western Reserve University, 1968.

Cooper, W. S. Expected Search Length: A Single Measure of Retrieval Effectiveness Based on the Weak-Ordering Action of Retrieval Systems. *American Documentation,* 1968, **19,** 30–41.

Cooper, W. S. The Potential Usefulness of Catalog Access Points other than Author, Title and Subject. *Journal of the ASIS,* 1970, **21,** 112–127.

Coyaud, M. *Introduction à l'Étude des Langages Documentaires.* Paris: Klincksieck, 1966.

Coyaud, M., and Siot-Decauville, N. *L'Analyse Automatique des Documents.* The Hague: Mouton, 1967.

Craig, J. A. *et al.* DEACON: Direct English Access and Control. *Proceedings of the 1966 FJCC, AFIPS Conference Proceedings,* 1966, **29,** 365–380.

Cros, R. C., Gardin, J. C., and Lévy, F. *L'Automatisation des Recherches Documentaires; Un Modele Général: Le* SYNTOL 2nd. ed. with new preface, 1968). Paris Gauthier-Villars, 1964.

Cuadra, C. A. (Ed.) *Annual Review of Information Science and Technology.* Vol. 1, 1966; Vol. 2, 1967, New York: Interscience; Vol. 3, 1968; Vol. 4. 1969; Vol. 5, 1970. Chicago: Encyclopedia Britannica.

Cuadra, C. A., and Katter, R. V. The Relevance of Relevance Assessment. *Levels of Interaction between Man and Information, Proceedings of the ADI,* 1967, **4,** 95–99. (a)

Cuadra, C. A., and Katter, R. V. Opening the Black Box of Relevance. *Journal of*

Documentation, 1967, **23,** 291–303. (b)

Cuadra, C. A., Katter, R. V., Holmes, E. H., and Wallace, E. M. *Experimental Studies of Relevance Judgements.* Final Report, Vol. 1, Project Summary; Vol. 2, Description of Individual Studies. System Development Corporation, Santa Monica, California, 1967.

Curtice, R. M. Experiments in Associative Retrieval. *Progress in Information Science and Technology, Proceedings of the ADI,* 1966, **3,** 373–383.

Curtice, R. M., and Jones, P. E. Distributional Constraints and the Automatic Selection of an Indexing Vocabulary. *Levels of Interaction Between Man and Information, Proceedings of the ADI,* 1967, **4,** 152–156.

Curtice, R. M., and Jones, P. E. *An Operational Interactive Retrieval System.* Arthur D. Little Inc., Cambridge, Massachusetts, 1969.

Dale, A. G., and Dale, N. Some Clumping Experiments for Associative Document Retrieval. *American Documentation, 1965,* **16,** 5–9.

Damerau, F. J. An Experiment in Automatic Indexing. *American Documentation,* 1965, **16,** 283–289.

Dattola, R. Experiments with a Fast Algorithm for Automatic Classification. In *Information Storage and Retrieval.* Report No. ISR-16. Department of Computer Science, Cornell University, 1969.

Dattola, R. T., and Murray, D. M. An Experiment in Automatic Thesaurus Construction. In *Information Storage and Retrieval.* Report No. ISR-13. Department of Computer Science, Cornell University, 1967.

Dennis, S. F. The Construction of a Thesaurus Automatically from a Sample of Text. In *Statistical Association Methods for Mechanized Documentation.* Stevens, Heilprin, and Giuliano (Eds.), Washington, D.C. National Bureau of Standards, 1965.

Dennis, S. F. The design and testing of a fully automated indexing-searching system for documents consisting of expository text. In Schechter (Ed.), *Information Retrieval–A Critical View.* Washington, D.C.: Thompson, 1967.

Dinneen, F. P. *An Introduction to General Linguistics.* New York: Holt, 1967.

Dobrovol'skij, M. I., and Verevčenko, A. P. (A Descriptor Type Information Retrieval System for Searching Documents on Varied Subjects). *Vsesojuznaja Konferencija po Informacionno-Poiskovym Sistemam Avtomatizirovannoj Obrabotke Naučno Texničeskoj Informacii,* 3rd, Moscow, 1967, 295–300.

Dobrovol'skij, M. I., *et al.* An Automation of Document Retrieval by the MINSK 22 Computer. *Vopr. Naučn. Prognozir.,* Moscow, 1969, 84–88. (*A.J.* 70.7.151).

Doyle, L. B. Semantic Road Maps for Literature Searchers. *Journal of the ACM,* 1961, **8,** 553–578.

Doyle, L. B. Indexing and Abstracting by Association. *American Documentation,* 1962, **13,** 378–390.

Doyle, L. B. Some Compromises between Word Grouping and Document Grouping. In Stevens, Heilprin, and Giuliano (Eds.), *Statistical Association Methods for mechanized Documentation.* Washington, D.C.: National Bureau of Standards, 1965.

Doyle, L. B., and Blankenship, D. A. Technical Advances in Automatic Classification. *Progress in Information Science and Technology, Proceedings of the ADI,* 1966, **3,** 63–71.

Druk, T. M. (Using UDC for Coordinate Indexing). *Naučno-Texničeskaja Informacija,* *Ser. 2,* 1968, **11,** 22–27. (*A.J.* 69.4.69).

Earl, L. L. Experiments in Automatic Indexing and Extracting. *Information Storage and Retrieval,* 1970, **6,** 313–334.

Earley, J. An Efficient Context-free Parsing Algorithm. *Communications of the ACM,* *1970,* **13,** 94–102.

Edmundson, H. P., and Wyllys, R. E. Automatic Abstracting and Indexing—A Survey and Recommendations. *Communications of the ACM,* 1961, **4,** 226–234.

Euratom, *EURATOM Thesaurus: Indexing Terms Used within Euratom's Nuclear Documentation System.* Euratom, (2nd ed.) Brussells: 1966.

Experim. Sistema Anglo-Russk. Avtomatič. Perev. Patent. Dokumentacii. Moscow, 1970.

Fairthorne, R. A. Basic Parameters of Retrieval Tests. *Parameters of Information Science, Proceedings of the ADI,* 1964, **1,** 343–345.

Fairthorne, R. A. Some Basic Comments on Retrieval Testing. *Journal of Documentation,* 1965, **21,** 267–270.

Fairthorne, R. A. Morphology of 'Information Flow.' *Journal of the ACM,* 1967, **14,** 710–719.

Fairthorne, R. A. Empirical Hyperbolic Distributions (Bradford-Zipf-Mandelbrot) for Bibliometric Description and Prediction. *Journal of Documentation.* 1969, **25,** 319–343.

Falkov, F., and Alebastrova, A. (An Automatic Indexing Method). In *Primenenie Universal'n. Vyčisl. Mašin v Rabote Organov Inform.,* Moscow, 1970. (*A.J.* 70.12.107).

Fangmeyer, H., and Lustig, G. The Euratom Indexing Project. *Information Processing 68: Proceedings of IFIP Congress 1968.* In Morrell (Ed.), Amsterdam: North-Holland, 1969.

Fangmeyer, H., and Lustig, G. Experiments with the CETIS Automatic Indexing System. In *Handling of Nuclear Information.* Vienna: International Atomic Energy Agency, 1970.

Farradane, J. Concept Organization for Information Retrieval. *Information Storage and Retrieval,* 1967, **3,** 297–311; 312–314.

Farradane, J., Datta, S., and Poulton, R. K. *Report on Research on Information Retrieval by Relational Indexing, Part 1: Methodology.* City University, London, 1966.

Fillmore, C. J. The Case for Case. In Bach and Harms (Eds.), *Universals in Linguistic Theory.* New York: Holt, 1968. pp. 1–88.

Fischer, M. The KWIC Index Concept: A Retrospective View. *American Documentation,* 1966, **17,** 57–70.

Foskett, D. J. Informatics. *Journal of Documentation,* 1970, **26,** 340–369.

Freeman, R. R. The Management of a Classification: Modern Approaches Exemplified by the UDC Project of the American Institute of Physics. *Journal of Documentation,* 1967, **23,** 304–318.

Freeman, R. R., and Atherton, P. File Organization and Search Strategy using UDC in Mechanized Reference Retrieval Systems. In Samuelson (Ed.), *Mechanized Information Storage, Retrieval and Dissemination.* Amsterdam: North-Holland, 1968. pp. 122–152.

Friedman, J. Directed Random Generation of Sentences. *Communications of the ACM,* 1969, **12,** 40–46.

Furth, S. E. Automated Retrieval of Legal Literature: State of the Art. *Computers and Automation*, 1968, **17**, 25–28.

Gaifman, H. Dependency Systems and Phrase-Structure Systems. *Information and Control*, 1965, **8**, 304–307.

Gardin, J. C. *SYNTOL*. Vol. 2 of Artandi (Ed.), Rutgers Series on Systems for the Intellectual Organization of Information. 1965. Graduate School of Library Service, Rutgers, The State University, New Brunswick, New Jersey.

Gardin, N., and Lévy, F., *Documentary Lexicon for Scientific Information*. Groupe d'Étude sur l'Information Scientifique, Association Marc Bloch, Paris, 1969.

Gaster, K. Thesaurus Construction and Use: A Selective Bibliography based on Material in the Aslib Library in July 1967. *Aslib Proceedings*, 1967, **19**, 310–317.

Gerasimova, A. G., Giršberg, Ju. V., and Šenderov, V. Z. Automatic Indexing System Based on a Bilingual Thesaurus. ICEREPAT, Stockholm, 1967. (*A.J.* 70.2.80).

Gifford, C., and Baumanis, G. J. On Understanding User Choices: Textual Correlates of Relevance Judgements. *American Documentation*, 1969, **20**, 21–26.

Gillum, T. L. Compiling a Technical Thesaurus. *Journal of Chemical Documentation*, 1964, **4**, 29–32.

Giršberg, Ju. V., and Šenderov, V. Z. (A Description of an Automatic Indexing System Integrated with an Automatic Translation System). In *Experim. Sistema Anglo-Russk. Avtomatič. Perev. Patent. Dokumentacii*). Moscow, 1970. (*A.J.* 70.9.105).

Giuliano, V. E. The Interpretation of Word Associations. In Stevens, Heilprin and Giuliano (Eds.), *Statistical Association Methods for Mechanized Documentation*. Washington, D.C.: National Bureau of Standards, 1965.

Giuliano, V. E., and Jones, P. E. *Study and Test of a Methodology For Laboratory Evaluation of Message Retrieval Systems*. Arthur D. Little Inc., Cambridge, Massachusetts, 1966.

Gladkij, A. V., Rybakova, M. V., and Sedko, T. I. An Outline of a Semantic Language for Transcription of Mathematical Texts. *JPRS* **13254**, 1962.

Glasersfeld, E. Von. 'Multistore', a procedure for correlational analysis. Report No. ILRS-T10-650120. Instituto Documentazione della Associazione Mecannica Italiana, Milan, 1965.

Gleason, H. A. *An Introduction to Descriptive Linguistics*. New York: Holt, 1961.

Goffman, W. On the Logic of Information Retrieval. *Information Storage and Retrieval*, 1965, **2**, 217–220.

Goffman, W. An Indirect Method of Information Retrieval. *Information Storage and Retrieval*, 1968, **4**, 361–373.

Goffman, W., and Newill, V. A. A Methodology for Test and Evaluation of Information Systems. *Information Storage and Retrieval*, 1966, **3**, 19–25.

Good, I. J. Categorisation of Classification. In *Mathematics and Computer Science in Biology and Medicine*. London: Medical Research Council, 1965.

Gorobcov, V. M. On the Feasibility of Constructing a Model IR System with a Hypothetical Thesaurus. *Vopr. Naučn. Prognozir.*, Moscow, 1969, **8**, 184–190. (*A.J.* 70.7.116).

Goroxov, S. A. 'SETKA-3' Automated IPS on the MINSK-22 with the Use of the Socket Associative-Method of Organization of Information. In *All-Union Con-*

ference on Information Retrieval Systems and Automatic Processing of Scientific and Technical Information. (Transl.) Wright-Patterson Air Force Base, Ohio: 1969.

Gotlieb, C. C., and Kumar, S. Semantic Clustering of Index Terms. *Journal of the ACM,* 1968, **15,** 493–513.

Green, C. Application of Theorem Proving to Problem Solving. In Norton and Walker (Eds.), *Proceedings of the International Joint Conference on Artificial Intelligence.* Bedford, Massachusetts: MITRE Corporation, 1969. pp. 219–239.

Green, C., *et al.* BASEBALL: An Automatic Question-Answerer. In Feigenbaum and Feldman (Eds.), *Computers and Thought.* New York: McGraw-Hill, 1963.

Griaznixina, T. A., Pšeničnaja, L. E., and Skoroxod'ko, E. F. *(An Information Retrieval System).* Kiev: Nauka Dumka, 1964.

Griffiths, T., and Petrick, S. On the Relative Efficiencies of Context-free Grammar Recognizers. *Communications of the ACM,* 1965, **8,** 289–300.

Grinina, R. F., and Sokolova, A. V. (A Comparison of Subject and Descriptor Type IR Languages). *Naucnye i Texniceskie Biblioteki SSSR,* 1970, 3–4, 48–58. (*A.J.* 70.9.115).

de Grolier, E. *A Study of General Categories Applicable to Classification and Coding in Documentation.* Paris: UNESCO, 1962.

de Grolier, E. Quelques Travaux Récents en Matière de Classification Encyclopédique. *Bulletin des Bibliothèques de France,* 1970, **15,** 99–126.

Gross, M. *A Computer Program for Testing Grammars On-line.* MTP-102. MITRE Corporation, Bedford, Massachusetts, 1968.

Harper, K. E. Measurement of Similarity beween Nouns. Rm-4532-PR, Rand Corporation, Santa Monica, California, 1965.

Hays, D. G. Parsing. In Hays (Ed.), *Readings in Automatic Language Processing.* New York: American Elsevier, 1966. pp. 74–82.

Hays, D. G. *Introduction to Computational Linguistics.* New York: American Elsevier, 1967.

Heald, J. H. *The Making of TEST: Thesaurus of Engineering and Scientific Terms.* Project LEX, Office of Naval Research, Washington, D.C., 1967.

Heald, J. H., *et al. Manual for Building a Technical Thesaurus.* Project LEX, Office of Naval Research, Washington, D.C., 1966.

Herbrand, J. Recherches sur la Théorie de la Démonstration. *Travaux de la Société des Sciences et des Lettres de Varsovie.* Classe III, Sciences Mathématiques et Physiques, **33,** 1930.

Hersey, D. F., and Hammond, W. Computer Usage in the Development of a Water Thesaurus. *American Documentation,* 1967, **18,** 209–215.

Hillman, D. J. The Notion of Relevance (1). *American Documentation,* 1964, **15,** 26–34. (a)

Hillman, D. J. On Concept-Formation and Relevance. *Parameters of Information Science, Proceedings of the ADI,* 1964, **1,** 23–29.(b)

Hillman, D. J. Mathematical Classification Techniques for Non-Static Document Collections, with particular reference to the Problem of Relevance. In Atherton, (Ed.), *Classification Research: Proceedings of the Second International Study Conference.* Copenhagen: Munksgaard, 1965.

Hillman, D. J. Negotiation of Inquiries in an On-Line Retrieval System. *Information Storage and Retrieval,* 1968, **4,** 219–238.

Hillman, D. J., and Kasarda, A. J. The LEADER Retrieval System. *Proceedings of the 1969 SJCC, AFIPS Conference Proceedings,* 1969, **34,** 447–455.

Hockett, C. F. *A Course in Modern Linguistics.* New York: Macmillan, 1958.

Hockett, C. F. Grammar for the Hearer. In Jacobson (Ed.), *Structure of Language and Its Mathematical Aspects.* Proceedings of Symposia in Applied Mathematics 12. Providence: American Mathematical Society, 1961. pp. 220–236.

Holst, W. A User-Oriented Information System, Operational on a Regional Basis within the Scandinavian Countries. *Information Storage and Retrieval,* 1970, **6,** 101–125.

Hoppe, A. Maschinelle Verarbeitung der Sprache auf Basis einer kommunikativen Grammatik. *Studium Generale,* 1969, **22,** 310–338.

Hutchins, W. J. Automatic Document Selection without Indexing. *Journal of Documentation,* 1967, **23,** 273–290.

Ide, E. *Relevance Feedback in an Automatic Document Retrieval System, Information Storage and Retrieval.* Report No. ISR-15. Department of Computer Science, Cornell University, 1969.

(International Forum on Informatics). Papers for the 1969 F.I.D. Congress. 2 vols. Moscow: VINITI, 1969.

Ivanova, N. S. (On Automatic Thesaurus Construction). *Naučno-Texničeskaja Informacija, Ser. 2,* 1969, **6,** 17–20. *(A.J.* 69.11.67).

Ivanova, N. S., and Moskovič, V. A. Automatic Compiling of Thesauri on the Basis of Statistical Data. ICEREPAT, Stockholm, 1967. *(A.J.* 70.1.96).

Ivanova, N. I., Leont'eva, T. M., and Margaritov, V. B. (Aspects of the Development of an Automated Retrieval System in Chemistry and Chemical Industry). In *International Forum on Informatics.* Moscow: VINITI, 1969. *(A. J.* 70.3.161).

Ivie, E. L. *Search Procedures based on Measures of Relatedness between Documents.* Doctoral Thesis, MAC-TR-29, Massachusetts Institute of Technology, 1966.

Jackendoff, R. S. Quantifiers in English. *Foundations of Language,* 1968, **4,** 422–442.

Jackson, D. M. *Automatic Classification and Information Retrieval.* Ph.D. Thesis, University of Cambridge, 1969.

Jacobs, R., and Rosenbaum, P. *English Transformational Grammar.* Waltham, Massachusetts: Blaisdell, 1968.

Jardine, N. Algorithms, Methods and Models in the Representation of Complex Data. *The Computer Journal,* 1970, **13,** 116–117.

Jardine, N., and Sibson, R. The Construction of Hierarchical and Non-Hierarchical Classifications. *The Computer Journal,* 1968, **11,** 177–184.

Jardine, N., and Sibson, R. *Mathematical Taxonomy.* New York: Wiley, 1971.

Jones, P. E., and Curtice, R. M. A Framework for Comparing Term Association Measures. *American Documentation,* 1967, **18,** 153–161.

Jones, P. E., Giuliano, V. E., and Curtice, R. M. *Papers on Automatic Language Processing.* Vol. 1, Selected Collection Statistics and Data Analyses; Vol. 2, Linear Models for Associative Retrieval; Vol. 3, Development of String Indexing Techniques. Arthur D. Little Inc., Cambridge, Massachusetts, 1967.

Jones, P. E., Curtice, R. M., Giuliano, V. E., and Sherry, M. E. *Application of Statistical Association Techniques to the NASA Document Collection.* Arthur D. Little Inc., Cambridge, Massachusetts, 1968.

Jordan, J. R. A Framework for Comparing SDI Systems. *American Documentation,* 1968, **19,** 221–223.

Kagalovič, N. M. (Evaluating the Performance of Descriptor-type Document Retrieval Systems). *Naučno-Texničeskaja Informacija, Ser.* 2, 1969, **7,** 30–32. (*A.J.* 69.12.90).

Kaplan, R. M. *The MIND System: A Grammar-Rule Language.* Memorandum RM-6265/1-PR. Rand Corporation, Santa Monica, California, April 1970.

Karasev, S. A. (Automatic Indexing Methods and their Classification). *Naučno-Texničeskaja Informacija, Ser.* 2, 1970, **4,** 19–26. (*A.J.* 70.11.111).

Kasher, A. *Data Retrieval by Computer: A Critical Survey.* Hebrew University, Jerusalem, 1966. Reprinted in Kochen (Ed.), *The Growth of Knowledge.* New York: Wiley, 1967.

Katz, J. J., and Fodor, J. A. The Structure of a Semantic Theory. *Language,* 1963, **39,** 170–210. Reprinted in Fodor and Katz (Eds.), *The Structure of Language.* Englewood Cliffs, New Jersey: Prentice-Hall, 1964.

Kay, M. *Large Files in Linguistic Computing.* P-3136. Rand Corporation, Santa Monica, California, 1965.

Kay, M. *Experiments with a Powerful Parser.* RM-5452-PR. Rand Corporation, Santa Monica, California, 1967.

Kay, M., and Martins, G. R. *The MIND System: The Morphological-analysis Program.* RM-6265/2-PR. Rand Corporation, Santa Monica, California, 1970.

Kay, M., and Su, S.Y.W. *The MIND System: The Structure of the Semantic File.* RM-6265/3-PR. Rand Corporation, Santa Monica, California, 1970.

Keen, E. M. Evaluation Parameters. In *Information Storage and Retrieval.* Report No. ISR-13. Department of Computer Science, Cornell University, 1967.(a)

Keen, E. M. Suffix Dictionaries. In *Information Storage and Retrieval.* Report No. ISR-13. Department of Computer Science, Cornell University, 1967.(b)

Keen, E. M. Thesaurus, Phrase and Hierarchy Dictionaries. In *Information Storage and Retrieval.* Report No. ISR-13. Department of Computer Science, Cornell University, 1967.(c)

Keenan, S., and Terry, E. *Retrieval of the 1964 Laser Literature using MIT's Project TIP.* Information Division, American Institute of Physics, New York, 1968.

Kellogg, C. H. A Natural Language Compiler for On-line Data Management. *Proceedings of the 1968 FJCC, AFIPS Conference Proceedings,* 1968, **33,** 473–492.

Kent, A., and Lancour, H. (Eds.) *Encyclopedia of Library and Information Science.* New York: Marcel Dekker, 1968–.

Kent, A. K. Performance and Cost of 'Free Text' Search Systems. *Information Storage and Retrieval,* 1970, **6,** 73–77.

Kessler, M. M. Bibliographic Coupling Between Scientific Papers. *American Documentation,* 1963, **14,** 10–25.

Kessler, M. M. A Comparison of the Results of Bibliographic Coupling and Analytic Subject Indexing. *American Documentation,* 1965, **16,** 223–233. (a)

Kessler, M. M. The MIT Technical Information Project. *Physics Today,* March 1965, 28–36. (b)

Kessler, M. M. *TIP System Applications.* Technical Information Project, Massachusetts Institute of Technology, 1967.

King, D. W., and Bryant, E. C. A Diagnostic Model for Evaluating Retrospective Search Systems. *Information Storage and Retrieval,* 1970, **6,** 261–272.

Königová, M. (Using Mathematical Methods for the Evaluation of Surveys). *Metodika a Technika Informaci,* 1968, **10,** 10; 37–50. (*A.J.* 69.6.49).

Kozačkov, L. S. (Relevance in Informatics and the Science of Science). *Naučno-Texničeskaja Informacija, Ser. 2,* 1969, **8,** 15–18. (*A.J.* 70.2.8). (a)

Kozačkov, L. S. (Some Aspects of Constructing Document Search Patterns). In *(Automation of Information Activities and the Problems of Applied Linguistics).* AN USSR Naučn. Sovet Po Kibernet. Kiev. In-t Kibernet, 1969. (*A.J.* 70.5.136).(b)

Kraus, D. H. *Scientific and Technical Documentation and Information in Bulgaria; . . . Czechoslovakia; . . . Hungary; . . . Romania; . . . Yugoslavia,* School of Information Science, Georgia Institute of Technology, 1968. (a–e)

Kravec, L. G., Moskovič, V. A., and Šenderov, V. S. Automatic Indexing of Patent Information. ICEREPAT, The Hague, 1966. (*A.J.* 70.1.90).

Kuhns, J. L. The Continuum of Coefficients of Association. In Stevens, Heilprin and Giuliano (Eds.), *Statistical Association Methods for Mechanized Documentation.* Washington, D.C.: National Bureau of Standards, 1965.

Kuno, S. The Predictive Analyzer and a Path Elimination Technique. *Communications of the ACM,* 1965, **8,** 453–462.

Kuno, S., and Oettinger, A. G. Multiple-Path Syntactic Analyzer. In Popplewell (Ed.), *Information Processing–1962.* Amsterdam: North-Holland, 1963. pp. 306–312.

Kurbakov, K. I. (On the 'Mirror-Image, Principle for Information Classification Systems). *Vopr. Naučn. Prognozir., Moscow,* 1969, **8,** 57–61. (*A.J.* 70.7.92).

Kurbakov, K. I., and Boldov, V. G. (Accurate Relevance Evaluation—a Sine Qua Non of Retrieval Language Comparison). *Naučno-Texničeskaja Informacija, Ser. 2,* 1968, **8,** 15–18.

Kuznecov, A. V., Padučeva, E. V., and Ermolaeva, N. M. (An Information Language for Geometry and an Algorithm of Translation from Russian to Information Language). *Mašinnyj Perevod i Prikladnaja Lingvistika,* 5 & 6, Moscow, 1961; also in *Lingvisticeskie Issledovanija po Masinnomu Perevodu,* Moscow: VINITI, 1961.

Kuznecov, A. V., Padučeva, E. V., and Ermolaeva, N. M. On an Information Language for Geometry and a Translation Algorithm from Russian into this Information Language. *Information Storage and Retrieval,* 1963, **1,** 147–165.

Kuznecov, O. A. (On Pertinence in Information Systems). In Symposium SEV, *Teor. Osnovy Inform.* Moscow: VINITI, 1970. (*A.J.* 70.11.132).

Lamb, S. M. *Outline of Stratificational Grammar,* Washington, D.C.: Georgetown Univ. Press, 1966.

Lancaster, F. W. *Evaluation of the Medlars Demand Search System.* National Library of Medicine, Bethesda, Maryland, 1968. (a)

Lancaster, F. W. *Information Retrieval Systems: Characteristics, Testing and Evaluation.* New York: Wiley, 1968. (b)

Lancaster, F. W. On the Need for Role Indicators in Post-Coordinate Retrieval Systems. *American Documentation,* 1968, **19,** 42–46. (c)

Lancaster, F. W. MEDLARS: A Report on the Evaluation of its Operating Efficiency. *American Documentation,* 1969, **20,** 119–142.

Lancaster, F. W., and Climenson, W. D. Evaluating the Economic Efficiency of a Document Retrieval System. *Journal of Documentation,* 1968, **24,** 16–40.

Lance, G. N., and Williams, W. T. A General Theory of Classificatory Sorting Strategies: I, Hierarchical Systems. *The Computer Journal,* 1967, **9,** 373–380. (a)

Lance, G. N., and Williams, W. T. A General Theory of Classificatory Sorting Strategies: II, Clustering Systems. *The Computer Journal,* 1967, **10,** 271–277. (b)

Langendoen, T. G. *The Essentials of English Grammar.* New York: Holt, 1970.

Langleben, M. M. (Experience with Adaptation of Linguistic Concepts and Linguistic Terminology to the Description of Artificial Language). *Vsesojuznaja Konferencija po Informacionno-Poiskovym Sistemam i Avtomatizirovannoj Obrabotke Naučno-Texničeskoj Informacii,* 3rd, Moscow, 1967, 170.

Laxuti, D. G., *et al.* Semi-Automatic Translation from Natural Language into the Descriptor Language of Grow-Non Grow Systems (Automatic Indexing). *Vsesojuznaja Konferencija po Informacionno-Poiskovym Sistemam i Avtomatizirovannoj Obrabotke Naučno-Texničeskoj Informacci,* 3rd, Moscow, 1967, 111.

Lazarescu, G. (An Evaluation of Roles as Retrieval Tools in Analytical Chemistry). In *International Forum on Informatics,* Moscow: VINITI, 1969. (*A.J.* 70.3.143).

Leimkuhler, F. F. The Bradford Distribution. *Journal of Documentation,* 1967, **23,** 197–207.

Leimkuhler, F. F. A Literature Search and File Organisation Model. *American Documentation,* 1968, **19,** 131–136.

Leont'eva, T. M., and Margaritov, V. B. (A Method of Constructing and Using a Descriptor Dictionary). *Naučno-Texničeskaja Informacija, Ser.* 2, 1968, **8,** 19–22. (*A.J.* 69.1.79).

Lerman, I. C. *Les Bases de la Classification Automatique.* Paris: Gauthier-Villars, 1970.

Lesk, M. E. Performance of Automatic Information Systems. *Information Storage and Retrieval,* 1968, **4,** 219–238.

Lesk, M. E. Word-Word Associations in Document Retrieval Systems. *American Documentation,* 1969, **20,** 27–38.

Lesk, M. E., and Salton, G. Relevance Assessments and Retrieval System Evaluation. *Information Storage and Retrieval,* 1969, **4,** 343–359.

Levien, R. E., and Maron, M. E. *Relational Data File: A Tool for Mechanized Inference Execution and Data Retrieval.* RM-4793-PR. Rand Corporation, Santa Monica, California, 1965.

Levien, R. E., and Maron, M. E. *Relational Data File: Experience with a System for Propositional Data Storage and Inference Execution.* RM-5947-PR. Rand Corporation, Santa Monica, California, 1969.

Lévy, F. *Compatibility between Classifications and Thesauri: Evaluation of a First Study in the Field of Information Storage and Retrieval.* Computing Centre, Maison des Sciences de l'Homme, 1967, Paris.

Lewis, P. A. W., Baxendale, P. B., and Bennett, J. L. Statistical Discrimination of the Synonymy/Antonymy Relationship between Words. *Journal of the ACM,* 1967, **14,** 20–44.

Lindsay, R. K. Inferential Memory as the Basis of Machines which Understand Natural Language. In Feigenbaum and Feldman (Eds.), *Computers and Thought,* New York: McGraw-Hill, 1963.

Lipetz, B.-A. Information Storage and Retrieval. *Scientific American,* 1966, **215,** 224–242.

Litofsky, B. *Utility of Automatic Classification Systems for Information Storage and Retrieval.* Doctoral Thesis, University of Pennsylvania, 1969.

Locke, W. N. Computer Costs for Large Libraries. *Datamation,* 1970, **16,** 69–74.

Londe, D. L., and Schoene, W. J. TGT: Transformational Grammar Tester. *Proceedings of the 1968 SJCC, AFIPS Conference Proceedings,* 1968, **32,** 385–393.

Lovins, J. B. Development of a Stemming Algorithm. *Mechanical Translation,* 1968, **11,** 22–31.

Luhn, H. P. *see* Schultz, C. K. (1968a)

Lustig, G. A New Class of Association Factors. In Samuelson (Ed.), *Mechanized Information Storage, Retrieval and Dissemination.* Amsterdam: North-Holland, 1968. pp. 213–224.

Lynch, M. F. Subject Indexes and Automatic Document Retrieval. *Journal of Documentation,* 1966, **22,** 167–185.

Lynn, K. C. A Quantitative Comparison of Conventional Information Compression Techniques in Dental Literature. *American Documentation,* 1969, **20,** 149–151.

Lyons, J. *Introduction to Theoretical Linguistics.* Cambridge, Massachusetts: Cambridge Univ. Press, 1968.

MacNaughton-Smith, P. *Some Statistical and Other Numerical Techniques for Classifying Individuals.* London: Her Majesty's Stationery Office, 1965.

Mandersloot, W. G. B., Douglas, E. M. B., and Spicer, N. Thesaurus Control—The Selection, Grouping and Cross-referencing of Terms for Inclusion in a Coordinate Word List. *Journal of the ASIS,* 1970, **21,** 49–57.

Markov, A. A. *Theory of Algorithms.* Works of the Mathematical Institute (IMEI), Academy of Sciences of the USSR. Vol. 42. (Transl. by the Israel Program for Scientific Translations, 1961.)

Maron, M. E. Automatic Indexing: An Experimental Enquiry, *Journal of the ACM,* 1961, **8,** 404–417.

Maron, M. E., and Kuhns, J. L. On Relevance, Probabilistic Indexing and Information Retrieval. *Journal of the ACM,* 1960, **7,** 216–244.

Martyn, J., and Vickery, B. C. The Complexity of the Modelling of Information Systems. *Journal of Documentation,* 1970, **26,** 204–220.

Mathews, W. D. The TIP Retrieval System at MIT. In Schecter (Ed.), *Information Retrieval: A Critical View.* Washington D.C.: Thompson, 1967. pp. 95–108.

McCarthy, J., *et al. LISP 1.5 Programmer's Manual.* Cambridge, Massachusetts: MIT Press, 1963.

Meetham, A. R. Communication Theory and the Evaluation of Information Retrieval Systems. *Information Storage and Retrieval,* 1969, **5,** 129–134.

Melton, J. L. Automatic Language Processing for Information Retrieval: Some Questions. *Progress in Information Science, Proceedings of the ADI,* 1966, **3,** 255–263.

Melton, J. S. The Semantic Code Today. *American Documentation,* 1962, **13,** 176–181.

Mesnik, V. M. Mechanized IPS for a Varied Fund Developed and Introduced by the Upper Volga TsBTI. In *All-Union Conference on Information Retrieval Systems and Automatic Processing of Scientific and Technical Information.* (Transl.) Wright-Patterson Air Force Base, Ohio, 1969.

Mextiev, D. I., and Kuznecova, E. K. Certain Questions of Machine Preparation of Indexes for Current and Retrospective Retrieval of Scientific and Technical Information Materials. In *All-Union Conference on Information Retrieval Systems and Automatic Processing of Scientific and Technical Information.* (Transl.) Wright-Patterson Air Force Base, Ohio, 1969.

Mills, J. *The Universal Decimal Classification.* Vol. 1 of Artandi (Ed.), Rutgers Series on Systems for the Intellectual Organization of Information. Rutgers, The State University, Graduate School of Library Service, New Brunswick, New Jersey, 1964.

Mills, J. Library Classification. *Journal of Documentation,* 1970, **26,** 120–160.

Mixailov, A. I., Černyj, A. I., and Giliarevskij, R. S. *(Fundamentals of Informatics).* (2nd ed. Rev. and Suppl.) Moscow: Nauka, 1968.

Mixailov, A. I., *et al.* (Eds.) *On Theoretical Problems of Informatics.* F.I.D. 435. Moscow: VINITI, 1969. (a)

Mixailov, A. I., Černyj, A. I., and Giliarevskij, R. S. (Informatics: Its Scope and Methods). In *Theoretical Problems of Informatics.* F.I.D. 435. Moscow: VINITI, 1969. (b)

Montague, B. A. Testing, Comparison and Evaluation of Recall, Relevance and Cost of Coordinate Indexing with Links and Roles. *American Documentation,* 1965, **6,** 201–208.

Morozov, V. V., and Šemakin, Ju. I. (Experience in Developing a Methodology for Translating Document Contents and Requests in the Polytechnical Subject Field into a Descriptor-type IR Language). *Vopr. Naučn. Prognozir., Moscow,* 1969, **8,** 164–171. (*A.J.* 70.7.107).

Moskovič, V. A. (The Morphological Structure of the Word in Natural and Retrieval Languages). *Vsesojuznaja Konferencija po Informacionno-Poiskovym Sistemam i Avtomatizirovannoj Obrabotke Naučno-Texničeskoj Informacii,* **3rd,** Moscow, 1967, 401–409. (a)

Moskovič, V. A. Typological Classification of Information Retrieval Languages and Transcriptions. ICEREPAT, Stockholm, 1967. (*A.J.* 70.2.74). (b)

Moss, R. Minimum Vocabularies in Information Indexing. *Journal of Documentation,* 1967, **23,** 179–196.

Moys, E. *A Classification Scheme for Law Books.* London: Butterworths, 1968.

Mulvihill, J., and Brenner, E. H. Ranking Boolean Search Output. *American Documentation,* 1968, **19,** 204–205.

Nadtočij, A. I., *et al.* A System of Automatic Differentiation of Distribution of Information (SARI-1) on Constant Inquiries Developed in TsBNTI AKIAE. In *All-Union Conference on Information Retrieval Systems and Automatic Processing of Scien-*

tific and Technical Information. (Transl.) Wright-Patterson Air Force Base, Ohio, 1969.

NASA, *NASA Thesaurus: Subject Terms for Indexing Scientific and Technical Information.* (Prelim. ed.) Scientific and Technical Information Division, Office of Technology Utilization. National Aeronautics and Space Administration, Washington, D.C., 1967.

National Library of Medicine. *Medical Subject Headings.* Department of Health, Education and Welfare, Public Health Service, Washington, D.C., 1968. (Also *Index Medicus,* Jan. 1968, **9** (No. 1, Pt. 2).

Naumyčeva, K. I. (The Frequency Distribution and Information Assessments of a Keyword Vocabulary). In Symposium SEV, *Teor. Osnovy Inform.* Moscow: VINITI, 1970. (*A.J.* 70.11.92).

Needham, R. M. A Method for Using Computers in Information Classification. In Popplewell (Ed.), *Information Processing 62: Proceedings of IFIP Congress 1962.* Amsterdam: North-Holland Publ., 1963. **pp. 284–287.**

Needham, R. M. Automatic Classification in Linguistics. *The Statistician,* 1967, **17,** 45–54.

Needham, R. M., and Sparck Jones, K. Keywords and Clumps. *Journal of Documentation,* 1964, **20,** 5–15.

Neville, H. H. Feasibility Study of a Scheme for Reconciling Thesauri Covering a Common Subject. *Journal of Documentation,* 1970, **26,** 313–336.

Niblett, G. B. F., and Price, N. H. Mechanized Searching of Acts of Parliament. *Information Storage and Retrieval, 1970,* **6,** 289–297.

O'Connor, J. Mechanized Indexing Methods and Their Testing. *Journal of the ACM,* 1964, **11,** 437–449.

O'Connor, J. Relevance Disagreements and Unclear Request Forms. *American Documentation,* 1967, **18,** 165–177.

O'Connor, J. Some Questions concerning 'Information Need.' *American Documentation,* 1968, **19,** 200–203. (a)

O'Connor, J. Retrieval of Answer-Providing Documents. *American Documentation.* 1968, **19,** 381–386. (b)

O'Connor, J. Some Agreements and Resolved Disagreements about Answer-Providing Documents. *American Documentation,* 1969, **20,** 311–319.

Oswald, V. A. *see* Borko, H. (1967a).

Otradinskij, V. V., and Kamalov, K. Š. (Modern UDC-based Information Retrieval Languages). *Voprosy Kibernetiki i Vyčislitel'not Matematiki,* (Taškent), 1969, **31,** 81–90. (*A.J.* 70.2.68).

Otradinskij, V. V., and Kravčenko, N. D. (A Method for Indexing Full Texts). *Naučno-Texničeskaja Informacija, Ser. 2,* 1969, **7,** 16–22. (*A.J.* 69.12.79).

Otradinskij, V. V., and Vleduc, G. E. (A Technique for Document Text Compression Based on Aspect Descriptors). *Dokumentalist-69,* Vilnius, 1970. (*A.J.* 70.12.110).

Ovčinnikov, V. G. (Some Aspects of the Evaluation of Classification Systems Used in IR). *Naučno-Texničeskaja Informacija, Ser 2,* 1969, **7,** 23–29. (*A.J.* 69.12.69).

Overhage, C. F. J., and Harman, R. J. (Eds.) *INTREX: Report of a Planning Conference in Information Transfer Experiments.* Cambridge, Massachusetts: MIT Press, 1965.

Overhage, C. F. J. and Reintjes, J. F. Information Transfer Experiments at M.I.T. In Morrell (Ed.), *Information Processing 68: Proceedings of IFIP Congress 1968.* Amsterdam: North-Holland, 1969.

Padučeva, E. V. (Semantic analysis of natural language during translation into the language of mathematical logic), *Vsesojuznaja Konferencija po Informacionno-Poiskovym Sistemam i Avtomatizirovannoj Obrsabotke Naučno-Texničeskoj Informacii,* 3rd, Moscow, 1967, 156.

Padučeva, E. V. The Language of Mathematical Logic as a Semantic Model for Natural Language, *Social Science Information,* 1968, **7,** 27–39.

Parker, E. B. *SPIRES (Stanford Public Information Retrieval System).* 1968 Annual Report. Institute for Communication Research, Stanford University, 1968.

Pavličenko, N. D., and Raznikova, Ž. P. (A Mechanized IR System with Generic and Associative Relations Between Descriptors). *Ukr. N-i. In-t Naucno-Tex. Inform. i Tex.-Ekon. Issled.,* Kiev, 1970. (*A.J.* 70.9.152).

Perreault, J. M. (Ed.) *Proceedings of the International Symposium on Relational Factors in Classification* (1966); *Information Storage and Retrieval,* 1967, **3,** 177–410. (a)

Perreault, J. M. On the Articulation of Surrogates: An Attempt at an Epistemological Foundation. *Information Storage and Retrieval,* 1967, **3,** 177–189. (b)

Pevzner, B. R. (On the Automatic Translation of English Texts into the Language of the 'Pusto-Nepusto 2' System. *Naučno-Texničeskaja Informacija, Ser. 2,* 1969, **11,** 12–17. (*A.J.* 70.5.176).

Pokras, Ju. L. (A Descriptor Type IR Language in the Field of Specialization and Cooperation in Mechanical Engineering). *Naučno-Texničeskaja Informacija, Ser. 2,* 1969, **5,** 12–15. (a) (*A.J.* 69.9.74).

Pokras, Ju. L. (Avenues of Research into Relations in Descriptor-Type IR Languages). *Vopr. Naučn. Prognozir.,* Moscow, 1969, **8,** 159–163. (b) (*A.J.* 70.7.102).

Pollock, S. M. Measures for the Comparison of Information Retrieval Systems. *American Documentation,* 1968, **19,** 387–397.

Popova, N. A., and Jakubson, G. L. (Comparing the Effectiveness and Efficiency of Four IR Systems). *Naučno-Texničeskaja Informacija, Ser. 2,* 1969, **2,** 16–18. (*A.J.* 69.7.56).

Preparata, F. P., and Chien, R. T. *On Clustering Techniques of Citation Graphs.* Coordinated Science Laboratory, University of Illinois, 1967.

Project LEX, *Thesaurus of Engineering and Scientific Terms.* (1st ed.) Washington, D.C.: Office of Naval Research 1967. (Also Engineers Joint Council, 345 E. 47th St., New York.)

Prywes, N. S., and Litofsky, B. All-automatic Processing for a Large Library. *Proceedings of the 1970 SJCC, AFIPS Conference Proceedings,* 1970, **36,** 323–331.

Purto, V. A. (Automatic Reviewing on the Basis of Statistical Analysis of Text). *Doklady Konferencji po Obrabotke Informacii, Mašinnomu i Avtomatičeskomu Cteniju Teksta,* 1961, **1.**

Ranganathan, S. R. *The Colon Classification.* Vol. 4 of Artandi (Ed.), Rutgers Series on Systems for the Intellectual Organization of Information. Rutgers. The

State University, Graduate School of Library Service, New Brunswick, New Jersey, 1965.

Ranganathan, S. R. Hidden Roots of Classification. *Information Storage and Retrieval*, 1967, **3**, 399–410.

Raphael, B. SIR: Semantic Information Retrieval. In Minsky (Ed.), *Semantic Information Processing*. Cambridge, Massachusetts: MIT Press, 1968.

Rees, A. M. *The Evaluation of Retrieval Systems*. Comparative Systems Laboratory, Case Western Reserve University, 1965.

Rees, A. M. Evaluation of Information Systems and Services. In Cuadra (Ed.), *Annual Review of Information Science and Technology*. Vol. 2. New York: Interscience, 1967.

Rees, A. M., and Saracevic, T. The Measurability of Relevance. *Progress in Information Science and Technology, Proceedings of the ADI*, 1966, **3**, 225–234.

Reich, P. *The Relational Network Simulator*. The Linguistic Automation Project, Yale University, May 1968.

Reintjes, J. F. *et al.* Four papers constituting a Progress Report on Project Intrex, including Reintjes, J. F. System Characteristics of Intrex. *Proceedings of the 1969 SJCC, AFIPS Conference Proceedings*, 1969, **34**, 457–490.

Resnikoff, H. L., and Dolby, J. L. The Nature of Affixing in Written English. Part I. *Mechanical Translation*, 1965, **8**, 84–89.

Resnikoff, H. L., and Dolby, J. L. The Nature of Affixing in Written English. Part II. *Mechanical Translation*. 1966, **9**, 23–33.

Robertson, S. E. The Parametric Description of Retrieval Tests. Part I: The Basic Parameters. *Journal of Documentation*, 1969, **25**, 1–27. (a)

Robertson, S. E. The Parametric Description of Retrieval Tests. Part II: Overall Measures. *Journal of Documentation*, 1969, **25**, 93–107. (b)

Robins, R. H. *General Linguistics: An Introductory Survey*. London: Longmans, 1964.

Robinson, J. A. Automatic Deduction with Hyper-resolution. *International Journal of Computer Mathematics*, 1965, **1**, 227–234. (a)

Robinson, J. A. A Machine-oriented Logic Based on the Resolution Principle. *Journal of the ACM*, 1965, **12**, 23–41. (b)

Robinson, J. J. Methods for Obtaining Corresponding Phrase Structure and Dependency Grammars, *Proceedings of the Second International Conference on Computational Lingustics, Grenoble, 1967*.

Robinson, J. J., and Marks, S. *Parse: A System for Automatic Analysis of English Text*, RM-4564-PR, Rand Corporation, Santa Monica, California, 1965

Robison, H. R. Computer-Detectable Semantic Structures. *Information Storage and Retrieval*, 1970, **6**, 273–288.

Rocchio, J. J. *Document Retrieval Systems—Optimization and Evaluation, Information Storage and Retrieval*, Report No. ISR-10. The Computation Laboratory, Harvard University, 1966.

Rolling, L. A Computer-Aided Information Service for Nuclear Science and Technology. *Journal of Documentation*, 1966, **22**, 93–115.

Rolling, L. Compilation of Thesauri for Use in Computer Systems. *Information Storage and Retrieval*, 1970, **6**, 341–350.

Rolling, L., and Piette, J. Interaction of Economics and Automation in a Large-Size Retrieval System. In Samuelson (Ed.), *Mechanized Information Storage, Retrieval and Dissemination.* Amsterdam: North-Holland, 1968. pp. 367–390.

Romerio, G. F., and Cavara, L. Assessment Studies of Documentation Systems. *Information Storage and Retrieval,* 1968, **4**, 309–325.

Rosenberg, K. C., and Blocher, C. L. M. A Comparison of the Relevance of KWIC vs. Descriptor Indexing Terms. *American Documentation,* 1968, **19**, 27–29.

Rothenburg, D. H. An Efficiency Model and a Performance Function for an Information Retrieval System. *Information Storage and Retrieval.* 1969, **5**, 102–122.

Rozencvejg, V. Ju. (Machine Translation). In *Teor. Probl. Sov. Jazykoznanija.* Moscow: Nauka, 1968. (*A.J.* 69.4.47).

Rubinoff, M. and Stone, D. C. Semantic Tools in Information Retrieval. *Levels of Interaction between Man and Information, Proceedings of the ADI,* 1967, **4**, 169–174.

Rublev, Ju. V., and Invaniuškin, V. I. (A Method of Constructing a Multidimensional Reference Retrieval System with an Adjustable Matching Criterion). *Vopr. Naučn. Prognozir., Moscow,* 1969, **8**, 89–92. (*A.J.* 70.7.122).

Sager, N. Syntactic Analysis of Natural Language. In Alt and Rubinoff (Eds.), *Advances in Computers 8.* New York: Academic, 1967.

Sakai, I. Syntax in Universal Translation. *1961 Conference on Machine Translation and Applied Linguistics.* London: Her Majesty's Stationery Office, 1962.

Salton, G. (Project Director) *Information Storage and Retrieval.* Scientific Reports Nos. ISR-11—ISR-17. Department of Computer Science, Cornell University, 1966–1969.

Salton, G. *Automatic Information Organization and Retrieval.* New York: McGraw-Hill, 1968. (a)

Salton, G. Search Strategy and the Optimization of Retrieval Effectiveness. In Samuelson (Ed.), *Mechanized Information Storage, Retrieval and Dissemination.* Amsterdam: North-Holland, 1968. pp. 73–107. (b)

Salton, G. A Comparison between Manual and Automatic Indexing Methods. *American Documentation,* 1969, **20**, 61–71. (a)

Salton, G. Search and Retrieval Experiments in Real-time Information Retrieval. In Morrell (Ed.), *Information Processing 68: Proceedings of IFIP Congress 1968.* Amsterdam: North-Holland, 1969. (b)

Salton, G. Automatic Text Analysis. *Science,* 1970, **168**, 335–343. (a)

Salton, G. Automatic Processing of Foreign Language Documents. *Journal of the ASIS,* 1970, **21**, 187–194. (b)

Salton, G. Evaluation Problems in Interactive Information Retrieval. *Information Storage and Retrieval,* 1970, **6**, 29–44. (c)

Salton, G., and Lesk, M. E. Computer Evaluation of Indexing and Text Processing. *Journal of the ACM,* 1968, **15**, 8–36.

Sandewall, E. J. LISP-A: A LISP-like System for Incremental Computing. *Proceedings of the 1968 SJCC, AFIPS Conference Proceedings, 1968,* **32**, 375–384.

Saracevic, T. Quo Vadis Testing and Evaluation. *Levels of Interaction between Man and Information, Proceedings of the ADI,* 1967, **4**, 100–104.

Saracevic, T., and Rees, A. M. Towards the Identification and Control of Variables in Information Retrieval Experiments. *Journal of Documentation,* 1967, **23**, 7–19.

Schank, R., and Tesler, L. G. *A Computer Parser for Natural Language.* Memo No. AI 76, Stanford Artificial Intelligence Project. Computer Science Department, Stanford University, 1969.

Schneider, K. UDC in Mechanized Indexing and Information Retrieval. In Samuelson (Ed.), *Mechanized Information Storage, Retrieval and Dissemination.* Amsterdam: North-Holland, 1968. pp. 153–159.

Schultz, C. K. (Ed.) *H. P. Luhn: Pioneer of Information Science, Selected Works.* London: Macmillan, 1968..(a)

Schultz, C. K. *Thesaurus of Information Science Terminology.* Communications Service Corporation, Philadelphia, 1968..(b)

Sechser, O. (On Retrieval Languages with Syntax). *Metodika a Technika Informaci,* 1968, **10,** 10, 1–36. (*A.J.* 69.5.81).

Selye, H. *Symbolic Shorthand System.* Vol. 6 of Artandi (Ed.), Rutgers Series on Systems for the Intellectual Organization of Information. Rutgers, The State University, Graduate School of Library Service, New Brunswick, New Jersey. 1966.

Šemakin, Ju. I. (Some Aspects of Developing and Studying a Descriptor IR Language for General Technology). *Naučno-Texničeskaja Informacija, Ser. 2,* 1969, **6,** 8–13. (*A.J.* 69.11.66).

Seménova, T. A. (Experience in the Development of an Information Language for an Automated Search System. *Vopr. Naucn. Prognozir., Moscow,* 1969, **8,** 154–158. (*A.J.* 70.7.96).

Shapiro, S. C. *The MIND System: the Data Structure for Semantic Information Processing.* R-837-PR. Rand Corporation, Santa Monica, California, 1971.

Shapiro, S. C., and Woodmansee, G. H. A Net Structure Based Relational Question Answerer. In Norton and Walker (Eds.), *Proceedings of the International Joint Conference on Artificial Intelligence.* Bedford, Massachusetts: MITRE Corporation, 1969. pp. 325–346.

Sharp, J. R. *Some Fundamentals of Information Retrieval.* London: Andre Deutsch, 1965.

Shaw, T. N., and Rothman, H. An Experiment in Indexing by Word-Choosing. *Journal of Documentation,* 1968, **24,** 159–172.

Shera, J. H. The Sociological Relationships of Information Science. *Journal of the ASIS,* 1971, **22,** 77.

Simmons, R. F. Answering English Questions by Computer: A Survey. *Communications of the ACM,* 1965, **8,** 53–70; Reprinted in Kochen (Ed.), *The Growth of Knowledge.* New York: Wiley, 1967.

Simmons, R. F. Natural Language Question-Answering Systems: 1969. *Communications of the ACM,* 1970, **13,** 15–30.

Sinnett, J. D. *An Evaluation of Links and Roles Used in Information Systems.* Air Force Materials Laboratory, Wright-Patterson Air Force Base, Ohio, 1964.

Skoroxod'ko, E. F. (Semantic Models in Information Retrieval). *Vsesojuznaja Konferencija po Informacionno-Poiskovym Sistemam i Avtomatizirovannoj Obrabotke Naučno-Texničeskoj Informacii,* 3rd, Moscow, 1967, 319–327.

Skoroxod'ko, E. F. (The Information Retrieval System at the Institute of Cybernetics, Academy of Sciences of the Ukrainian SSR). In *International Forum on Informatics.* Moscow: VINITI, 1969. (*A.J.* 70.3.160).

Skoroxod'ko, E. F. (On the Adequacy of Representation of Text Contents by Means of an Information Language). In *Primenenie Universal 'n. Vyčisl. Mašin v Rabote Organov Inform.*, Moscow, 1970. (*A.J.* 70.12.95).

Šneiderman, Ja. A. (Development of a Descriptor Vocabulary for Materials Science). *Naučno-Texničeskaja Informacija, Ser. 2*, 1969, **9**, 17–23. (*A.J.* 70.3.129).

Soergel, D. Some Remarks on Information Languages, their Analysis and Comparison. *Information Storage and Retrieval*, 1967, **3**, 219–291.

Soergel, D. *Klassifikationssyteme und Thesauri*. Deutsche Gesellschaft fur Dokumentation, Frankfurt-am-Main, 1969.

Sokal, R. R., and Sneath, P. H. A. *Principles of Numerical Taxonomy*. London: Freeman and Co., 1963.

Sokolov, A. V. (Investigation of Information Losses and Information Noise in Descriptor Information-Retrieval Systems). *Naučno-Texničeskaja Informacija*, 1965, **12**, 23–28.

Sokolov, A. V., Byumenau, D. I., Grinina, R. F., and Sorkin, A. M. Experimental Investigations of Comparative Effectiveness of Manual and Mechanized IPS in the N.K. Krupskaja Leningrad State Institute of Culture. In *All-Union Conference on Information Retrieval Systems and Automatic Processing of Scientific and Technical Information*. (Transl.) Wright-Patterson Air Force Base, Ohio, 1969.

Sparck Jones, K. *Synonymy and Semantic Classification*. Ph.D. Thesis, University of Cambridge, 1964.

Sparck Jones, K. *A Small Semantic Classification Experiment Using Cooccurrence Data*. Cambridge Language Research Unit, 1967.

Sparck Jones, K. Automatic Term Classification and Information Retrieval. In Morrell (Ed.), *Information Processing 68: Proceedings of IFIP Congress 1968*. Amsterdam: North-Holland, 1969. pp. 1290–1295.

Sparck Jones, K. Some Thoughts on Classification for Retrieval. *Journal of Documentation*, 1970, **26**, 89–101.

Sparck Jones, K. *Automatic Keyword Classification and Information Retrieval*. London: Butterworths, 1971.

Sparck Jones, K., and Barber, E. O. What Makes an Automatic Keyword Classification Effective? *Journal of the ASIS*, 1971, **22**, 166–175.

Sparck Jones, K., and Jackson, D. M. Current Approaches to Classification and Clumpfinding at the Cambridge Language Research Unit. *The Computer Journal*, 1967, **10**, 29–37.

Sparck Jones, K., and Jackson, D. M. The Use of Automatically-obtained Keyword Classifications for Information Retrieval. *Information Storage and Retrieval*, 1970, **5**, 175–201.

Spiegel, J., and Bennett, E. A Modified Statistical Association Procedure for Automatic Document Content Analysis and Retrieval. In Stevens, Heilprin and Giuliano (Ed.), *Statistical Association Methods for Mechanized Documentation*. Washington, D.C.: National Bureau of Standards, 1965. (2nd ed. enlarged, 1970.)

Šreider, Ju. A. (A Mathematical Model of the Theory of Classification). *Naučno-Texničeskaja Informacija, Ser. 2*, 1968, **10**, 7–14. (*A.J.* 69.3.48).

Šreider, Ju. A., Arapov, M. V., Gorkina, N. S., and Padučeva, E.V. *Development and Application of Information Retrieval Languages*. Working Paper prepared for the ICSU/UNESCO Joint Project on the Communication of Scientific Information. Moscow: VINITI, 1969.(a)

Šreider, Ju. A., Arapov, M. V., Gorkina, N. S., and Padučeva, E.V. *Linguistic Problems of Scientific Information.* Working Paper prepared for the ICSU/UNESCO Joint Project on the Communication of Scientific Information. Moscow: VINITI, 1969.(b)

Stevens, M. E. *Automatic Indexing: A State of the Art Report.* Monograph 91. Washington, D.C.: National Bureau of Standards, 1965. (2nd ed. enlarged, 1970.)

Stevens, M. E. *Research and Development in the Computer and Information Sciences.* 3 Vols., Monograph 113. Washington, D.C.: National Bureau of Standards, 1970.

Stevens, M. E., and Urban, G. H. Evaluation of Automatic Indexing Using Cited Titles. In Stevens, Heilprin and Giuliano (Eds.), *Statistical Association Methods for Mechanized Documentation.* Washington, D.C.: National Bureau of Standards, 1965.

Stevens, M. E., Heilprin, L., and Giuliano, V. E. (Eds.) *Statistical Association Methods for Mechanized Documentation.* Symposium Proceedings (1964). Miscellaneous Publication 269. Washington, D.C.: National Bureau of Standards, 1965.

Stiles, H. E. The Association Factor in Information Retrieval. *Journal of the ACM,* 1961, **8**, 271–279.

Stokolova, N. A., and Tonijan, A. V. (Application of 'Standard Phrases' in Developing a Language for Explanatory Phrases in Chemical Indexes). *Naučno-Texničeskaja Informacija, Ser. 2,* 1970, **3**, 16–25. (A.J. 70.10.84).

Stokolova, N. A., and Vleduc, G. E. (On the Basic Principles of an Information Language for Searching the Titles of Chemical Publications). *Naučno-Texničeskaja Informacija,* 1966, **10**, 19–25.(a)

Stokolova, N. A., and Vleduc, G. E. (On the Basic Principles of an Information Language for Searching the Titles of Chemical Publications). *Naučno-Texničeskaja Informacija,* 1966, **11**, 25–30.(b)

Stone, D. C. *Word Statistics in the Generation of Semantic Tools for Information Retrieval Systems.* Moore School of Electrical Engineering, University of Pennsylvania, 1967.

Stone, D. C., and Rubinoff, M. Statistical Generation of a Technical Vocabulary. *American Documentation,* 1968, **19**, 411–412.

Swanson, D. R. Searching Natural Language Text by Computer. *Science,* 1960, **132**, 1099–1104.

Swanson, D. R. Research Procedures for Automatic Indexing. In *Machine Indexing: Progress and Problems.* Washington, D.C.: American University, 1962.

Swets, J. A. Effectiveness of Information Retrieval Methods. *American Documentation,* 1969, **20**, 72–81. (Report issued by Bolt, Beranek and Newman, Inc., Cambridge, Massachusetts, 1967.)

Tague, J. M. The Evaluation of Statistical Association Measures. *Progress in Information Science and Technology. Proceedings of the ADI,* 1966, **3**, 391–397.

Tague, J. M. *Statistical Measures of Term Association in Information Retrieval.* Thesis, Case Western Reserve University, 1967.

Tell, B. V., Larsson, R., and Lindh, R. Information Retrieval with the Abacus

Program. In *Handling of Nuclear Information*. Vienna: International Atomic Energy Agency, 1970.

'Thesauri': *Bulletin de l'Association Internationale des Documentalistes*. Special Issue on Thesari, **5**, 4, 1966.

Thorne, J. P., Bratley, P., and Dewar, H. The Syntactic Analysis of English by Machine. In Michie (Ed.), *Machine Intelligence 3*. New York: American Elsevier, 1968. pp. 281–309.

Toma, E. (Criteria for the Evaluation of Indexing Effectiveness. 2. Analysis of Some Formalized Vocabularies). *Studii şi Cercetări Docum.*, 1969, **11**, 121–137. (*A.J.* 70.5.124).

Tomasik-Bek, I. (Basic Information Retrieval Languages and the Effectiveness of Information: A Case Study in the Field of Medical Sciences). In Symposium SEV, *Teor. Osnovy Inform.* Moscow: VINITI, 1970. (*A.J.* 70.11.96).

Ullmann, W. A Generalized Method for Matching Arbitrary Logical Statements in Mechanized Retrieval Systems. *American Documentation*, 1969, **20**, 253–258.

Van Slype, G. Essai de Typologie des Langages d'Indexation. *Management France*, 1969, **5**, 40–47.

Vasilievskij, A. L., and Kravec, L. G. (A General Outline of the System for Automatic Translation of Items from the 'Official Gazette'). In *Eksperim. Sistema Anglo-Russk. Avtomatič. Perev. Patent. Dokumentacii)*, Moscow, 1970. (*A.J.* 70.9.82).

Vaswani, P. K. T. A Technique for Cluster Emphasis and its Application to Automatic Indexing. In Morrell (Ed.), *Information Processing 68: Proceedings of the IFIP Congress 1968*. Amsterdam: North-Holland, 1969.

Vaswani, P. K. T., and Cameron, J. B. *The National Physical Laboratory Experiments in Statistical Word Associations and their Use in Document Indexing and Retrieval.* Teddington, National Physical Laboratory, Middlesex, 1970.

Vaxabov, V. K. (Some Findings of Statistical Studies of a Descriptor Language). *Naučno-Texničeskaja Informacija, Ser. 2*, 1970, **4**, 27–31. (*A.J.* 70.11.93). (a)

Vaxabov, V. K. (Certain Statistical Regularities in Descriptor-Based Information Searching). In *Primenenie Universal'n. Vyčisl. Mašin v Robote Organov Inform.*, Moscow, 1970. (*A.J.* 70.12.123). (b)

Vaxabov, V. K., Mixajlova, A. A., Esilevskaja, L. M., and Kuteeva, T. S. Experience in Creating Information Retrieval Language Via Computer Technology. In *All-Union Conference on Information Retrieval Systems and Automatic Processing of Scientific and Technical Information*. (Transl.) Wright-Patterson Air Force Base, Ohio, 1969.

Vickery, B. C. *Faceted Classification Schemes*. Vol. 5 of Artandi (Ed.), Rutgers Series on Systems for the Intellectual Organization of Information. New Brunswick, New Jersey, Graduate School of Library Service, Rutgers, The State University, 1966.

Vickery, B. C. Bibliographic Description, Arrangement and Retrieval. *Journal of Documentation*, 1968, **24**, 1–15.

Vleduc, G. E., and Stokolova, N. A. (On a Method for Constructing Information Languages with Grammar). In *International Forum on Informatics*. Moscow: VINITI, 1969. (*A.J.* 70.3.124).

Voskovojnik, D. I., Vleduc, G. E., and Černjavskij, V. S. Basic Trends in the Development of Information Retrieval Systems. In *All-Union Conference on Information Retrieval Systems and Automatic Processing of Scientific and Technical Information.* (Transl.) Wright-Patterson Air Force Base, Ohio, 1969.

Vsesojuznaja Konferencija po Informacionno-Poiskovym Sistemam i Avtomatizirovannoj Obrabotke Naučno-Texničeskoj Informacii, 3rd, Moscow, 1967; for translations of selected papers SEE *All-Union Conference* . . .

Wall, E. Further Implications of the Distribution of Index Term Usage. *Parameters of Information Science, Proceedings of the ADI,* 1964, **1**, 457–466.

Wall, E. A Rationale for Attacking Information Problems. *American Documentation,* 1967, **18**, 97–103.

Wall, E. Vocabulary Building and Control Techniques. *American Documentation,* 1969, **20**, 161–164.

Watt, W. C. Habitability. *American Documentation,* 1968, **19**, 338–351.

Weiss, S. F. Syntax in Text Analysis. In *Information Storage and Retrieval.* Report No. ISR-16. Department of Computer Science, Cornell University, 1969.(a)

Weiss, S. F. Template Analysis and its Application to Natural Language Processing, In *Information Storage and Retrieval.* Report No. ISR-16. Department of Computer Science, Cornell University, 1969.(b)

Williams, J. H. Results of Classifying Documents with Multiple Discriminant Functions. In Stevens, Heilprin and Giuliano (Eds.), *Statistical Association Methods for Mechanized Documentation.* Washington, D.C.: National Bureau of Standards, 1965.

Williams, J. H. Computer Classification of Documents. In Samuelson, (Ed.), *Mechanized Information Storage, Retrieval and Dissemination.* Amsterdam: North-Holland, 1968. pp. 235–246.

Woods, W. A. Semantics for a Question-answering System. *Mathematical Linguistics and Automatic Translation.* Report No. NSF-19. Computation Laboratory, Harvard University, 1967.

Woods, W. A. Procedural Semantics for a Question-Answering Machine. *Proceedings of the 1968 FJCC, AFIPS Conference Proceedings,* 1968, **33** (Pt. 1), 457–471.

Woods, W. A. Transition Network Grammars for Natural Language Analysis. Cambridge, Massachusetts, 1970 [Author mimeo].

Wyllys, R. E. Extracting and Abstracting by Computer. In Borko (Ed.), *Automated Language Processing.* New York: Wiley, 1967.

Zunde, P., and Slamecka, V. Distribution of Indexing Terms for Maximum Efficiency of Information Transmission. *American Documentation,* 1967, **18**, 104–108.

AUTHOR INDEX

Numbers in italics refer to the pages on which the complete references are listed.

SUBJECT INDEX